Thee Jerusalem Gangster

Emad U Deen

Table of Contents

Al-Qur'an 4: 135...... "standing firm in justice, witnesses for Allah (God), even it be against yourselves or parents and relatives".

Dedications

I without a doubt want to the thank Allah (God) the creator of the heavens, earth and everything in between. I dedicate this book primarily to my late beloved mother who was a pillar of strength for me and the family. I miss her so much and she is always be in my thoughts and prayers. If I could have given her what life I have left and to take her place I would have done it without giving it a second thought but unfortunately death is something that is beyond our control. Mom you are my heart and soul, how I wish you were here with us, you could have met your granddaughter little Fouza. I am positive you two would have fallen in love with each other not just because she is your granddaughter but because she is so much like you. I hope and pray that you are looking down on me and you are pleased with what you see, Insha Allah (God willing). When Allah/God called you back to him it created a big void in my life that will never ever be filled! You were the strongest women I ever knew, you suffered much yet you always remained steadfast and was always thankful to Allah (God). I promise you my beloved mother that I will continue to stay on the straight path for the remainder of my time on this earth. I Thank you for always being there for me and never abandoning me, until we meet in the next life I will always love and miss you more than anything in this world. I also dedicate this book to my beautiful daughter little Fouza whom I love so very much and am thankful to Allah (God) for giving you to me. I pray that Allah (God) will guide you onto the straight path and give the opportunity to be her with you in this life to see you leading a healthy, clean, and successful life, Ameen. I pray that he associated you with the best of people and keeps evil people away from you, Ameen may the peace and blessings be upon our beloved Prophet Mohammad. I would also like to also dedicate it to my two sons who I don't see much of, I love you two and ask your forgivenes if I have wronged you. I wish you two the best future that life has to offer. Ameen Lastly to my boys (Thee Almighty Saints of Little Spain) who are no longer with us rest in peace.

Acknowledgement

First and foremost, I acknowledgement that it is only with the permission of Allah (God) that I have made it to this point in my life to be able to turn my life story into a book, Alhamdu lilahee rubu almeen (Praise be to Allah (God) Lord of the worlds). Also I am acknowledging all the individuals who gave me encouragement to write this book especially my guy/brother Farod L, AKA Farilla G Author of "True Gangsters Don't Fold". Finally, I cannot thank the Author of many books Demitrien Oliphant enough for always being there with help whenever I reached out to him.

My beautiful and beloved late mother on the left may Allah (God) have mercy on her soul. On the right is the beautiful love of my life Little Fouza may Allah (God) give her a life of purity, peace and success Ameen.

Jerusalem

Emad U Deen is my name, I was born close to the walls of the Old City of East Jerusalem on August 10, 1966 to a Muslim couple of Palestinian descent. We lived in the neighborhood of Sheikh Jarrah which is less than a quarter of a mile from the walls of the Old City of Jerusalem. At the time of my birth we were ruled and governed by the British along with the help of their proxy the Jordanians. Then almost a year after my birth the newly created State of Israel, which was created on one half of historical Palestine, invaded and expanded its territories by capturing the remaining parts of historical Palestine. This invasion took place in early June of 1967 in what is known as the Six-day war. We lived in a one-bedroom home without any electricity, running water or gas. My beloved mother stood at about 5' 2" and maybe a 105LB but was mentally the strongest person I would ever come to know. My mother's whole life was one big sacrifice, at an early age she was taken out of school as a young girl and handed over to her grandmother who lived in the City of Nablus to basically be a maid and a caretaker for her grandmother, she cooked, washed and cleaned at her grandmother's house while her brothers and sisters were free to go to school and get an education. Then when she became a woman she had to endure the biggest sacrifice of her life and that is to be married to my father who was a savage and a tyrant when it came to my poor mother. She always told me stories about how unbelievably crazy life was immediately after the Six day. My father and uncle were immediately put on the wanted list by the Israeli authorities for resisting the newly occupying government (Israel). The first time they came to our house looking for my uncle they shot through the doors in the house than looked behind them. They did this because they did not want to take any chances of being shot by uncle who may have been hiding behind one of those doors. Also, the door to our front yard which made of sheet metal that stood about six feet high was riddled with bullet holes from the guns of the Israelis. The interior of the house was black from being set on fire by the Israelis. According to my mother, my father and uncle were captured not long after the Israeli army visited our house. They kept my father in prison, but it was a different story for my uncle, he was exiled across the border to Jordan. I was told by grandfather that Israeli intelligence came looking for him (grandfather) in those early days but he was not home. They found my grandmother there and instructed her to tell my grandfather that he must go to Al meskubia (a police station) to answer some questions and if he did not go on his own they would return for him and arrest him. When he came home my grandmother gave him the message that was given to her by the Israeli intelligence. My grandfather did as they instructed and when he arrived at the police station he was instructed to sit down on a bench in the hallway and wait. While sitting there he heard screams, moans and the sounds of men being beat coming from the rooms down the hall from where he was seated. It was no secret by now that Palestinians were being tortured by the Israelis during interrogations. There was mass imprisonment without charges, beatings and torture was part of everyday life for the people of Palestine living under Israeli occupation and it did not matter if you were a Christian or a Muslim. My grandfather decided he was not going to wait around for a beating, so he got up and walked towards the exit. As he approached the exit an Israeli officer popped up and asked him "Where are you going old man"? My grandfather thought fast and told the officer that he was there to inquire about his son who had been arrested earlier in the day. The officer looked him up and down and then walked off allowing him to escape. After that day my grandfather was on the run, and he ran for about 18 months in the hills of Nablis and Qabbalan (a small village outside of Nablus where he was from) at times hiding in trees while Israeli soldiers were walking around looking for him. He was finally captured and received what he had been running from. He showed me the upper right side of his back where he had a baseball size knot, he told me it appeared after the beatings he received from the Israelis. It turned out that a Palestinian informant told the Israelis that my grandfather had buried some weapons in a water well and that was the reason for the Israelis wanted him for questioning. That informant also implicated my mother as being an accomplice with my grandfather and the Israeli intelligence come to our house and questioned my mother. When I inquired with my mother about this story she told me that they came to the house in their tan jeeps and started to question her while she was carrying me in her arms, among the Israelis was an Iraqi Jew who didn't like the way she answered the questions so he lifted his hand in the air in order to strike her but was stopped by a European Jew. That was not something my mother was expecting that a European would be more just than a Middle Easterner Iraqi Jew but that is what happened. My uncle Nabil was a teenager when he was first arrested and sent to prison in the Jordanian desert for shooting shattering the elbow of a British Officer with a slingshot near the walls of the Old City. For that my uncle was also shot in the ankle which left him with a slight limp for the rest of his life. He spent seven years in that desert prison without any visitation because it was not allowed. My aunt his younger sisters told me that when he was released and arrived home he was unable to tell one sister from the other because they had grown up so much in the seven years he was in prison. She said he was dressed in a suit jacket that was three times his size and the shoes he had on were not a pair but were two different shoes. As I said my uncle was exiled to Jordan after the Six-Day War but his stay in Jordan was short lived because he crossed the border along with four other Palestinians with the intentions of attacking the Israeli military in a freedom fighter operation. According to what I was told he and his comrades crossed the border on five camels but unfortunately at the time of their crossing there was a group of Western reporters in Israel doing a news piece on how Israel protects its borders after the Six-Day war and they were doing this in an Israeli military helicopter. As they were filming the border they spotted my uncle and his four comrades coming through. The Israelis in the helicopter immediately notified other Israeli military who arrived and there after a firefight ensued between both parties. By the end of the firefight three of my uncle's comrades were killed and the fourth was injured and captured along with my uncle. My father and uncle fought in the Six-Day War and my father's story was, they (Palestinians) only had a few WWI and WWII weapons. These were British guns that were rusted and in junk condition where the firing pins kept breaking on them. The only military that existed at the time to defend the Palestinians were the British and Jordanians. According to my father and other Palestinians, the British and most of the Jordanian military had disappeared off the face of the earth during the night before the invasion an indication that the takeover of the rest of Palestinian lands was planned in a conspiracy by the Zionists, British and the Jordanian authorities. My uncle was a member of Dr. George Habash 's PFLP (the popular front for the liberation of Palestine) Dr. Habash was very much respected and loved by both Palestinian Christians and Muslims alike. After my uncle's capture in the desert he was hauled into Israeli military court where he was prosecuted and was of course convicted then sentenced to 125 years in prison. Among those present in court on the Israeli side was none other than the famous Israeli general Moshe Deyan. According to family members and reporters Moshe Deyan told my uncle, "you shouldn't have come back, this is not your country anymore, it belongs to us Jews". My uncle gave the court a speech denouncing the newly created State of Israel and its occupation of historical Palestine. My uncle's story and his speech have been documented and printed in books and magazines relating to the Palestinian struggle against the occupation. By now all three men on my father's side were imprisoned by the Israelis which meant my grandmother was busy going from one courtroom to another and then from one prison to another, visiting either her husband or one of her two sons. Eventually my grandfather and father were released but every few months the Israelis would come to pick up my father for questioning regarding political activities by him and other

Palestinians whether it be demonstrations or political gatherings which were deemed illegal by the Israeli government. The correct terminology should be arrest rather than only questioning because he would disappear for two months, tree months, six months and even a year at a time. My grandmother (father's mother) whom I loved so much that words alone cannot describe the love I had for her. Fatimah was her name and she was from a small village in the West Bank near the city of Ramallah called Turmos Ayaa. She dressed in the traditional Palestinian thoob (dress) and a white headscarf. She visited my uncle once a month I believe, and she would take me with her on those visits. I remember she would make a basket of food the night before and the next morning about five or 6 AM we would head out to meet the bus near the Damascus Gate which transported us to the prison. After we boarded the bus an Israeli officer would board the bus holding a clipboard, on that clipboard was a list of the names of families who could visit their grandfathers, fathers and or sons. If your name was not called than you would have to exit the bus than you could try your luck next month. From there the bus would take us to the prison and at the time my uncle was in Ashkelon prison in the southern part of Palestine. When we arrived at the prison you would have to fill out paperwork and even than you still hoped and prayed your loved one was still at that prison because the Israelis would sometimes move prisoners without letting the family know. If he was moved, you would just have to sit outside the prison and wait for the other families to finish their visits hoping someone would have some information from other Palestinian prisoners on the where a bouts of your missing father or son because the Israelis were in no way going to give you any information. Most of the time we waited for hours to be able to visit our loved ones and the visit lasted for only about half an hour to 45 minutes at most. The visits in those days took place in a room with a concrete wall which had about 10 small mesh covered windows and a long bench to sit on facing that wall where visitors would sit and talk to their loved ones through that mesh covered windows. The prisoners were all there for political reasons, their only crime was that they were Palestinians who opposed the illegal occupation of our land either by words or by actions. You would have to fit in all you could about how life is now under the occupation in that short visit and at the same time be very careful that the Israeli guards did not hear you saying the wrong thing, or you might be arrested. I remember we visited my uncle one day and I happened to be wearing a red colored jacket, which I'm sure was given to us by somebody since we were too poor to afford much of anything at that time. My uncle asked me if I liked red, seeing that he seemed to want me to say yes, I said yes. At the time of the question I was too young to understand the meaning of that question but years later I learned that red was the color of communism and was also the color of the Popular Front for the Liberation of Palestine who followed Carl Marx's ideology. On one attempt to visit my uncle, my grandmother woke early and as usual we headed to the bus stop and boarded it as usual at the Damascus gate. As always, the Israeli officer boarded the bus with his clipboard and started calling off the names of people on the list who were allowed a visit but this time he finished calling the names without calling our name. My grandmother stood up and stepped into the center aisle of the bus with me following behind. She was slowly approaching the Israeli officer while trying to explain to him that her name was not called, that today was indeed her son's visitation day. The Israeli officer started screaming at her "if your name was not called that means there is no visit for your son, get off the bus". My grandmother, being a mother just like all mothers was a fighter, so she kept insisting that it must be a mistake. The Israeli officer was still screaming at her to get off the bus while walking towards us and us was walking towards him. Than we finally met, he reached and grabbed a hand full of her hair and preceded to pull her to the front of the bus. He yanked her so hard that she lost her balance and fell to the floor of the bus. As she fell, I gabbed and held on tight onto the bottom of her dress screaming and crying and he finally pulled her off the bus. I must have been somewhere around

6 or 7 years old at the time of this incident. My grandmother suffered much, and from that suffering and grief she had a stroke while visiting my aunt in the West Bank village of Tormus Ayaa. She was transported back to Jerusalem and was admitted into the Al Maqasid hospital which is located at the top of the Mount of olives in Jerusalem. I did not know at the time, but I am guessing she was in a coma do to the stroke. I was at the hospital when the Israeli military brought my uncle to see my grandmother. He arrived in a military Jeep with a black cloth hood over his head which they did not remove until he was inside of the hospital, he was shackled around his waist and ankles. I was standing at the door of her room when he walked past me with the two Israelis by his side. I remember watching my uncle as he tried to get a response from my grandmother, "Yumma yumma (Mother mother) it's me Nabil" over and over but there was no response, movement or anything else for that matter and a few minutes later he was led away by the Israelis to the military jeep and went back off to his prison cell. A few days later my father came home with a grief-stricken face and it was at this moment that my mother took me to our friends next door because she knew that look on my father's face meant that my grandmother had passed away. My father worked the front desk at the Al Maqasid hospital whenever he was not in Israeli prisons, so he was at work when he found out from the doctors informed him there is nothing else to do. My father was brutal when his temper flared up, and it didn't take much for him to go into a violent rage and give me and my mother a beating without any mercy as if we were his worse enemies. I remember some of the beatings in those early years and was told about others by my mother. One day my uncle, my mother's brother, aunt and their son were visiting when the subject switched from whatever they were talking about to children being smart in school. So, my uncle asked his son to say the ABCs and my cousin did them without making any mistakes. I was scared to death while my cousin was saying them because I knew when he finished my father was going to ask me to say them. As soon as my cousin said Z my father

looked over to me and said "now you say them" I couldn't say them I just did not know. For that my father scolded me in front of everybody and when my uncle and aunt left, he beat me and my mother for embarrassing him. My mother was able to get away from his beating and grab me by my hand and run to our next-door neighbors, a caring old couple who were like grandparents to me. Me and my mother hid there for a few hours until my father cooled down enough and it was safe enough for us to go home. During my father's many stints in Israeli prisons he was beaten and tortured and because he was in and out of Israeli prisons so much it was virtually impossible for him to support us. One of my aunts (father's sister) had been trying to help him migrate to the United States and there was a very good chance she could help him because she was an American citizen living in Puerto Rico at the time. In 1973 he was granted permission to migrate and it sure came at the right time because he was just released from Israeli custody and during that imprisonment, they had tortured him bad enough to cause his kidneys to become inflamed or something like that. when he was released that time, he skinny and looked very pale. That year in 1973 he migrated to the United states and my poor mother was left to fend for the five of us while pregnant with her sixth child. After my father left us and we didn't get much help from anyone in our relatives except for my grandfather (my father's dad) he did what he could which wasn't much since he himself did not have that much but he was all we had and appreciated having him. Some of our relatives were even ashamed of being related to us because we were so poor while most of them were leading pretty good lives. We received from the welfare or the UN a 100pound of flour, sugar, salt and a can of grease once a month. My mother would mix the flour and make bread and would than glaze it with grease and sprinkle sugar over it. That is what we ate for breakfast, lunch and dinner on most days for a long time. She had an arrangement with the local pita bread bakery to bake the dough for her. She would wake me up early in the morning at about five or 6 AM and send me to the bakery with the dough on a round aluminum tray and I would wait there at the bakery until it was done, which took about half an hour most of the time, and then I would take it back home. The bakery was about a half block from our house and at times it was a bit hectic navigating to that bakery while trying to dodge a small pack of dogs that roamed freely in that small neighborhood. At that time, I was going to a school in Jerusalem called Al Muttron, and really can't say how we were able to afford me going to that school. After my father's migration to the United States, my mother took on the task of paying for that school with whatever little money she had. The students at that school came from blue-collar and upper-class families who had money unlike my family. All the other students came to school with lunches every day, but I never had any lunch, I had no breakfast so by lunch time I was starving to the point that couldn't concentrate on school or anything else for that matter. Most of the time I would stay behind when the bell rang for the end of the launch recess and my reason for staying behind was to see if I could find a quarter or half a sandwich left behind by the other students, so I could eat it. It is common practice in the Middle East not to throw dread away or on the floor out of respect and being grateful to Allah (God) so if the students did not finish their sandwich, they would just leave what was left of the sandwich on the ledge of a short concrete barrier surrounding the walkway. I would try my best to make sure no one was watching. I would than snatch up whatever was left over of the sandwich and eat it as fast as I could before anyone seen me because I didn't want to be embarrassed and made fun of. Unfortunately, most of the time luck was not on my side because there weren't any leftovers for me to eat. When I was given home work there was nobody at home to help me with it given the fact that my mother could neither read or write. My aunt, my mother's youngest sister who was a teenager at the time was very smart in school would sometimes try to help me with my homework assignments, but she had no patience and if I made a mistake, she would beat me and even bit me hard enough to leave her teeth imprints on my body. By the end of that school year my grades were so bad that I was failing every class which understandably upset my mother so much that she swore that she was going to take me out of that school because I was wasting whatever little money we had without any good results. At the end of the school year in those early years my mother allowed me to go spend the summer at my grandmother's (father's mother) village called Turmos Ayaa in the West Bank. I spent the summer living with my grandmother's sister who I always addressed as grandmother which is the custom in the middle East. The practice is that anyone your mother and father's age is uncle and aunt, anyone your grandparents age is grandfather and grandmother it did not matter if you were related or not. Life in the village was so beautiful that I wished I could stay there for the rest of my life. The village called Turmos Ayaa was full of olive groves, almond trees, fields of grain, peach and plum trees. People including my grandmother had chickens, mules, donkeys, cows, goats, sheep and there was a horse or two. My grandmother would wake me very early in the morning after she had made a basket of food and we would head out to a piece of land she owned at the edge of the village where I would help her tend the crop of chickpeas until midday and then we returned home. Unfortunately, the summer my mother took me out of the Al Muttron school I was no longer allowed to go to the village anymore because she got me a summer job. I got my first job at the Pita bread bakery where we got our bread baked. My mother talked to the owner and he agreed to give me a job, I did not mind I knew my mother needed the help and it was a way of teaching me responsibility. The family who owned the bakery were from city of Al Khalil (Hebron) the city gets its name from Prophet Abraham peace be upon him, where God says Abraham is Khalilullah (Abraham is the friend of God). Prophet Abraham, our mother Sarah and Isaac, peace be upon them, are all buried together inside a mosque in that city. The family seemed like nice people and they had few of their own sons working there also. I was to report to work between 6 and 7 AM and I would work until 8 PM but on Friday sometimes it might be until 9 or 10 PM and on Sundays I worked until 5 or 6 PM. My pay was one Learra a day so that's seven Learras a week which equivalent to approximately two American dollars a week. This was an old bakery, so it was dark and very hot from the big oven and it was summer time which made it brutal and almost unbearable to work in there but like anything else you learn to adapt. Sometimes my job was to load baseball size dough on to a machine with rollers that flattened the dough into a circle and sometimes the dough would get stuck in the rollers and would need a little push to go through the rollers. One day as I was feeding the dough into the machine and the dough got stuck at the rollers. I attempted to push the dough with my fingers tips and the rollers caught my index and middle finger on the right-hand and smashed them flat up to my first knuckle. I felt the pain immediately, so I yanked my fingers back out ripping the skin on both fingers. I had blood pouring out of both fingers and both fingernails immediately turned black under the smashed finger nails. I was taken to the hospital and received stitches on my index finger and of course smashing my fingers meant nothing I was back at work the same day and the rest of the summer. Naturally, with the passing of time I got to know the owners very well, they were four brothers but only three owned the bakery and one brother was just a worker. The brother who was not an owner happened to be the oldest of the four and was a miserable human being and for some reason made it his business to treat me like a jerk, he was always mocking me or complaining that I wasn't moving fast enough. Even at the age of 8 or 9, I understood that something had to be seriously wrong with this 50-year-old man who felt it was necessary to pick on a little kid who was busting his ass during the summer to help his mother. Naturally as time passed, I started to hate him as much as he seemed to hate me but even more. The owner's sons who worked with me were older than I was except one who was about my age maybe a year older than me. One day me and the son who was my age were playing and for some reason he became upset and hit me, so I hit him back and he immediately started crying. As he was crying his father happened to come around the corner, the father asked him "why are you crying" and the son pointed to me and said, "he hit me". The father walked up to me without saying anything and punched me in my stomach, he punched me hard enough that he knocked the wind out of me. I grabbed my stomach, hunched over and fell to my knees trying to catch my breath and crying at the same time. The father was a muscular man who was a father of five who punched a child in the stomach without giving it a second thought. I was crying but it wasn't just from the pain but from the fact that this man should have been like an uncle to me maybe even a father figure given the fact that he knew my father was not around and my uncle was a hero in Israeli prisons not to mention the fact that my mother was alone. What hurt most is knowing that he punched me without a worry because he knew my mother was alone with no men around otherwise, he would have never done that! He was Palestinian and a Muslim who was supposed to protect us but instead this coward was assaulting me because I hit his son who hit me first. I never said anything about it to my mother but after that I hated that gutless coward who would have never laid a hand on me if my father and uncle were home. At the beginning of the school year my mother enrolled me and my middle brother in a school called Dar ul Awl ad (the house of young boys) an all boy school in Jerusalem. It was a school where you not only went to school there but we also lived there. She sent my three sisters to a school called Dar ul At fall (the house of children/girls) an all-girls school my sisters also lived at that school. My youngest brother for some reason was sent to a school in Rehaa (Jericho) same thing he lived there. In my school, from mingling with other students I learned much more about nationalism and that seemed to be what I became preoccupied with painting Palestinian flags which was an illegal act according to Israeli law and talking about fighting the evil occupiers of our land by throwing rocks at Israeli soldiers. I was also burning tires in the streets, to be frank by this time I did not care about education, my only dream was to one day become a freedom fighter and be just like my uncle. Everywhere you went there were Israeli soldiers carrying machine guns harassing people pretending our country belonged to them. I always volunteered to go out and burn tires because I was small enough to fit through bars on the windows of course there were other kids who fit through the bars, but many were too scared to do so. We would slip through the bars at about 5 or 6 am than jump down onto the roof of the school kitchen which was below our living quarters windows. From there we climbed down to the street and from there we would retrieve the tires. These tires were brought the night before from the industrial area down the street and placed in a field and were covered with brush to conceal them. We would place the tires in the middle of the street and poor fuel over them which we stole the night before from the fuel tanks of a hotel down than set them on fire. One day as we were at recess in the school playground an Israeli Jeep drove past, and someone threw a rock at it. The Jeep stopped and reversed then the soldiers got out of the Jeep and walked into the school playground pointing their machine guns in all directions, they then grabbed the closest kid to them. They asked the kid who was already crying who threw the rock, out of fear the poor kid turned around and pointed to the first kid behind him who happened to be my middle brother. Immediately my brother started to cry and scream my name "Imad, Imad" but the Israeli soldiers only paused for a second than made a threat "if another rock is thrown at us again, we are coming back into the school yard and beat and take someone to jail". After threatening us they turned around walked back to their Jeep got into it and drove off. I could not wait for them to leave and once they were gone, I ran up to the kid that pointed my brother out and kicked him so hard in his ass that his pants split at the seam between his legs than called him a snitch. By the end of the school year my grades were just as bad as the year before at the other school. As the year ended all of us kids were back home for the summer to be with mom. By this time my mother was working in an Israeli cookie factory, so we had to stay home alone and since I was the oldest I had to take care of my brothers and sisters. We weren't allowed to leave the house while my mother was at work and we dared not disobey her. The front sheet metal door that was riddled with bullet holes was no longer there it was replaced with another metal door and the black walls inside the house from the fire were painted over and no longer existed. One afternoon that summer not long after we got home from school, we were playing in our small front yard when there was a knock at the front door. We all looked at each other and wondered if we should answer and who it could be since we never really had many people including family members knocking on our door. I approached the door and opened it and there stood two ladies, one of them holding the hand of a dirty little kid who was wearing a pointed cotton beanie hat on his head, the kind that has a string on each side to tie below the chin. The ladies asked for my mother and I informed them that she was not home. One of the ladies pulled the boy's hand towards me and said here and they turned around and left leaving the little boy with us. I pulled him by the hand and into the yard and he never said a word, he just followed me, and I shut the door behind me. We all went into our one-bedroom house, the little boy still said nothing as I sat him down at the edge of the bed and then we all stood around looking at him. Someone said "he looks hungry" so I retrieved an orange and handed it to him, he glanced at the orange than took a glance at us and immediately grabbed it and placed the orange into his mouth and bit into the peel of the orange. I grabbed the orange from him and peeled it then handed it back to him and he ate it like a wild animal. We spent the next few hours staring at him and whispering amongst each other about who this kid was. We heard the front door open which meant mom was home, so we ran to meet her screaming that two ladies had dropped off a little boy while she was at work. My mother walked into the house and seen the little kid sitting on the edge of the bed and immediately tears started running down her cheeks and she started saying, "my love my love come here" while walking towards him. She grabbed and hugged him, and it was at this time that we realized this little kid was our little brother. We just stood there quiet and in a bit of shock just watching, that was not the way he was when we parted a little under a year ago. She undressed him and took his beanie hat off and it became clear why they had him wearing a winter beanie hat in the hot summer. He had a baseball size knot in the center towards the back of his head with a small hole in the middle of it which looked infected. My mother was there for some time squeezing pus out of it through the little hole. Within the next few days I went back to my summer job at the bakery and of course same hours and same pay. Unfortunately, my father who migrated to the US had somehow forgotten he had a wife and six children back in Jerusalem because he never sent my mother any money, I am guessing he was living it up in the US. I really can't say much about most of our relatives back home whether on my father's side or my mother side they just pretended we did not exist and probably would have been satisfied if we did not exist at all. The only ones who helped us were my father's dad and my mother's mom who would pack the leftover food into a basket and let me take it home with me whenever I visited her. It was no secret most of our relatives were embarrassed of us simply because we were poor, hell we heard them say so a few times in front of us. My uncles (mom's brothers) were upset that my mother had a job and was now working to feed her children. They felt that she had shamed them because it was right for their sister to work because she was a woman. Nevertheless, none of her brothers ever gave her any help but only criticized her for working in order to survive and feed her six children. The only time her two younger brothers remembered her was when they got into an argument with their older brother and left the house where they all lived and had nowhere else to go. They would come spend a night or two by us and when they went back home we would see them again. I also heard them on many occasions taunting my mother about her husband being a crappie husband and father by forgetting about his wife and children as if it was somehow my mother's fault. They would also rather see her, and her six children starve to death rather than shame them by getting a job. Whenever my mother had a little extra money, she would surprise me when she came home from work with a small paper bag containing a mixture of ground nuts and sugar, these small things I can never ever forget about her. It was during these years that I experienced my first panic attack, one evening as my mother was visiting the old couple next door, I started to get this feeling doom and fear came over me. My heart was racing, and my mind was telling me I was going to die than everything around me seemed to be closing in on me. I ran out of the house and into the front yard and started to scream for my mother to come home. My mother came running into our front yard and took one look at me than   hugged me and asked, "Maalek Yekhi" (what's wrong honey)? I told her that I was going to die but she kept assuring me that I was fine all the while rubbing my head and hugging me. She eventually calmed me down than took me into the house and made me a hot cup of tea and continued to comfort me until all the fear was gone. Even though we our religion was Islam we did not know much about it and honestly as for the adults in our household they themselves were ignorant about Islam. As I learned much later in life about many Muslims, just because someone comes from a Muslim nation and is born into a Muslim family that does not mean he or his family know much about Islam! I will say this, my mother always mentioned Allah (GOD) and his beloved messenger Muhammad, peace be upon him, she truly and honestly loved Islam. I loved going to the Dome of the rock that sits on the grounds of mosque Al Aqsa (the holy sanctuary) which is the third most holy site on earth for all Muslims Mecca being first and Medina being second in Hijaz (Saudi Arabia). I played there with my friends in the courtyard and as far as I am concerned that is the most beautiful place on earth. Jerusalem in general had a special feel to it, it has a feeling of holiness that cannot be explain. One day I was walking my cousin home after playing in the court yard of the Dome of the Rock, we had to walk down a narrow street facing the Mount of olives which had a few businesses on it. As We past one of those business a young guy in his mid-twenties was using a metal grinder on a metal gate so we stood there watching for a few minutes as the sparks shot in all directions and that looked awesome to us kids. He lifted his grinding mask up and noticed that we were standing there watching him. He lips broke out into a big proud smile and asked "how are you young men doing" after we answered he put his mask on and went back to grinding on the gate. I walked my cousin the rest of the way to his house and then headed home myself. The next day I heard the bad news, that the welder we were watching the day before was shot 15 or 16 times by an Israeli soldier at about five or 6 AM while on his way to work in revenge for what another Palestinian did during that night to an Israeli soldier. That poor guy left behind a young wife and a new born child such was life under the occupation. We Palestinians the Israeli occupation to be free while the Israeli side fights us to break our will to fight and to be in total control without any resistance. After that summer break my mother found out about a school in the city of Bethlehem so she enrolled me and my younger brother in it. It was a Palestinian Christian school and its name was Al Injeeliai Al Lotharia again this was a school where some of the students went home and others lived there. The school where the classes were held was in Bethlehem but the building where we slept in was about a mile away in Beit Jalla. The Christians of Bethlehem are a proud people with deep roots in Bethlehem and are very nationalistic. They loved Palestine and most of them were staunch supporters and followers of late Dr. George Habash who was the leader of the PFLP movement. The actual school was about a block or so away from the church of Nativity, where it is believed that our beloved Prophet Jesus Christ peace be upon was born. Most of the students at the school were Christians with maybe a maximum of 10 Muslim students in the school at the time. The building we slept in only had two Muslims there and that was me and my middle brother. We were treated no different than the Christian students and not once in the year that we were there did we ever feel that we were being discriminated against because we were Muslims. I made many friends just as my brother did with most of the kids there. My soccer playing skills were beyond good so when we played soccer in small teams everybody would fight to have me on their team. The school paid a local Imam to come in on Friday for the purpose of teaching us how to read the Quran, but he did not show up on most Fridays. Some of the students who were locals invited us to their homes and their families welcomed us with open arms, feeding us and treating us as their own children. That's one thing I loved about living in Palestine, Christians and Muslims treated each other as brothers never noticing what the other person's religious beliefs were. I can honestly say those days in Bethlehem were some of the greatest memories of my life in my beloved homeland Palestine. In that school I started doing very well in my classes I even received an award once for academic achievements the award was a small magnetic chess game. Bethlehem and Beit Jala are two beautiful small cities with small rolling hills. I remember one morning waking up and had to use the restroom which was in a small building outside of the main building that we slept in. I stepped out the door and a breeze hit me which was kind of cool and warm at the same time and I have never ever felt that breeze ever again to this day in my life. At the end of the year the school took us on a long field trip to the northern part of Palestine/Israel we visited the Sea of Galilee, Haifa, Jaffa, Tel Aviv and Jabbel E Shiekh (Mountain of Shiekh) which is beautifully snowcapped and overlooking southern Lebanon on one side and Syria on the other. The view of the Mediterranean sea's blue water is breathtaking, a site I regularly yearn for but have come to except and understand the fact that I may never be able to see from the shores of Palestine during my lifetime and that truly weighs have on my heart. After that year in Bethlehem ended, we all went back home to be with mom and like the summer before I went back to my job at the bakery. Our mother had been to the USA visiting our father while we were at school and she had been preparing for our migration to the US. We were waiting for approval to migrate to the US, so we could be united and be a complete family once again. During that summer, I came home from work one day and my mother informed me that we (the boys) had received approval to migrate to the US. The time of migration would be in late August, I was so excited and happy that I felt like I was walking on clouds thinking about going to the US and be done with this miserable poor way of living and not having a father. I day dreamt daily about going to that beautiful place called the US of A that I had heard so much about. All the freedoms and no more living under threat and being treated like a prisoner like we do now in our own homeland by the Israelis. I had heard other Palestinians describe the United States of America as paradise on earth, a country where dreams are made, and the streets paved with gold. The week before I left Jerusalem, as I was walking out of the bakery, I was confronted by a few teenage boys with their father nearby and these guys were trying to bully me for some stupid reason. The sons were years older than me and happened to live next door to the bakery where I worked. I was upset but I just kept walking and did not respond to their comments, When I arrived home my mother could see I was upset about something, so she asked what happened. I was pretending like nothing was wrong with me, but she could see it in my face, so she persisted and insisted that I tell her until I gave in and told her. I remember her face turning red and she did not hesitate for one second, she grabbed me by my hand and walked me back to the bakery where the group was still standing in their front yard. My mother started screaming at them, reminding them that my uncle was in prison as a hero serving a 125year sentence for the Palestinian cause and my father was exiled for the same reason. She called them cowards for picking on child whose father and uncle are Palestinian heroes. She told them that they were very fortunate that my father and uncle were not there. She than spat on the floor in their direction then turned and walked away pulling me by my hand behind her. Not one person in that group dared open his mouth, rather they all hung their heads in shame because they knew she was correct about everything she had said. I informed the owner of the bakery that I would be leaving the next week that this will be my last week of work. The owner wished me luck and told me to tell my father that he sends his best. On that Sunday, he handed me my pay which would have been as usual 7 learras. When I got home, I unfolded the money to give it to my mom and found that he had given me only six learras beating me out of a day's work. I don't know if he did that intentionally or not, but he never made that mistake before. The day came for us boys to leave for the US, we took a taxi from Jerusalem and headed to the Lud airport which is now called Ben-Gurion airport. At the airport, my mother found a Palestinian couple who were traveling to Chicago and asked them if they would look after us and deliver us to our father in Chicago. This practice was not unusual among Palestinians traveling abroad, the couple agreed, and for that my mother was very thankful. My mother hugged and kissed us directed us to take care of each other and said she would see us in a year or so. If I knew than what I know now nothing on this earth and I mean nothing on this earth could have made me leave Jerusalem. I had no idea that this day would be the last time I see Masjid Al Aqsa and the end of simple but beautiful life, a life of real happiness, innocence and purity. There would be no more playing soccer ball because in the 70s it was not a popular sport in the United States. There would be no more climbing fig trees trying to find a branch that was best suited for making a slingshot in order to hunt small birds. Finally, we made our way and were now approached the Israeli airport security officers where they check our papers than allow us to head to the planes. The man we were with was at the front with our papers speaking to the Israeli officers and then turned around and pointed to me and my two brothers than showed our papers to the officers. After that the officer stepped off to the side to check something after looking at our papers they came back and pulled the man, his family and the three of us out of line than took the guy to a small room where he was questioned for about ten minutes. Finally, the man emerged from the room sweating and his face red as a tomato, he walked up to his wife and in a whisper said "shyaboonee" (they turned my hair gray) an Arabic saying when someone gives you hell. He told his wife that the Israelis were asking him how he knew us, what's his relations to my father and uncle and they told him that now they would be keeping a close eye on him. I was standing close enough to hear all of this and his final words were "we should have never agreed to take them". Shortly thereafter we boarded a KLM airplane for Amsterdam and then on to Chicago. The only thing I knew is that I was headed to paradise when really, I was headed to a place that would become a living hell for some years to come. No matter how poor we were in Jerusalem it was still better to live there than the life we were headed for. Knowing what I know now I would prefer to have been shot and killed by an Israeli soldier rather than have left Jerusalem. I always think "only if I could bring time back" but we all know that life does not offer that option!

Me on the far left and my beloved grandmother along with my two sisters and brother in Jerusalem, I think this was sometime in 1971 or early 1972.

Chicago

We arrived in Chicago on August 25, 1978 it was a bitter sweet day as we were going through the security lines one could look up at the Windows of the upper level where family members were looking down to see if their loved ones had arrived. My brothers and I were looking up at those windows to see if we could find our father and we found him but next to him noticed a blonde woman standing really close to him, they were both talking to each other and were waving at us. I immediately figured out that this woman had to be his girlfriend and at that point I turned to my brothers and instructed them not to waive back at them and none of us waived back. We finished through the security and stepped out of the doors to meet my father and the blond lady who was in fact his girlfriend. We picked up our luggage and hugged then walked over to the parking garage where his car was parked and headed home. As I mentioned before I heard from people who had been to the USA that the streets were paved with gold and I honestly believed that they were paved in gold. Never for a minute did I think that it was figuratively speaking and the statement about the streets being paved in gold was referring to the so many opportunities a person has at making it in this land of milk and honey. As we proceeded home I remember thinking to myself wow where is the gold in the streets and why are the streets so dirty looking. In Jerusalem, even though we were poor everything was clean there were sweepers that walked up and down the streets with brooms and garbage cans. But then again looking at the size of Chicago and the number of people one could understand how it would be so hard to keep clean. We drove past downtown Chicago and the city skyline was enormous and breathtaking to say the least I had never seen buildings that big made of glass in my life. We finally arrived home which happened to be on the south side of

Chicago on 65th Street and Western Ave. considering what we just left it's easy to say that the apartment we now lived in was like living in a castle. It had thick white carpet, couches, a refrigerator with food, a bathroom with shower with hot water, a telephone and a color television set that was on 24 hours a day if you choose to watch it. Back home when we took a bath mom put a round steal tub in the middle of the one-bedroom house and heated water in a big pot than poured it in the tub, giving a bath one at a time. Other than the streets in some areas being dirty I can say that much of what I heard about the USA was true, grocery stores so big that you can get lost in there for a minute or two, new and used car dealerships everywhere. Shopping malls the size of small cities and at night businesses were lit up with fast moving flashing lights which made the night to come alive. That summer our father showed us a good time by taking us to the beautiful Chicago lake front, Wisconsin Dells, Pensacola Florida to visit his friends, and New York city where we had relatives. Of course, we did all these things in the company of that blonde woman and it did not take long for us to overlook how wrong it was to have this woman living with us but even if we did abject what could possibly do about it. As for this blond woman she was actually a very nice lady, but that meant nothing any when thinking about my mother and I have to say I did not blame her. My father was to blame for this blatantly disrespecting my mother by having a woman living with us. Where we came from this was not allowed and unheard of to have a girlfriend let alone have her living in your house with your kids while having a wife. I understood than why he had forgotten about us and that was because he was too busy enjoying himself chasing women which took time and money to do. Unbeknownst to me the neighborhood we moved into was the Marquette Park area which happened to be one of the most racially tense areas in Chicago at that time. Blacks were not allowed to cross Western Avenue and they did not dare go one block west of Western

Avenue and other small minority groups were abused also. The Marquette Park area is where the late Dr. Martin Luther King marched and was attacked during the 60s. It was right out in the open there was a building on 71st St. a block west of Western Avenue which had a big white sign and painted on it was a big black Nazi swastika in the center with bold black letters that read **"WHITE POWER"**. This sign was professionally done, this wasn't just some scribbling on the wall with a can of spray paint and it was on the wall of the second floor too high for someone to just walk up and paint it. We were registered at Marquette grammar school where the students were predominantly European Americans with some Hispanics and a few Palestinians. When we started school, we could not speak a word of English, hell I think we only knew how to say hello and nothing else. It became immediately clear that Palestinian students were constantly being bullied, made fun of, spat on and in some cases physically assaulted by other students. It did not take long for tension to build up between me and white students. I guess they figured they had just received another Arab kid to bully around, but they were sadly mistaken when they made that assumption. They would say things to me which I did not understand but I knew from their demeanor it was nothing friendly or nice. Within no time I started to understand and speak the English language at least enough to now know what was being said to me. They called me names such as camel jockey, sand Niger and towel head. The term camel jockey was somehow supposed to be offensive yet no matter how hard I tried I could not see what was so offensive about someone riding a camel even though I had never been on one myself. Hell the only camel I ever seen in Jerusalem was the one used to take tourists on rides and that was it. I thought to myself, I just left a tough life behind something these spoiled kids know nothing about, yet these clowns think they were going to scare me? I already knew and made my mind up that there was no way I was going to allow them to treat me as they treated other Palestinian kids in that school! There was no way on God's green earth I was not going to accept any mistreatment no matter what I had to do even if it meant fighting these kids all day every day! I had wished for things to be different, but these kids were cruel so there had to be a reaction to their actions and to me that was violence because that seemed to be the only thing they understood! The weather in Chicago was starting to change winter was coming with a big surprise. In my 12 years of living in and around Jerusalem I had only seen snow once as far as I could remember and that did not last but a day or so before it vanished. We had already experienced the bitter cold of November and December but in January 1979 we were given a beautiful surprise by nature in the form of a snow blizzard. I had never seen that much snow in my life, enough snow to buried and crippled a great big City like Chicago. My brothers and I were neck deep in snow, it was unbelievably beautiful, and we loved everything about it. Back at school I was fighting on a regular basis I had so many fights that first year. If I was to put a number on the fights I had, I would say around 50 fights and I would not be exaggerating one bit, hell it might have been higher than 50. There was a Palestinian American kid in the school that I did not personally know who seemed to be always running away from other students from his grade which I believe was the eighth grade. I despised that Palestinian kid because he was a coward, being bullied by European and Hispanic Americans and never fighting back but instead just run away with a ridiculous looking smile on his face. I can still remember his face and how embarrassing it was that he was a Palestinian and a big coward at that. One morning a few months after we started school as we were waiting in front of the school for the bell to ring me and a white kid exchanged words. Within a minute or two I had three or four of his white friends surround me except one of them who looked Hispanic to me. I knew that I was going to have to fight, that I was going to have to make the first move to show them that out numbering me meant nothing at all. so, I made up my mind that my first move was to kick the Hispanic kid in his balls than move on from there to the next kid. I chose Hispanic kid simply because I could not believe that he stood there before me, a person of Brown color trying to oppress and bully me with those European kids. After kicking him in his balls he went down and then the other three jumped on me and I did what I could to fight back. I will say that I did not do too bad because they were hurt as much as I was. A school official came out and broke up the fight and by that time I was only tussling with the kid that I originally had the argument with. The official grabbed me and him and escorted us to the principal's office. I was angry and kept looking for a window of opportunity to present itself, so I could attack that white kid in the office, but I was unable to while in the principal's office. I did get that opportunity when they were taking us to our classrooms, the kid was walking about 5 feet in front of me and a male teacher was escorting us with his hand on my shoulder while walking next to me. I kept trying the free my shoulder from his light grip, so I could charge and attack the kid walking in front of us. Finally, he looked down at me and I said to him "I'm okay" and as soon as he got comfortable I bolted away from him. I ran up to the kid and quickly faced him then punched him so hard on the left side of his face that the right side of his head bounced off the wall locker three times. He grabbed his head in immediately started screaming and crying like a little girl yet an hour before he was a tough kid trying to bully me. I screamed something at him and bolted out of the front door than ran home. By the end of the school year most kids knew not to mess with me, not because I could beat them all up but because they knew I was not going to accept any bullying and would fight in a heartbeat. During that year I always had a fat lip or a shiner and so did the other person who attempted to bully me. One of the Palestinian kids named Mahmood was also new to the country like myself came to me one day and said "Imad there is this white kid who picks on me when I head home after school". I asked him to point the kid out and he did. I approached the white kid and told him that Mahmood was my cousin, that he had better leave him alone and if he picked on him again there was going to fight him. A few days later Mahmood came to me and said, "you scared this guy because he does not bother me anymore". That first year was a very rough year and by the end of the school year I knew how to speak and understand English well. Summer came, and my mother and sisters were due to arrive in the States but up to that point my father had not beat us much. I had seen his temper flare up once or twice but no heavy beatings. Before my mother and sister's arrival we had to move to a bigger apartment in order to accommodate the rest of the family. We moved to 66th and Artesian which was right around the corner from where we lived, and it was in this new apartment that I received my first major beating from my father. One day I had an argument with a Palestinian girl at school, but it was nothing big and somehow the girl's mother had gotten a hold of our home telephone number. That evening at about 5 or 6 PM as I was sitting at the kitchen table the telephone rang and my father answered it. I think he was on the telephone for a few seconds than hung up the telephone looked at me and asked, "you called her bitch"? That was the last thing I remember but none of the beating I received that evening. He beat me so bad that I passed out for something I did not do because I never called that girl a bitch, hell it was just a silly argument. My brothers told me what happened that evening, they said once I pasted out my father tried to wake me and snap me out of it for hours but was only able to totally do so. They said I kept mumbling things and not making any sense what so ever, that I was unable to hold myself up in a sitting position. Nothing worked he even tried putting me to sleep but they said I kept mumbling and saying things that made no sense.

Finally, Joan convinced him to take me to the hospital which he did and that is where I woke up a day or two later. When I woke up my father and Joan were standing by my bedside and my father was looking like he was very scared. He asked me how I was feeling and that he had a present for me which turned out to be a BB gun rifle. He then looked at me with a sad face and told me, "when the doctors ask you what happened tell them you fell down the steps of the back porch". It was easy to figure out even at that age that the BB gun rifle was sort of a bribe to keep my mouth shut not that I would have said anything against my dad for what he did. When the doctor asked me what happened to me, I told them exactly what my father had instructed me to say, that I fell down the steps of the back porch and they believed me. My mother and sisters arrived in Chicago and we went to O'Hare airport to picked them up and headed home but now without my father's girlfriend Joan who was gone but not forgotten by my father. My poor little innocent sisters were so happy to see their father but they had no idea what they were in for just as we didn't. From that day forward our daily lives were filled with insults, intimidations and beatings, hence living a nightmare. Immediately after my mother and sisters arrived my father began to beat my mother and us kids up on a regular basis for the smallest issue. The beatings would sometimes last for hours where he would beat one of us and then move on to the next kid until he got to my mother and sometimes he would just start with my mother first and move on to us. He would kick punch and body slam any one of us and did not matter to him if it was boy or girl. He once beat my poor mother so bad that he paused to catch his breath and then grabbed her by her ears lifted her off her feet and head butted her while we watched cowering in different corners of the living room. I was the oldest, I was 13 years old at the time so there really wasn't much I could do but if I could bring time back, I would have done something. I certainly would not hesitate to kill him and save my mother from years of living with agony and pain. He had a 41 Magnum Black Hawk hand gun that was given to him as a present by Joan and he was very proud of that gun. He was always bragging about that stupid gun, he did it so much that I can't count the times I heard him talk about how powerful this gun was, and how they stopped producing it because of its power. It was embarrassing to me when he did that especially when you looked at his friends faces as they listened to his bullshit. They had a look on their faces that clearly said, "THIS GUY IS AN IDIOT" and I know my mother felt that same way because she said as much to me. He sat us down at the dinner table one night after he beat my mother up and for dessert, he placed his prize possession the 41 Magnum on the table then gave us some food for thought when he said, "eat your dinner but when you're done, I'm going to shoot and kill all of you". As you can tell he did not follow through and execute his plan, big man was just tormenting a helpless and fearful mother and her 6 children. That was part of his mental abuse which sometimes came before or after the beatings. One day he decided that he was going to leave us and go live with Joan which was music to my ears and I was praying that he would actually never come back but I knew deep inside that this was just another way to torment us by leaving for a day or two and then come back with more physical and mental abuse. By this time, he was already poisoning my poor sister's mind, who was the oldest of the girls, with his madness. So, he decided to take her with him when he left us, and the poor girl had no choice in the matter even if she did not want to go with him. He had been using her to spy on all of us including my mother. She was reporting everything we did and said when he was not home, but it did not take us long to figure out what she was doing. We stopped saying or do anything when she was around, we also did our best not to get on her bad side. I think we were all at the news of him leaving us and started discussing what we were going to do about making a living.

We discussed getting some government assistance until we could figure out how to make living, hell if we survived in Jerusalem without him we could surely do it here in this land of milk and honey. Unfortunately for us within a day or two he was back, he telephoned the house early in the morning and threaten us that he was on his way home to beat everybody up. That of course scared the hell out of everyone including my mother, I remember all of us frantically running throughout the house trying to get our things together in order to make our escape to school. A few of us left first and rest followed but my youngest brother was slow in getting ready and as soon as he finished putting his shoes on he heard my mother say that my father was parking the car in front. The poor kid ran to the back porch and jumped from the second-floor window onto the backyard grass and amazingly enough he didn't break an arm or leg and that is just how much we feared him. As for my poor mother she had to stay and face that Demon because she had no place to go. My father went into the house and found no one there, so he went back out and got into his car to drive up and down the streets looking for us like a maniac, it wasn't like any other kids were out there because it was too early. Little did he know we were watching him through the bushes in front of people's homes and that is where we were hiding. It was a new year now at school and I was not worried about anyone messing with me, but this year my three sisters were at the school with us and they did not speak a word of English. Male students knew by now not to mess with me, but females were another story because they figured they could bully my sisters and I would nothing about it. One day after school one of the Palestinian American girls came running to me frantically to tell me that some white girls were planning on beat up my oldest sister when she came out of school. I thanked her and stood there waiting for my sister to come out of school and when she did I walked up to her and instructed her to stay close to me. We couldn't have taken 4 or 5 steps when some girls were approached fast from behind us, so I turned around to face them at the same time I pulled my sister behind me. It was three European girls and they were big girls who were older than me and my sister. I informed them that if they laid a hand on my sister that I was going to fight them as if they were boys. The prettiest one of the three tried to shove me aside and go past me to get at my sister and without giving it a second thought I cocked my right arm back and punched her dead square in the nose. Blood started to run out of her nose and she fell to the ground screaming. The other two girls took off running and I lost it, I got on top of her and punched her a few more times until finally somebody pulled me off her then I grabbed my sister and ran home. I will be the first to admit that beating on a girl is not something to be proud of, but I was left with no choice not to mention what I had to go through the year before. No can pass judgement on me in this situation, one would have to be there to understand the position I was put in. If I had not reacted, they would have lashed out violently against my sister without any mercy and not only that, but they would have continued to pick on her. The next day when I entered my class I was immediately sent to the principal's office and when I got there I found the girl I punched already sitting there with two black eyes and a swollen nose. As we sat there outside the principal's office the girl started talking to me and apologized, telling me that the whole thing was the other two girls' idea and that my sister had not done anything to them. She also apologized in front of the principal and admitted that she was in the wrong but that was no help for me the principal suspended both of us and sent us home. I will admit that by this time from all the physical and mental abuse administered by my father towards the whole family and especially my mother I was seriously thinking about killing him and was constantly fantasizing about how great life would be without him in our lives. One day we got invited by one of my father's relatives for lunch then as we were sitting there on the table the relative's husband showed my dad his gun. As soon as I seen that gun, I thought to myself "the first chance I get, I'm going to steal that gun" to kill my father with. I made up my mind that when my father hits my mother I was going to shoot and do my best to kill him. Everybody went outside to the backyard, but I stayed behind by making an excuse of having to use the restroom. When the coast was clear I went straight to where the gun was and took it and grabbed a few bullets. I stuck the gun in my waist, it was a small 380 automatic hand gun which was easy to conceal. I went outside and did my best to act normal and not show any signs of being nervous. Later that day I called my sister Fatimah to the side and showed her the gun than said to her "look we don't have to worry anymore, the next time dad hits mom I'm going to shoot and kill him" but to my surprise her eyes filled with tears and she immediately started shaking crying and said "NO". Her reaction blew me away and scared the hell out of me because I honestly never expected that type of reaction from her and thought she would be glad to hear what I told her. At that point I realized that maybe I was the only one felt that we would be better off if our father was dead. Even though all my brothers and sisters hated the way our father treated us and especially how he treated our mother it seemed that I was the only one who wanted him dead and gone. So now I could not possibly do it all courage was gone so I was stuck with this gun because there was no way I could return the gun it. I had to get rid of the gun before I got caught with it so with the help of a guy, I sold it for $85 to somebody at the flea market. There was no way I was going to attempt shooting him after the reaction I got from my sister, there just was no way. At the time the Arab community was scattered between 55th St. and 63rd St. from Western Avenue to a few blocks west of Kedzie. The Arabs of the time did not have much to do with the religion of Islam even though 99% were Muslim if not all. The source of income for most of those Arabs was grocery stores/liquor stores among the African-American communities. Many of those Arab business owners were killed during robberies committed by African-Americans and just to be clear Arab Muslims should have never been in those communities selling products forbidden by Islam. Many others who stayed in that type of business would later in life lose their families, but others took that dirty blood and started other businesses such as real state and used car dealerships. There was Arab nationalist clubs for each political group such as Fatah or PFLP and so on but nothing Islamic as far as I can remember. Sometime in the beginning of 1980 my mother started encouraging my father to purchase this small grocery store which was up for sale in the back of the yard area. At the time, my dad was penniless and we at this point were living check by check. He never was able to save up any money from the many years of working because he was blowing it away on himself and women. The only option was to go out and try to borrow the $25,000 from other Palestinian friends which was not going to be an easy task given my father's reputation as a womanizer and not much of a business man. They tried to obtain the money from a few friends, but things weren't looking good because his friends felt he would blow the money away and they would never get their money back but my mother was not the type of person who gave up easily. She kept pushing and pushing until she made it happen by persuading some of his friends to borrow them some of the money and even used whatever money she had from working at the cookie factory back home. An agreement was reached to purchase a business called "JOE'S STORE" a small grocery store located on 4404 South Wood St. in the back of the yard area. When purchasing a business from another Palestinian it is normal for the seller to stay on in the business with the new owners for two weeks in order to teach you the business but more important to acquaint you with the neighbors. After all, this was a small neighborhood store and the seller would introduce the new owners as his relatives in order to pass down the relationship he had developed with the neighbors. The store was in an old frame 2flat building, half of the first floor was the store and the rear half was a small 2bedroom apartment. The second floor was split in two apartments, a front apartment and a rear apartment. The owners were Palestinian an uncle and his two nephews who were in their 20s. The plan was, after the two weeks they would move out of the apartment and we would move into it. One night after closing the store during the two weeks of training, we were sitting in the rear apartment with the uncle and his two nephews. My father starts bragging to them about one of his old girlfriends who was from the state of Wisconsin whose name was Janice. He had a letter from her recorded onto a cassette tape and in it she was crying and talking about how much she loved him and cared for him. I knew about the tape and had heard small parts of it many times as he had played it for other people in bragging. I could never stomach sitting there listening to it for more than a minute and the fact that he would play it in front of our mother and us was disgusting to me. I never heard the whole message, nor did I care to hear it. As far as I was concerned it was downright embarrassing to watch my dad brag about this cassette tape. As far as I was concerned that tape meant nothing to me so about a month before he attempted to play it for the guy and his nephews, I recorded over her message with music from Television shows of the 70s such as CHIPS Highway Patrol and the opening music of Hawaii 50. He placed the cassette tape into the tape player, pushed play and to his surprise instead of Janice's cries there was the music of those TV shows for all to hear. He was fuming inside which was easy to see on his facial expression. I could sense the rage brewing inside of him and at that point I already knew without a doubt that the gates of hell were going to open for and I was going to receive a severe beating. He already knew who the guilty party was, and as soon as we got into the car, he started by first screaming about how I destroyed his tape and how I embarrassed him in front of those people. After the screams he started swinging at me hitting me in the head with his fist as I sat trapped in the backseat of the car and then he turned his rage to the windshield of the car cracking it with every punch he landed. The yelled and beat me all the way from 44 Street to 66 Street and into the house until he was satisfied. The thought of wanting to kill him was heavy on my mind again or that God would take me away because there was no way I was going to kill myself. I decided to steal another gun, this time from the people we were purchasing the store from, but this time I was caught and of course received the beating of my life. I wonder how he would have felt if he knew that I stole the guns to kill him. Only two people knew the reason why I was stealing these guns and that was me and my beloved sister Fatimah who never ever said a word to anyone.

The Back of the Yard's Neighborhood

It is 1980 and we were now living in the rear apartment while operating the store. The people in the new neighborhood were by far much more welcoming than the people in the Marquette Park area. At least that can be said for the three blocks east of the store, on the other hand the two blocks west of the store were a bit hostile towards us. I ran the store during those days, I was back working just as I did back home and missing out on my childhood. My father kept his Job as a machinist at Rockwell international, so I run the store while my mother cooked and cleaned the apartment. As for my brothers and sisters, they were all younger than me and they did what kids usually do. My mother would wake up early in the morning to open the store and shortly thereafter wake me up to get myself ready to go downstairs and tend to the store. The store hours were 7 AM to 10 PM so those were my work hours and of course I ask my mother if I could go out later in the day, but she would always say "let's wait and see when your dad comes home from work". Waiting for my father to home was a waste of time I already knew the outcome, he was not going to let me go out. I never blamed my mother because there was nothing she could say or do about anything. There was only one dictator running that house and it was my father. He came home from work and walked into the store with a mean look on his face never saying hi, hello or anything good just a miserable look on his face. I hated to see his car pull up because it was like doom and gloom had just arrived. The beatings continued nothing changed but most people had no idea about that side of him, it was so disgusting to watch how he acted in front of people which was like he is this honorable, righteous and caring person. I wish people had known how he really was, maybe just maybe someone would have been able to stop him from beating my mother. As for me by this time I felt no pain when he hit me, I was already numb by that time. Anyway, it was 1980 and domestic abuse was not that big of a deal during those days as a matter of fact the attitude of most people was that it was no one's business what happened in other people's homes. One day my mother said something that upset him which did not have to be anything big, it could something as simple as not agreeing with what he was saying. As usual he would start by calling my mother and call her family names and then he would beat her like a maniac. I did not witness this beating but was told by my sister and it was different he punched my mother in the left eye so hard that blood ran out of her eye instead of tears but that did not stop him it only gave him more empowerment and he kept beating her until she was able to get away and run out of the house to find a spot to hide. It is these thoughts that eat me up and make me hate myself for not killing him when I had the chance but that was long ago and of course the time has passed and we all know I cannot bring time back or I would. The school year was about to start, and we were now registered at Seward school located on 46th and Hermitage two blocks south of where we lived. I was in the seventh grade and was assigned in Mr. D's class where I made friends with two Mexican American kids, one named Robert the other named Fred and these two became my best friends. I couldn't hang out with them much after school because I had to work but nonetheless they were my best friends. Seward school and the people of the neighborhood in general were much different than the people of the Marquette Park area even though these neighborhoods were only 20 blocks from each other a mere five-minute drive yet were like two different worlds. The students at Seward school did not care if your name sounded Arabic or Polish nor did they care what part of the world you were from where they accepted you! After living in the

Marquette Park area, I had developed some hate for European Americans and understandably so, but that hate disappeared because the European Americans I met in the back of the yards were very friendly and like everyone else did not display any racism. And as far as school work was concerned nothing changed, I still did not care to do it because it was easy not to. I had spent so much time concentrating on defending myself and others during our stay in the Marquette Park area that I was way behind and felt it would take too much to try and play catch up. Whenever we had testing or the S.A.T test I would just guess all the answers and be the first one done with test. I still had a couple of fights even at Seward school, but it wasn't for someone trying to be a bully or because of my race, it was fights over stupid shit. I remember one fight I had with this white kid whose nickname was Rocky, you'd think I would have had an idea why he was nicknamed Rocky. I never connected the name Rocky with the character played by Sylvester Stallone in the movie Rocky, but I would surely soon find out why he was called Rocky. Me and Rocky had an argument one morning before school started so I called him out to fight, but Rocky was not looking to fight rather it was me who was being an asshole and a bully this time. I guess from all the fights I had at Marquette school and won I figured I could just pick a fight with anybody and win. But there was a difference this time because I was the bully and aggressor. Rocky and I agreed to wait until they opened the school doors and from there we would make our way into the bathroom and settle things before class starts. The doors opened and we went into the bathroom, Robert and Fred followed us in and as soon as we entered the bathroom Rocky and I went straight at it. Rocky got the best of me and then we split up and I went after him, but he got the best of me again and again. The more he got the best of me the more I wanted to fight him but finally we had to stop and make it to class so we both gave up and parted ways but, on that day, I received a reality check. That year I started to sneak my father's car out for joy rides I just got to the point where consequences meant nothing nothing to me. I was getting beat along with the rest of my family anyway so might as well get a beating for something, not to mention the fact the I was a prisoner in that store. One day at about noontime I took the car for a quick joy ride and was about three blocks from my house when I looked up and seen a black detective car behind me. I did my best to keep my cool but was scared and nervous at the same time. I was hoping the detective car would fade away, but the opposite happened. They started flashing their lights for me to stop and at that point I panicked and pushed the gas pedal as far as it could go. I turned the corner so fast that the car started to slide sideways and before I knew it, I lost control and crashed into a parked pickup truck. I hit the pick up so hard that it was now sitting on the hood of my father's car. I opened the car door and took off running and one of the detectives gave chase on foot, but I was too fast for him. After running for a block, I ran into a gangway and hide under a set of stairs for a few minutes until I felt it was safe to come out. I ran home and begged a neighbor to please go home with me because my father was going to kill me because I just crashed his car. By the time I got home my father was gone to the crash site, the police found out the address of our house and went to my house. My father went to the crash site with the police and in those days the police were much more understanding and lenient than they are these days. The officers made out the report which stated that my father was driving the car at the time of the accident because they found out that I took the car without permission. The shocking thing was, I didn't receive a beating but only some yelling and scolded the hell out of me and even threatened to send me back home. As the school year was coming to an end I was starting to understand the neighborhood better. A lot of the people in the neighborhood came from big families and some of those families were related to each other through marriages. That just made the neighborhood so much better everybody knew everybody and most of the people were close friends even if they had different ideologies. For the most part everybody got along but as we all know nothing in life is perfect and you had your problems here and there but no big deal nothing a fist fight could not fix. The borders of our neighborhood started at 43rd St and ended on 47th St. then it was Ashland Avenue from the eastern border and Damon Avenue was the Western border. We only had a few problems with a few white kids from those two blocks west of our house, but they were silly problems more comical and not serious at all. For example, one day this kid in his late teens named Gordon came to the store with a cloth attached to a stick it as if it were a banner and he started singing "free our hostages" referring to the hostages being held in Iran. I thought to myself "what an idiot" for mistaking Iranians/Persians for being Arabs but this was a very common misconception by most Americans. That summer came and went while I was trapped in the store which seemed like 24 hours a day 7days a week especially after wrecking my father's car. The Start of the school year was here now and I was in the eighth grade. By that time, I was already making friends with a few members of the neighborhood gang known as the Saints. A few were in my 8th grade class one was called Gringo and the other one was Fat Rick and I got along with both kids. They were normal kids other than the fact that they dressed like gangbangers. In those days gang bangers dressed a certain way and for the most part no one else dressed as they did. A few people may have come close to the dress code but majority of the people living in gang infested neighborhoods who were not involved in gang banging wanted nothing to do with the dress code because they did not want to be mistaken for gang members. I met another Saint called Santo in a totally different way, we had words in the school yard than he reached under his jacket and pulled out a sawed-off shotgun and pointed it at me and threatened to shoot me but after a few seconds he put the shotgun back in his jacket and took off running. He didn't have to go far because he lived kitty corner from the school. Thinking back on the incident I don't remember being scared or having thoughts of running in order to escape but stood there. I remember looking at him and listening to his threats but the only thing I remember was admiring the shotgun he was pointing at me. Later I found out that Santo was constantly in and out of juvenile detention and not long after the incident between me and him Santo was back in juvenile detention. Also, in the neighborhood were two party crews one called "Thee Boyz of 45th", the other "Party Boys of 45th" but these two groups were well liked in the neighborhood and even catered to especially by those running the neighborhood park (Davis Sq., Park). The Saints on the other hand were the out casts because they were gang bangers. My father had purchased a motorcycle small dirt bike for me a red Yamaha GT 80. I would ride the motorcycle through the neighborhood and every now and then get chased by the police, but they couldn't catch me because I would go into a dirt field behind the neighborhood known as Damen Field where the police could not go. My father did attempt at times to be a loving father by purchasing his wife and his children some materialistic things as if that was going to compensate us for his physical and mental abuse that he was still committing. Sure, I accepted the gift and was happy to receive it from him but also hoped he stopped the beatings and mental abuse. I mean there was no way we were going to say, "no we don't want it because you physically and mentally torture the shit out of us" or something like that besides we worked in the store and made the money. Without a doubt he Would have destroy whatever he may have purchased if he sensed a bit of displeasure. I saw my father destroy TVs, refrigerators, cash registers, chairs, doors and whatever else was in his way during those rage episodes. I was starting to drift away from Robert and Fred and to leave started to hang out with some of the young guys who considered themselves Saints any chance I got. One evening as I was hanging out in front of one of Saint's house on 45th and Hermitage we noticed two guys walking towards us but when they got to the corner of 46th they made a right turn. We followed and stop them on 46th and Pauline, with me was Fat Rich, Mo and two other kids. We knew these two guys had to be gang bangers by the way they dressed so I addressed them "what you be about" a term used to inquire about a person's gang affiliation? They said they did not belong to any gang, but we knew they were lying, as I already explained in those days only gang bangers dressed the way they were dressed. They were coming from the neighborhood south of ours which belonged to the Latin Souls, 22 boys and Satan disciples so I accused them again of being one of the three, but they kept denying it. I didn't like the look on the face of the kid standing closer to me, so I swung and punched him in the face. The other kid who was standing to my left jumped back about a foot reached in his hoodie sweat jacket and pulled a revolver out and aimed it at the side of my head and squeezed the trigger three times before I could make a move. I heard the "click click click" but no boom, this was 1981 and guns in the hands of gang bangers at the time were pretty much junk. The two guys took off running towards 47th St. and my friends were already about 100 feet away before I moved a muscle. As I said the reason why that gun did not fire is because guns and ammo were old and unreliable in those days plus Allah (God) did not call for me hence it was not my time to go. I did not have any fights at school that year and the only beatings going on was the ones being handed down was by my father to the whole family. Than towards the end of the year near graduation time I noticed a kid picking on a special Ed kid who used to pick up aluminum cans around the neighborhood who never ever bothered a soul. I approach the kid who was the aggressor and asked him to leave the special

Ed kid alone, but he just ignored me and kept on harassing and making fun of the him. It reminded me of the kids being picked at Marquette school so the next thing I knew I was pounding the aggressor in the face without any mercy. There was blood all over the place from his nose and mouth especially on the windbreaker I was wearing that I had to throw it away before I got home. The next day I went to school as usual but when I got to my classroom my teacher told me that I had to go see the lady teacher in the classroom next to door. That was the classroom of the kid I beat up the day before. I walked over to her class and knocked on the door, when she saw me, she stepped out of classroom and started to scold me about the incident. I tried explaining to her what happened but the only thing she kept saying was "do you know that he had to get six stitches inside of his mouth, he can't speak or eat". Than for her last statement she said "you can forget about going on the field trip to Springfield Illinois with the rest of your class" which really meant nothing to me. So, my class went to the field trip without me, and the amazing thing was that they allowed me to graduate even though I was failing in all subjects. School ended, and I was at the store working as usual while every other kid my age enjoyed the summer, but I hung out with some of the younger Saints whenever I got to escape the store even if it was just for an hour. In those days hanging out with kids who were already Saints did not mean you were a member because one had to be initiated into the gang. The process of initiation was to walk through the line and this line is made up of 4 to 5 guys on each side. The person being initiated had to walk in between while the guys while being kicked and punched. It was in your best interest to make it through as fast as you could without falling because if you did the whole group would pile up on you and beat you mercilessly. Back in those days gang bangers were already tough and most of the time the person was not interested in academics. You were already tough then you became a gang banger not the other way around which seems to have become the case some years down the line. As I said for the most part guns were junk and good ones were not as readily available in the late 70s or early 80s as they are now. You had to face your enemy close up with your fist on most occasions and if you did not have the heart and guts for that then naturally you wanted no part of being a gang banger and neither did the gang want any part of you. I am not saying that every single gang member in Chicago now a day is soft and not tough, but I am saying a lot of guys getting hooked up with gangs these days and for some time now have no business being hooked up. Being able to shoot people and getting a tattoo on your face are not the only thing that make you a standup gangster there is loyalty, trust and not betraying your brothers by informing on them. It was now time for me to go to high school and I was designated to Kelly high school which is located on Archer Avenue and California Street. At Kelly, I met people from many different neighborhoods, there were a few freshmen students who were from a street gang called Satan's Disciples from 42nd Street and Artesian. I also met other Disciples from other branches like 24th and Rockwell, 21st and Oakley and 63rd street. There were a few Saints at Kelly Crazy Joe, Bobby D, China man and Little dirt ball, two of them may have even been seniors at the time and were laid back for the most part. Without a doubt the Disciples had the most members, so they were the majority as far as Street gangs were concerned but the European Americans were the majority at the school. I became very good friends with two of the Satan Disciples Bee and Slick who were in my division class. From the start, I was cutting all my classes but would always make sure I made it to my division class. Everybody knew if you attended division than you would be marked as present for the whole day and no one from the school would contact your parents. I was everywhere with my new Disciple friends we visited their branches on two four and two one which I had mentioned above and met other Disciples.

I kicked it off pretty good with a Disciple from 21st and Oakley who was called Pee Wee. I remember him asking me what my nickname was so I said I didn't have one, he looked at me and said, "bro your nickname is Demon". I had been thinking for some years now that I was cursed because of the hand I was dealt in this life so when I heard Pee Wee say I should be called demon that played right into my thinking. I had just made 14 years of age and in my foolish thinking I thought that I must be doomed that maybe I was born on Aug 6 of 66 rather than Aug 1st, hence three 666s and that I was a part of something evil which would explain the situation I found myself in. Some years later I purchased a big painting of a Devil siting on a toilet smoking a cigarette which I hung in my bedroom over my bed and my brothers and sisters would ask me "how do you sleep in that room". Even though I sometimes hung out with the Disciples and considered them my good friends that in no way meant I a Satan Disciple because I already considered myself a Saint. Most people would later know me as Devil from the Saints and the name demon faded away. While hanging with the Disciples I had no problem with helping them against their arch enemy the Latin Kings if something went down. Like most gang bangers at the time I carried a permanent marker and I would make my mark where ever I went S I. N (Saint Nation). My Satan Disciple friends knew that I lived in a Saint neighborhood and they knew I was representing the Saints because I never hid it from them. I marked the walls in front of them and they never said anything until tensions started to build up between the two gangs at school. One day, Pee Wee was visiting Kelly high school and when I stepped out of school, he approached me and said, "what's up Demon I thought you were going to roll D, what's up bro"? I gave him the business politely by saying, "there is no way I would be anything other than a Saint". I also told him I did not see a problem with our friendship since there really was no war between the Saints and the Disciples at the time. He didn't seem to like what I said and started walking away than turned around and said, "fuck that shit bro, D love" but I just walked back into school. As I crossed the street to go back into the school I looked back and found Pee Wee mad dogging me and mumbling something to another Disciple called Pumps. When I walked into the school I ran into a Disciple I knew called Little Rabb in the hallway so I approached him and said, "look bro me and Pee Wee just had words because of my affiliation with the Saints and now he's mumbling shit, if he has a problem with that let him know we can handle the shit like men". Little Rabb told me he was going out to where Pee Wee was and he would rely the message to him. The next period I was told to go outside so me and Pee Wee can go head up (have a fist fight). I went outside and the Disciples were standing in a group near the bleachers next to the baseball field. As I approached Pee Wee started to walk towards me saying "what's up mother Fucker come get some" and from there we started to fight as we were fighting his boy Pumps walked up on the side of me and sucker punched me on the side of the head. Just than a Chicago police squad car which sometimes patrolled the school was coming up the street, so we were warned and stopped fighting than walked off in different directions. Even after that a 22 Boy named Sak who I was cool with tried getting me to become a 22 Boy but as with Pee Wee, I told him the same thing and that was the end of that. I was still cutting my classes but was no longer hanging out with the Disciples. I was not hanging around with the Saints at Kelly because all of them were going to their classes and were trying to graduate so they had no time for screwing up. I had another friend who was in a gang called the Spanish Chancellors from 28th street. I cut school with him one day, on that day we went to his house in Bridgeport and when we came back to school later that day as I got off the bus on Archer Avenue, I noticed my father's car parked in front of the school, but he was not in it. I ran into the school from the side door and came out through the front. By the time I came out he was already sitting in the car waiting for me. I got into the car and he gave me a dirty look then said, "every day you come to school but the teachers never see you in class so where are you going and what are you doing"? I did not even bother to answer him and just looked straight ahead. As he drove, he noticed that the left sleeve of my sweat jacket was pulled over my hand, so he told me to pull it up. Earlier that day I had written ST. N on my hand with a permanent marker when he saw the writing, he called me an animal for writing on my hand, but he never asked what it meant. He told me that I was not going back to school since there was only a month or so left for school to end and I was failing every class so badly that there would be no way to make my grades better. He scolded me non- stop even after we got home and told me that I wasn't going anywhere that the only thing I should look forward to is working in the store! Shortly after school ended bad news came from back home that my grandfather on my dad's father who I loved dearly was on his deathbed. My mother spoke to me and asked me if I could handle taking care of the store and watch over my brothers and sisters while her and my father went back home to see about my grandfather. I assured her that I would take care of everything that she could count on me. My father's demeanor took 180° turn towards me now, he was treating me nice as if we were friends, but I knew that it was a big act. At that time there was nothing anyone could say to convince me that my father did not hate me. My parents purchased plain tickets and flew back home, and they were supposed to be gone for only two weeks but they ended up staying there for a total of 27 days because my mother's father also passed while they were there. I opened the store on time and did not close it any earlier than I was supposed to. I took care of my brothers and sisters and made sure they were doing what they were supposed and let them to go out and have fun like other kids. They were still in school but there were only a few days left before the school year ended. During those 27 days I kept the store stocked and put to the side all the profit money made to the side. Everything was going fine even though I did go out at night and gang bang with my brothers the Saints of 45th. As in every gang everybody nicknames, Stony, Malo, Henio, Mustang, Sir Player and so on. The gang was made up of all ages ranging from 13 years old to as old as 50 and the older members had been in the gang since their teen age years. About four days after my parents left a guy I knew came into the store with a Smith and Wesson 38 detective special revolver which he wanted to sell, and I bought it along with some bullets. I got to use the gun once against the 48th street boys but a few days later my sister Fatimah came home from swimming at the park pool crying. I asked her what was wrong with her? She said Joe L was making fun of her and calling her a camel jockey. I told her not to worry that I'll take care of it and would make sure he never bothered her again. I was furious at what she told me, my blood was boiling to the point that I would have killed Jim if he was standing in front of me at that time. Joe L was related to Santo the one who pulled the sawed-off shotgun on me in the school playground. To me at that point I didn't care who Jim is related to because he was wrong for fucking with my sister. Deep inside I wanted to kill him but that was out of the question but beating him up and scaring him was another thing. I was already putting work in for the nation against oppositions, especially against our arch enemies the Latin souls and 22 boys of 51. A few days later, shortly after I opened the store early Sunday morning, lo and behold Jim walked into the store. The 38 was under the cash register counter where I kept it close to me. He walked to the milk cooler which was at the back of the store and I came out from behind the counter and calmly walked to the front door and locked it. I had already placed the 38 in my waist and when he came back to the counter, I walked up to him grabbed him by his shirt put the 38 right under his nose and said, "what the fuck did you say to my sister at the pool, who are you calling a fucking camel jockey you mother fucker"? He was shaking and winning, then while still holding the gun to his face I threatened him that the next time he fucks with someone in my family he's going to get what's inside the gun and pushed him towards the front door. I told him to get the fuck out and didn't allow him to purchase the gallon of milk he had come in for. Within 10 minutes Chicago police officers came into the store and placed me under arrest. They searched the store and found the gun than took me to the police station charged me assault with a deadly weapon and position of firearm. Since the crime was committed with a gun there would be no release from the police station. I had to see the judge which would happen the next day, so I was transported to the juvenile detention center on 11th and Hamilton to spend the night. At the detention center, I met with a case manager who looked at me and said, "getting arrested at your age for a crime with a gun, you're starting your life out on the wrong foot, just want you to know that" but at the time of her statement that did not mean anything to me because I was a teen age kid who thought I knew it all. Throughout my life her statement has always played in my head every time I found myself in some kind of trouble. That case manager hit the nail right on the head when she made that statement. The next day a family friend the son of the owner of El Milagro tortillas sent their family attorney to represent me in court who was able to get me released. My mother would call from Jerusalem to check on us whenever she could and I assured her everything was fine. There was no way I was going to tell her about me being arrested because she was already dealing with enough in her life. She called me a few days later to tell me that my grandfather (her father) had passed away and so did my other grandfather (dad's father). My parents returned from Jerusalem and found the store clean fully stocked and the profits there in their hands. It was the end of July and the next day after working half a day I asked my mother, even though I knew she couldn't make that decision, if I could go out hoping by some miracle she would just say yes and allow me to go. That was just me Wishfully thinking but unfortunately, she said "honey, ask your father please". So I built up the courage to go upstairs where my father was sitting on the couch with his feet resting on the center table, I walked as close as I could to him and said "dad can I go out for a little while" he looked at me and gave me that nasty look he always gave me and said, "you have no feelings, my father just passed away and you're asking to go out, get out my face" than he shoved the center table towards me with his feet. I thought about his statement for a second "my father passed away" as if his father was not related to me. My mind was made up and I did not care what the consequences were going to be. I had enough of his shit and if my mom was not going to remove us from around him than I was going to remove myself. At that young age I managed a small business took care of five children for almost a month, and sure I had one problem but in all I didn't do too bad and here is my father having a fit because I asked him to take a break for a few hours. I had it up to my ears with his bullshit, so I turned around and walked out the door not caring what the consequences were going to be. I did not care that I had no money in my pocket or a place to sleep, the only thing I knew was that it felt as if I had died and went to heaven to be free from him and the madness. I had become acquainted with four brothers Big A, K O, Problem and Little Problem who were all Saints. These four lived on 48th and Troop street in a neighborhood belonging to one of our enemies the 48th street Boys. These brothers cruised around the neighborhood all day long in a brown and beige Ford club wagon van blasting disco hot mix music from WBMX radio station. They saw me hanging out in the neighborhood a few hours after I left my house, so they picked me up. I hung out with them all day and most of the night then they found out that I was not going home, knowing I had nowhere to go they took me in. Now I was staying with them and it was non- stop gang banging day and night. As soon as we woke up, we would get cleaned up than put on our gang colors which are baby blue and black then we would head out to the neighborhood. As I had said before guns were hard to come by in those days, they weren't impossible to get but it was difficult to get our hands on them. We had a few guns mainly single shot sawed off shotguns and 22 caliber pistols and we were somewhat careful with them in order not to lose them to the police. Gang banging was tough in them days because it was mostly fist fighting, using baseball bats, chains or whatever else you could get your hands on hence the term humbug. From the moment we left their house to the moment we returned, there was not a dull moment in our gang banging adventures. We would sneak into neighborhoods surrounding ours and smash those we caught slipping (not paying attention) from other gangs like the Latin souls, Bishops, 22 boys and the 48th street boys who are now known as the La Raza street gang. It did not matter who they were, we just wanted to inflict as much pain and damage on our enemies as we could. We fucked up a lot of people, but we knew that they were definitely gang bangers. As I said there was a dress code for bangers which consisted of Dickey pants, converses All-Stars (Chuck Taylor's) with the laces tied a crisscrossed style, muscle shirts and bandannas usually your gang colors and there was the war sweaters (the old high school sweaters made up of your gang colors) but if it was dress-up time for parties it would be baggy pants, Stacy Adams, a dress shirt, Blazer leather coats and for some people gangster brims. I was now on my own living with a family of gang bangers who were known as a family of trouble makers and heavily involved in the Saints street gang. Sad to say I was happier than I had ever been in years, so I thought. We spent our day cruising around the neighborhood listening to disco music, chasing girls and inflicting pain on our enemies in their own neighborhoods. That summer some new guys were supposed to get initiated into the gang and even though I was considered a Saint I had not been through initiated yet. We met at the basketball courts in the park and the line was formed then the new guys went through, so I got ready for my turn but one of my older boys called Cochise pulled me to the side and whispered to me "not you". When he seen the confusion on my face, he said that I was already putting in more work for the nation than some of the boys who had been Saints for a long time. I didn't stay away from home long, my mother found me and talked me into going back home but that would not be the first or the last time that I would leave home. One day in the summer of 1982 as me and my father were standing in front of our store, so he said to me, "there are some young men your age and older who are volunteering to go to Beirut/Lebanon to fight alongside their Palestinian brothers against the Israelis, do you want to go"? I did not hesitate for a second in saying, "yes" he then said, "good now you have to convince your mother". I knew that was going to be a hard task to do and there was no chance she was going to agree to me going. A few minutes later my mother came out of the store and walked over to us and my father told her "your son wants to go to Lebanon to be a freedom fighter". My mother's face instantly turned red and she was very clear in what she said "if you think you're going to send my son to get killed for those crooks, referring to Arafat and his bunch you are wrong, as soon as my son gets on a plane to go fight I will also be getting on a plane with the rest of the kids after I divorce you". After listening to what she said he became angry and started calling her names as usual. If he could have beat her into agreeing he would have but he knew it would do him no good. My mother would die before agreeing to sending me to fight in Lebanon. I hated being home, I hated working in the store and all that hate was because of my father it was living in hell on earth. I would rather go to Lebanon and fight with the very likelihood of being killed rather than live with him and that is the honest to God truth. A few days later my mother told me that my cousin, the one who knew his ABCs, was coming from Jerusalem to stay with us for good which was a great surprise because he lived such a good life there. By this time my family was doing okay financially, we weren't rich or anything like that but we were okay living a blue-collar life style or maybe a notch or two over. My cousin's father was doing well financially when we were penniless back home, but he never ever helped us out. This was the same guy who was embarrassed of being our uncle because we were too poor for him but now, we are good enough to have his son live with us. After my cousin arrived, it didn't take long for me to see why his father sent him to live with us. All he talked about was about the drugs they were smoking back home and a bunch of other retarded shit which he thought sounded cool. He talked as if he was proud of his drug use which sounded stupid coming from a kid who was pampered and never had to struggle who never received a beating from his dad. This was the same kid who I used to watch being fed with a spoon by his mother at the age of 9 or 10 and insisted that his mother tell him a story while feeding him, never being offered a bite of food by any of them as if I was invisible. He was a pain in the ass than and he was trying to be now, he was still weak and gutless just as he was when we were kids. I would have to stick up for him and even fight on his behalf because a spoiled little coward. He tried to cling to me but me and him had nothing in common and I was on another page a page that might cost him his life. I knew he was too soft, and I didn't want anything to happen to him because at the end of the day I would be to blame, his family would make him out to be an angel. On one occasion, I caught him walking down the street in the neighborhood dressed in some gang banging clothing I had at home and he looked downright silly. Whenever I returned home, I would be back working at the store helping my mother. During one those times I purchased a 22 caliber Browning rifle, a Winchester type where the clip which holds the bullets is a tube under the barrel, you pull a rod out and load the 22 rounds through a small port. My cousin knew where I kept the gun so one morning as I was running the store he and my sister were in the back apartment. Suddenly, I heard my sister screaming "stop, stop" so I ran up the short set of steps and found him pointing the rifle at my sister's head. I rushed him and yanked the rifle away from him then I asked him what the fuck was his problem. He immediately stuck his hand in his pant pocket and came up with a bunch of bullets then said, "there's nothing in the gun". I asked if he was sure and he said yes while showing me the bullets again. I pointed the gun at his legs and he took off running into the store, so I followed aiming the gun at his leg then finally squeezing the trigger, lo and behold the gun went off putting a hole through his pants in his right thigh. He started hopping up and down on one leg moaning, groaning, and screaming. I screamed at him over his cries "I thought it was empty, you could've killed my sister". My sister was watching the whole thing and almost went into shock she was shaking and crying because I shot him but not because he could have killed her. I helped him hobble his way behind the milk cooler where the sink was right next to the stairs leading to the back apartment than told him to pull his pants down so I could see his wound. I looked at his wound and it was not bad there was a small hole, but no blood was coming out of it. I knew enough to know that it was a flesh wound and he was not going to die from it. He asked me to call an ambulance but I told him to sit down and wait for my mother to come home. When my mother came back, I told her I shot my cousin in his leg and he was okay. Understandably so, my mother's face turned pale and she started screaming at me. I immediately walked around the counter and was out the door and back on the streets as usual because there was no way I was going to stick around and wait for my father to come home and must listen to the bullshit he had to say. After I left they took my cousin to the ER and made up a story about him being a victim of a drive-by shooting. They bandaged him up at the hospital and sent them home without the need of any medications. After I was gone my mother found out the full story from my sister but was still pissed at me for having the gun in first place. I was back on the streets again gang banging and hanging out all night long on the streets, chasing girls. We drank drank but I myself was not much of a drinker because I did not like the taste or the smell of it! Sometimes when I was unable to go to Big A's house, I would sleep on the park bench or in my boy Puma's van and would clean myself up in an abandoned building in the neighborhood that only had cold running water which did not matter because it was summer time. After a short stay on the streets I was once again back home and working the store as usual. This time I found out from a next-door neighbor that my cousin who also worked in the store when I was away had been buying our neighbors electronic gifts such as radios, watches, etc. It doesn't take a rocket scientist to figure out what this cock sucker was doing. I knew that this prick had no money because his dad was not sending him any, so he had to be stealing cash out of the register from the store. I confronted him and he admitted to me that he did steal money from the cash register but asked me not say anything to my mother. There was no way I was going to agree to that for two reasons, the first one is he was stealing from my mother and the second was if I left again, he was going to do the same thing after I was gone. As soon as I got the chance I told my mother everything my cousin was doing. As I was telling her he walked into the store and my mother looked at him and said in Arabic "shame on you for stealing from your aunt, do I not give you whatever I give my kids"? I was standing next to her behind the counter and he was standing directly across from us on the other side of the counter. He looked at me and said an insulting Arabic saying, "may your religion be cursed". I lost it and ran around the counter and as I was approaching him I said, "you're stealing from my mother you pig and you think I'm going to cover up for you" then punched him in his left Eye so hard that it instantly swelled up and started to turn black and blue. Not long after that incident he was sent back home to his own family where his thieving coward ass belonged. But before he was sent back to Jerusalem, he got into two incidents with people at the store and as usual I had to come to his aid. He was standing in front of the store while I was working in the store when I heard arguing coming from outside. I walked out the store and found him tussling with two guys our age who had just moved into the neighborhood a month or two before. Immediately I joined the fight, my cousin left the fight and ran into the store leaving me to fight the two guys on my own but within minutes he was out of the store brandishing one of my guns. The two guys seen the gun and took off running, I ran over to my cousin grabbed the gun and pointed in the direction of the two guys who were running than squeezed the trigger, but nothing happened because the gun was not loaded. A few days later there was another example proving that my cousin was an idiot, again he brought out a gun without it being loaded. The second incident was started by me rather than him, a girl had just moved into the neighborhood from the north side of Chicago and she was very hot, and I always made it my business to hit on her when she came to the store. One day she walked into the store with a guy so I asked the girl if that was her boyfriend which caused the guy to immediately respond to my inquiry, "yea I am and what the fuck is it to you"? That's all it took for me to go into a rage, within a second, I was around the counter and on the guys ass, but his girl got between us. My cousin was with me in the store when this happened and of course he ran upstairs and retrieved a 25 automatic and was immediately back down in the store. Her boyfriend seen my cousin with the gun, so he turned around and ran out the store. But this time my cousin had the gun in one hand and the clip in the other than by the time my cousin handed me the gun with the clip her boyfriend was already out into the street. I immediately gave chase and by the time I hit the sidewalk he was already turning the corner, by the time I got to the corner he was almost at the alley where I aimed at him and fired once and no more. There was no way I was going to hit him that far with a 25 automatic that much I knew. I am not blaming my cousin for the incident but I am blaming him for bringing down the gun there was no reason for him to retrieve a gun in either of those incidents and I take the blame for using them but in a state of rage there is no such thing as rational thinking. One day as I was cruising around the neighborhood in my father's car listening to music with a few of my boys there was a kid standing on the front porch of his house at the top of the steps on 44th and Hermitage. The kid was throwing Little Rocks at cars that were passing by and as we passed, he threw one at my car and missed. I immediately stopped and reversed the passenger in my car told him to stop that shit than we drove off. Than as we came back around a few moments later he did the same thing but this time I stopped the car and ran up the steps and slapped him in the back head and told him that he better not do that shit again. A year or so later a fire erupted in my neighborhood which burned down four or five houses to the ground and a family of five or six people died in one of the 2nd floor apartments. This fire happened on the same block where the kid threw rocks at my car and the boy's father told the cops that I may have started the fire in retaliation for his son throwing rocks at my car. So that statement put the Bomb and Arson division detectives from 11th and state, Chicago police headquarters on my tail. They were out looking for me leaving business cards everywhere they could, and they also left a card at my boy's Big A's house on 48th and Troop instructing his family to tell me that I better call them immediately. When I found out, I called the detectives and asked why they were looking for me and if they wanted me, I was at the house on 48th and Troop.

When I called the detectives, I had no idea what they wanted me for and I knew for sure whatever it was it had nothing to do with me because the card they left behind had bomb and arson not gang crime or homicide. About half an hour later they showed up at the house, I came out and they instructed me to get in the backseat of the car which I did. They asked me what I knew about the fire on Hermitage, I gave them a look that said, "what the hell are you talking about" then gave them a simple answer, "I don't know anything about it". One of the detectives turned to look at me and said, "we hear it was you who did it because of the little boy who threw a rock at your car sometime back". Hearing that made me sick to my stomach, but I kept my cool and told them that they were wasting their time talking to me about it because there was no way in hell that I would set someone's house on fire because a stupid little kid threw a rock at my car. We went back and forth for a minute or two and I was sure they knew that I had nothing to do with that fire, but they thought they could get me to admit to the shit but eventually, they told me to get to the fuck out of the car and left. Six or seven months later I heard that a firebug was arrested on the north side for starting a fire and he also confessed to a bunch of other fires including the one in my neighborhood. The summer ended, and it was the same story throughout the summer I would leave and go live with my boy's family on Troop street who were now my best friends or at least that is what I thought at the time. I decided that I would go back to Kelly high school and I honestly had good intentions but within a couple weeks I was already having static with the Satan Disciples, the 22boys and stone Chicanos who were all allies of each other. There was a new member of the Saints whose nickname was Little B who was also going to Kelly high school at the time. One morning Little B approached me and told me that a kid in school kept harassing him because he joined the Saint. That kid who was harassing Little B was an associate of the Disciples but not a member. During my lunch period, I was standing in the lunch line talking with Little B when I noticed the kid who was harassing him standing in the same line about six or seven people ahead of us. I walked up on the side of him than sucker punched him and proceeded to beat the shit out of him. As luck would have it the police officer who worked at school was standing near and he seen the whole thing. I was arrested and transported to the police station on 61st and Racine they held me there for a few hours then released me. The next day while at school three Disciples and one Chicano caught me in the staircase between the guys and girl's gym. They jumped me, even with four of them attacking me I held my own ground and at the end of the attack I felt a sense of pride because I was still standing. I put up a hell of a fight against four guys who were bigger than me and that made them stop their attack and walk away. As I was walking away from them my mind was racing, trying to figure out what to do to get back at them right then and there. I did not want to wait for another day to sneak up on them in their areas to serve them. They walked into their gym class and I walked out into the hall way. I made my way to my locker and left in it what belonged to the school and took out my personal belongings. I decided at that moment that this would be my last day at that school. One of the Disciples called Toes who I knew before he had become a Disciple was assigned to woodshop during that period so I walked down the hall to the back of the school and down the stairs to woodshop. I looked through the window and there he was, I caught his attention and waved for him to come out of class. He stepped out, I told him that his boys jumped me, that I wanted him to give me a 2 x 4 and if he didn't then I would take it out on him. I already knew he was a coward, like I said I knew him before he became a Disciple. He walked back into class and grabbed a small piece of a 2 x 4 and handed it to me then as I started to walk away, he said "man bro please don't tell anybody I gave that to you". As I kept walking, I assured him that I wouldn't and not to worry because there was not going to be any talking. Unfortunately for Toes a few years later I heard that he was shot killed by the Latin kings. I walked back up to the second floor and as I was walking towards the gym, I stumbled into school security who was a retired Chicago police officer named O Malley. It was during class which meant I had no business walking down the halls of the school at that time. O Malley asked, "Where you headed son" I had the small 2 x 4 tucked under my sweat jacket in my right arm pit and the gym doors were only 15 feet behind him so I kept walking past him fast without saying anything until I got to the gym doors. I could feel him following behind me now, so I rushed through the gym doors and I saw the two Disciples and the Stone Chicano standing there. I started yelling, "Saint love, come on mother Fuckers jump me now, DK Chicano killer". The Stone Chicano ran into the office so did one of the disciples but the last one (Pumps) didn't he was actually walking towards me and the police officer was almost upon me. Unfortunately, I had no choice but to exit that situation and leave the paybacks for another day because within a second or two O' Malley would've had his hands on me and then I would have had to break free by fighting that old man which was not something I needed to do. I went home and told my father that I was not going back to school again that I would just work in the store rather than go back to school. Of course, that was music to his selfish ears but as for me it would be a decision that I would regret when I got old enough to understand. High school is an experience no teenagers should miss out on it's probably the best part of ones' life. I would encourage every teen to stay in school but not just for the experience of being but to get the best education one can get whatever school you go to because a good future depends on it. Now it would be work in the store from opening to closing seven days a week because of my bad actions and non-conformist behavior. It is kind of comical to say my bad behavior next to my father's behavior a husband who beats his wife and his kids savagely, cheats on his wife regularly and denies that God exists was like the pot calling the kettle black. We would work and he would spend, fishing boats, new car every year and if it didn't suit him he would trade it in within a week and lose thousands on the deal. He would go on fishing trips with his buddies from his job in which he was the one footing the bill as always. Luckily for him he had a wife and a son who were slaves busting their asses so he could have fun. He should have insisted on sending me away to an alternative school and trust me I would have been more than glad to go. I had my driver's license already which was basically bought for a little over a $100. In those days, it was common in the city of Chicago to buy your way through most situations, traffic stops, traffic court, the DMV and so on. I went to a driving school in my neighborhood but of course I still had to study for the written test and pass it. To make sure the whole thing would go smooth sailing with the road test, I was instructed to place a $20 bill under the passenger floormat for the driving instructor and when I went for the road test with the instructor, he would than retrieve it. The instructor entered the vehicle gave me his instructions and at the part of the test where you perform how you would Park the vehicle in an uphill position the instructor reached down and pulled the $20 from beneath the floormat. My father helped me obtain the license not for my enjoyment but because needed the car to run errands for the store. What he didn't know was that I was using the car for gang banging also and not just for running errands. I would pick up some of my boys and gang bang while running those errands. We would run past Kelly high school and try to catch same Disciples or their allies snoozing and when we did, they got served. Like most people gang banger also get the thought of wanting to do right in this life   because we all want to live a long life. It was obvious that there were only two outcomes for people like myself if I continued to head in that direction and those were prison or death. For example, I signed up for boxing and a photo was put on the front page of the back of the yards Journal along with other guys from the neighborhood. I was training a lot and we were even weighed in on the north side for tournaments which would have taken us to the Golden gloves fights. One night I went out jogging for a few miles and when I returned home I was drenched in sweat. When I walked into the store my father was standing there, he gave me his usual dirty look and asked where I had been and what I was doing. I told him that I was out jogging training for boxing, he started to scold me and went on to accuse me of lying, that I was out there hanging out with my gang banging buddies. His shit he said made me sick to my stomach, he can clearly see that I had been running, my sweatshirt and sweatpants were drenched in sweat, so it was obvious to see. I left home again because there was no use with this guy (father) than dropped out boxing was back on the streets gang banging. I am not saying I was going to be the next Muhammad Ali or anything like that, but it was the only positive thing I had going for me at the time. There is, something to mention and that is during the early 80s I was probably one of a very few Palestinians who were involved in Chicago street gangs. I say that because I did not meet any full-blooded Palestinians who were gang members in those days. Me and my boy Problem would go on missions (Gang hits) we would get dropped off on 48th and Western where some Satan Disciples lived and that's where we would start lite (shoot) those guys up, run down to 49th and Western than climb onto the railroad tracks, which ran east and west. From there we would head east on the tracks making our way back to our neighborhood or to Problem's house. Along the way, we would come down off the tracks and hit the next gang than run back up the tracks and do the same thing in every neighborhood along the way. We would hit the 22 boys, the Latin souls, the Bishops than the 48th St. boys and at times we would catch the Satan Disciples at Troop Park on 49th and

Troop which was only a block away from where Problem lived. One day late at night, me and Problem and his girlfriend were walking to his house, as we reached 48th and Bishop a 1975 or 76 two door Chevy Impala pulled up to the curve screeching its tires from hitting the brakes hard. My boy Problem recognized the vehicle as belonging to one the Bishops street gang. Problem was carrying a 22 revolver, I yelled out to him to shoot the guy but he was hesitating to do so. The driver was reaching under his seat, so I told Problem to give me the gun which he did and I immediately open fire on the driver and he grabbed for the gear shifter on the steering column. He got the car into reverse and stomped the gas pedal; the rear tires were screeching as he was reversing then the vehicle went out of control and slammed into the street light pole on the corner. We were already running and making our way Problem's house which was about three blocks away. We waited to hear sirens but nothing and we never heard anything any mention about the incident. On another occasion, me and Problem had an old 12gauge sawed-off shotgun which was a bolt action in our passion and I mean this thing was old and junky. We waited as usual until it was late at night to hit the streets in search of our enemies. I stuffed the shotgun in my waist and down my pants leg than went out into the night. We planned on hitting the Bishops of 48th so we walked from his house and headed west on 48th street but when we got to Loomis street which is the block before Bishop. There was a bunch of bikers out there that night with their girlfriends and they had their bikes parked next to each other in a row and there must have been about 10 or 15 of them. As we approach them, I told Problem let's cross the street before one of these mother fucking bikers says something stupid to us. We had no beef with these bikers so we crossed the street and sure enough when we were directly across from them one of the white girls yelled out "hey amigos" I looked at her and said "I ain't no fucking amigo". Immediately she took offense to how I answered her and started to yell profanities at us. It was obvious they were drunk and had no idea what they were about to get themselves into, and some of the bikers were now also shouting profanities at us. I turned to Problem and told him I was going to shoot at the mother fuckers and before he could say anything I was in the middle of the street pointing the shotgun at them. One of the girls screamed, "fuck he's got a gun" they were all starting to hit the ground and right at that moment I squeezed the trigger. The 12gauge went off shooting out a flame shot from the short barrel and the sound of it was deafening in between the old buildings. The screams of fear from the group echoed in all directions after the shot gun going off. I pulled the bolt on the gun back and the other shell under the bolt in the little clip flew out with the empty shell, so I turned around in search of Problem, but he was already turning the next corner on Bishop street. He had the other shells with him, all I had is what was in the chamber and the one in the clip which was now on the ground somewhere, I ran after him while yelling at him to give me the shells so I could shoot at them again but he kept yelling back "No come on, come on". Problem was ahead of me by 50 or 60 feet, we ran to 49$^{th.}$ then we climbed up on the railroad tracks to doubled back to Problem's house when we spotted some Satan Disciples at Troop Park and by then I obtained a shell from Problem and already placed it in the chamber. I yelled down to them "Saint love" and they started to represent back "Disciples, D love" which was my cue to open fire down on them and that caused them to scatter and run like roaches. From there we made our way to Problem's house and laid low for the rest of the night. This is how our nights and days were spent, one day as we pulled up on 47th and Loomis, Little Problem seen a kid at the bus stop who according to him was a 48th St. boy. Little Problem said, "that's the mother Fucker who keeps fucking with me at school" we were inside a cargo van which had a sliding door. I slid the door open and jumped out and of the van and immediately coldcocked the kid in the jaw. I punched him hard enough that I almost knocked him out then as I jumped back into the van while yelling back at him "Fuck with my boy Little Problem again and you got more than that coming next time". Years Later Little problem would be shot in the head and killed by a Satan Disciple. Not long after that incident with the 48th street boy a few Satan Disciples came our neighborhood attempting to shoot one of us and that night me and Problem prepared ourselves to go into their neighborhood and get some paybacks. We made our way to Troop Park at about 2am and noticed a group of guys hanging out at the basketball courts. I snuck up on them while armed with a pistol and represented to them "Saint love D K" and in return they started to represent back "Disciples". I was standing in the middle of the street and had not produced the pistol yet. One of the SDs tried sneaking around the park house building to throw a beer bottle at me and as he did, I pulled out the pistol and open fire on him. He fell back and started screaming which was my cue to take off and got ghost. I don't know what type of injury he had, and I wasn't going to hang around to try and find out. Any time me and Problem went out to do a burn I was always the burner (shooter) and he was the lookout. I honestly loved those guys like they were my blood brothers and would have given my life for them. But there was a problem because I loved them blindly and was not paying attention to what was going on around me. I never thought at the time how the police were finding out about things I did with Problem and his brothers, but I was the only one being targeted by the Chicago police gang crime unit for questioning or arrest. Case in point, the kid I punished for Little Problem did not know who I was, but he knew who Little Problem was and somehow gang crime found out my name than arrested and charged me for punching the kid and breaking his jaw. By now I had a pretty rough reputation and I was becoming more brutal, fuck with me and you're going to have plenty of shit on your hands. One day I saw a guy beating his wife while his two little daughters were screaming and crying on 45th and Hermitage. I was standing with Problem about seven houses away from where the guy was beating up his wife. I told Problem I was going down there to beat the fuck out of the guy, Problem looked at me and said, "don't waste your time Bro, after you help her she's going turn on you and stick up for her husband". It really didn't make a difference to me if she stuck up for her husband after I helped her. I grew up watching my father treating my mother the same exact way and there was no way this guy wasn't going to get a beating from me for what he was doing to his wife. I ran down there and gave the guy five or six good blows, he let go of his wife and was covering his head with his arms and cowering without trying to put up a fight. Of course, the wife got between me and her husband, so I walked away in order not to give her and her two children anymore grief. Not to brag but no one dared Fuck with my family in the neighborhood in those days, my boys (the Saints) didn't because they respected me even if one of my brothers was in the wrong and others did not out of pure fear. On one of my many away from home episodes, I ran into my middle brother one day and he told me about a conversation he had with a grown guy from the neighborhood , I cannot remember who the guy was, but my brother said the guy told him, "I saw your brother Imad walking down Hermitage the other day and I was scared to cross his path so I crossed the street". I was becoming eviler and more destructive by the minute, I could care less what the outcome was going to be whether prison or death! During the summer the church of the immaculate heart of Mary on 45th and Ashland always had a carnival for a week or two. That summer of 1983 I walked into that carnival with a few Saints and about 10 minutes later, a Spanish looking lady walked up to me and put her hand out to shake mine so I put mine out and as we shook hands she introduced herself "I am officer so and so we know who you are! If we have any trouble in here, we know you are the cause of it, and we want to let you know that we are watching you". In those days, Chicago street gangs were split in two organizations, one under the six-pointed star which were known as "Folks" and the other side was under a five-pointed star and were known as "People" and that's how Chicago gangs were split up. For example, in the Latin communities some of those riding under the six-point star were Satan Disciples, Two Six, Latin souls, Ambrose, 22nd St. boys, Maniac Latin Disciples, Spanish Cobras, Imperial Gangsters and many other organizations and in the black community those riding under the six- point star and were cousins to the Latin Folks were Gangster Disciples, Black Gangsters, Black Disciples, Mad Black Souls and others. On the other side, gangs riding under the five-pointed star in the Latin community were the Latin Kings, Bishops, Latin Counts, Latin Brothers, Deuces, Unknowns, Stone Kent and others and within the black community those riding under the five-pointed star were many different factions of the Vice Lords the Black P stones MCs and so on. This type of organizing was established within the walls and fences of the Cook County jail and the Illinois prison system. Gang bangers imprisoned in the Department of corrections from different gangs became united and become allies against common enemies. Certain people were recognized as leaders, committees were formed, treasurers, advisors and enforcers. Laws were created to govern these organizations and were to be studied and remembered but most of all obeyed by those incarcerated. These rules were strongly enforced in Illinois Department of corrections and were also carried out to the streets of Chicago but not followed and enforced by all gangs on the streets as much as they were in the joints (prisons). The leaders of these organizations were well known personalities who were loved and very much respected at that time. Personalities such as King Hoover who headed the Gangster Disciples, Milwaukee King Shaky who headed all the Latin folks within the Illinois

Department of Corrections at that time, Prince Ferny head of the Maniac Latin Disciples, King Tuffy head of the Spanish Cobras, Boonie head of the Black Gangsters, Little Davey head of the Two Six, Jeff Fort head of the El Rukns, the Inca Lord Gino head of all the Latin Kings and of course there were many other such leaders. I can talk about these things dealing with Chicago gangs these days but there was a time when I would have not talked about it in the open but now everything has been exposed by informers who have betrayed their Leaders, brothers and nations so I am not giving away anything that has not been exposed the RATS. As for us Saints of 45th well, we were renegades which meant we did not belong to either side on the streets of Chicago, our fight was with everyone except for one. That gang was our other branch in South Chicago on 87th and Houston which was started by two of the boys who were brothers. That branch started out as Saints then evolved into Saint Spanish Gangster Disciples and from there to Spanish Gangster Disciples (SGD) which meant they were connected to the Latin Folks. Back in them days they would come to our house parties and we would go to theirs and on a few occasions, they handle things for us on our end and we did the same for them. But it was understood that if one of us Saints of 45th, was arrested and sent to the county or state prison then we would ride with the Latin Folks under the six-point star! Other saints who were already incarcerated were riding Folks and once upon a time a message was sent out to us by them about the possibility of joining the ranks of the Latin Folks on the streets. That suggestion was put to a vote and failed, almost every one of the boys was against the idea of joining forces with anyone so we remained renegade. As for me honestly speaking I felt that we should have hooked up with the folks because I feared later generations of our boys would turn People (ride under the five-pointed star). I truly hated everything anything that was associated with the Latin Kings. The main reason the boys did not want to hook up with the Folks was that they did not want any other gangs roaming around our neighborhood which was expected once you united with the Folks or People. They were free to come in and out of your neighborhood because you were now allies. At any given time, you could drive into the Latin Souls neighborhood and find Disciples, Two Six, or Ambrose hanging around with the Latin Souls and the thought of that did not sit well with the boys at all. One hot summer day me, Big A and Problem drove into the neighborhood in a 1976 Chevy Malibu station wagon which belonged to another Saint. As Always Big A was the driver and we came down 46 Street and made a right on Hermitage heading north. I was sitting in the backseat, as I looked forward through the wind shield I noticed three guys riding bicycles on the street about half a block ahead of us. I noticed the riders waving their hands in the air and for a minute I thought I was seeing things, so I had to do a double take because I thought the guys were making the Latin Soul sign with their hands. After a second look I knew for sure those guys were Latin Souls riding through my neighborhood on bicycles disrespecting us which I must admit took a lot of balls. They made it to the corner before us and split up one kept straight the other one went to the left and the last one went right on 45th St heading east. I told Big A to run them, but they were already at the corner where went in different directions and we went after the one that made a right turn. Big A turned the corner and sped up and as he got almost next to the bike, he swerved the car into the bike, so we would sandwich and smash the Latin Soul between our car and the parked car. When a human's life is threatened, we sometime get supernatural powers and this kid got some at that point. He was on was so scared he lifted his legs up released the bicycle and jumped onto the hood of the parked car as we smashed the bicycle between both cars. He went over the roof than jumped off and took off with skipping a beat and took off running up 45th St. He got to Pauline street made a right and headed south trying to make it back to his neighborhood which was a little over two blocks away. Me and Problem were already out of the car and giving chasing on foot, but this kid was fast running for his life. We finally Caught up to him on 46th and Hermitage right in front of the funeral home, we proceeded to give him the beaten of his life. I grabbed him by the hair and smashed his face into the corner of the building which was made of limestone, we kept beating and kicking him trying to cause him as much damage as we could. Eventually he was knocked out and someone from the corner building was yelling down from the third floor for us stop before we kill him, or they were going to call the cops. We left him there laying on the floor bloodied from the beating with a few ice pick holes that Problem took away from him and used it against him. That same summer of 1983 Santo was released from juvenile prison, the same Santo that pulled the shotgun on me in grammar school. When he got out, we were introduced to each other and it was like nothing ever happened between us. We kicked it off well and became closer than blood brothers. I was driving my father's car, so I picked up Santo and Chico who was a down ass Saint who put in a lot of work for the nation. We went for a cruise looking for our enemies in their area, our first stop was Hoyen Park in Latin Soul territory where they were known to hang out at times. We walked into the park house and found a few guys playing pool at the pool tables. I walked up to them and asked "what you be" one of them answered "nothing" but they dressed like gang bangers which meant he was lying So, I punched him in the eye and then represented my nation and disrespected the Soul nation but they said nothing at all. A few minutes later we were on 47th St. and Paulina where we noticed a 48th St. boy hang around, so we tried creeping up on him, but he noticed us and took off, but we caught him after a short chase and he received a beating in the middle of the day for all to see. Within minutes we were on 48th and Justine where we caught another 48th St.

boy and he received a hell of a beating which included a baseball bat. We later heard that the second 48th street boy was in a coma but later came out of it. That night about 2 AM while at Davis Sq., Park I ran into one of my boys Called Stoney who was a go-getter who was feared by many people, he pulled me to the side and said "Man bro you gotta slow down you're doing too much shit out here", he was older than me and was just looking out for me. For Stoney to say that to me it meant I was fucking up and out of control. When Stoney said that to me it only made me want to more, it was like putting gasoline on the fire. On a beautiful summer night as I was cruising in the neighborhood with Big A and Problem, we passed up a yard party at an older Saint's house. As we passed somebody threw a can of beer towards our vehicle not knowing who we were. We circled the block and pulled up by the party, one of the older Saints named Cochise approached the car. I asked him who threw the beer can as we passed the party and he told me who it was. He tried calming me down because I was hot, he said the guy was a guest and asked me not to do anything until the end of the party which I agreed to do so out of respect. As the party wound down I came out of the car and walked towards the yard holding in my hand a switchblade. As I entered the gate the older Saint who was hosting the party named G stopped me and said, "please put the knife up bro don't stab the guy, fuck him up but don't kill the fucking guy". G put his hand out and I gave him the knife, from there I walked into the yard towards the guy who was leaning against the fence. I grabbed a full closed can of beer and lined it at his face as hard as I could. The can struck him in the face so hard that it exploded open then from there I proceeded to beat the living shit out of him until he passed out. There is a lot of things that I can talk about from those days but there are some things that I cannot, things I will have to take to the grave with me. I was nuts back then and I knew it but I never really knew how nuts and it is people who brought it to my attention years later for example, many years later I received a friend request from a guy with an Arab name on face book who obviously knew me but I had no idea who the guy was. Even though many of the people on his friend list I knew I still had no idea who he was, but he had to be from the neighborhood that much I knew. As soon as I accepted his friend request there was a message in my inbox from him,

N Awan; "what's up brother, I remember you Emad, you had everybody in the neighborhood fearing you I have nothing but respect for you. How have you been?

As it turns out, this guy was a young boy while I was running around back in the day when I was a gang banging. There is no a doubt that I had a very menacing reputation in those days. when I read his message, but it wasn't just him many other people have made similar statements to me which made me realize that I had been a much more menacing individual than I thought. Hearing these things being said about me does make me proud but neither am I ashamed because I played the hand that I was dealt the only way I knew how. I'm not a big guy but size does not really mean shit because there were plenty of guys out there who were plenty tough regardless of their size. I am in no way pretending to say that I was the toughest gang banger on my side of town, but I am saying that in those days I was not accepting shit from anyone and was giving out plenty of shit to those who were trying to send shit my way. What set people like me apart from other guys was that we were willing to do things that others were not willing to do. For instance, one day someone recognized a guy who was working in a hot dog stand in the neighborhood as a 22nd street boy. The boys confronted the individual, but the owner of the hotdog stand locked the window of the stand and called the police to escort the guy out of the neighborhood. I showed up on the scene as the police were escorting the guy out to their squad car and as they did, he had a smile on his face that said "ha ha I'm getting away" he thought he was Scott free, but he was sadly mistaken. I broke through the crowd and punched him in the mouth knocking out part of his front tooth which left a scar on my knuckle that is still there to this day. Situations like that did not stop people like me from doing something like that because the police were present. There were a lot of crazy gang bangers out there whose names were ringing bells, you couldn't let them catch you snoozing, or it was lights out for you. As I said I was closest at the time to those brothers who I did a lot of dirt with, Big A, Problem and Little Problem and there was the third brother called K O who was a real stand up at one time, or at least that's what everyone thought. He was given the name K O because he would always knockout anyone he punched. Unfortunately, a time came when rumors were circling that K O might be giving information to the cops about our activities in the neighborhood, but no one could say for sure that he was actually doing that. I saw him one evening when I first heard the rumor, I was in my father's car and with me were Cochise, Chico, another one of the boys called Sir Player and one other person who I can't really recall so I pulled the car over to the curb next to him and said;

Me; "K O what's up bro, going for a ride to the lakefront, roll with"?

K O; long pause with a suspicious look on his face, "Na I'm ok bro"

Me; "come on bro role would us man, you ain't doing nothing we'll go up there check it out and rollback"

K O; He smiles and says" Fuck it that's cool let's roll."

As we approached him, I told the boys in the car "let's take this mother Fucker to the Cabrini greens projects and throw his ass out up there". They had also heard the same rumor that I heard, and they agreed without any abjections with my plan. I remember someone saying, "fuck it let's do it maybe they'll do his ass in up there". So, K O got in the backseat and off we went to the northside where the Cabrini Green projects were located. When we got there, I pulled the car over and said I needed to take a piss, and everyone said the same thing than got out of the car except K O, he knew something was up. He was just sitting there so I said,

Me; "K O get out and take a piss before we head back to the hood bro"

K O; "I'm straight bro I took one before I met up with yous"

I looked at Cochise and Chico then back at K O and said,

Me; "man get the fuck out of the car mother Fucker"

K O; "come on bro, what's up"?

I told him he had two options, the first which would be his best bet was to get out the car on his own or the second option and that to get dragged out of car which includes a beating. He chose the first option and got out of the car than we jump back into the car and drove of heading back to the neighborhood hoping he would catch a beating from somebody. The Cabrini green projects in those days were a very dangerous place to be in for out siders, hell it was dangerous for the police. Unfortunately, K O made it out of Cabrini green in one piece but from that day on he was an outcast just out of suspicion. One late evening as I was hanging out on 45th and Hermitage with another Saint called Slay who lived in the house we were standing in front of and down the street from us were a few Saints hanging out in front of another Saints house. All the sudden we heard a big commotion coming from where they were standing, and it looked like they were facing a group of maybe 10 or more gang bangers who were a block deep in my neighborhood who were there to attack my boys. There were maybe five of us on the block so I asked Slay if he had any burners (guns) in the house but he said, " no, one of the boys picked up the shotgun earlier in the day and took it to Marshfield" then he jokingly said that he only had a starter gun which fires 22 blanks used for foot racing at the park. In those days, I didn't give a fuck about consequences of my actions, I told him "fuck it give it to me" he looked at me like I was crazy and said "what". I told him to get it and he ran into his house and got it and as soon as he came out, I took it and charged towards the enemy, who I later found out were Latin Souls and 22nd street boys, yelling "Saint love" then fired a shot here and there of the blank bullets at them. My boys were between me and the enemy, so I yelled out to them to get down as I charged the other guys and my boys did hit the ground fearing they would get hit from my gun fire. They had no idea, nor would they ever suspect I was firing a gun with blank bullets but the was the only game plan I could come up with in what seemed be like second. Those gang bangers seen me charging at them, did an about-face and ran as fast as they could out of our neighborhood. That evening I was upset because the gun in my had was not real because at that time I wanted to drop (shoot) them for disrespecting us by coming into our neighborhood like that. Minutes later when my boys gathered up, they were shocked that I did that with a starter gun. But my plan worked and all it took was some courage to carry out. Also, a civilian named Raul came out of his house and fired a single shot from a sawed-off shotgun at them after they were already running from me. Of course there were plenty of time when I thought about the road I was headed down and the madness of it all and I wanted to do right by myself but I felt like I was too far gone at the time and felt like there was nothing out there for me to cling to that was positive and I tried. For example, I once walked into the United States Marine Corp office on 46th and Ashland and asked if they would enlist me. The recruiter looked at me and asked what school I went to, I said I was a dropout and if there was any way they could take me into the military. The recruiter looked at me and said "No" that I would have to go to school and graduate first and there was no way that was going to happen. I turned around and walked out filled with disappointment and hopelessness I wished they would have taken me right than there. Also, in those days I signed up for automotive body and

Fender at Washburn vocational school but there was a long waiting list, this was a public vocational school. Unfortunately, by the time I was called, which I believe was about a year later, the school was getting ready to shut down due to loss of funding by the government. Most of my boys were of Mexican descent and were of the Catholic faith, it was odd for me to watch them do the crucifix on their body every time we passed a church. I thought to myself "fuck we were out in the streets robbing, assaulting and if we had to killing people yet these guys think God would want to have anything to do with them". Even on Ash Wednesday most of them walked around with a cross made of ashes on their foreheads. As for me I had stopped believing in a God or anything to do with religion at all for some time now. A few times as we drove around the neighborhood I would pull the car I was driving up on the sidewalk right in front of the church and throw all my trash out at the front doors of the church. Once I pulled up in front of holy cross church while the priest was out there than spit on the ground towards him. They never liked me doing that but I never gave a fuck and would taunt them about being gang bangers and religious at the same time. One evening I was at Big A's house and wanted to go to the neighborhood, so I asked him to drop me off on 45th and Hermitage by Mo's house. When he dropped me off, I walked into Mo's house who was also a Saint. A few minutes later the van was back in front of house and Big A was yelling for me to come out of the house. When I went out there, I found that someone had shot at the van and put a bullet hole in the side of it. If he hadn't dropped me off when he did that bullet would have struct me in the head. We never really found out who took that shot at him, but it did not faze me at the time that I had just missed death by mere minutes, that my life was spared by God and I took it as being lucky that day. Sometime in 1984 a kid called Curly who was a Saint moved back to Chicago from California and Curly was a real cool kid. He owned a 1975 Chevy Monte

Carlo, one day he let me use the car and I had with me three other Saints, so we decided to go to the Bridgeport neighborhood to see if we could run into a street gang called Spanish Chancellors that we were cool with. Many of the people in Bridgeport were Italian American and among some of their teenage kids there was a crew of kids who called themselves Hitmen Dagos. These white kids came from families who had money and plenty of city of Chicago connections, so they were not considered a street gang. It was misting that evening and the streets were wet, I drove towards Bridgeport through the stockyards to Halsted Street then made our way to 31st St. then took 31st to Wallace Street. When we got to Wallace some of the Hitmen Dagos were on the corner standing in front of the pharmacy, as we turned the corner they noticed us and we got into a shouting match with them and then we proceeded to look for the Chancellors but they were nowhere to be found so we decided to head back to the neighborhood. I took Wallace to 31st, not thinking about those Italian kids that we just had words with, then went to make a right turn and as soon as I turned the corner those Hitmen Dagos were laying in the cut for us they started to bomb the vehicle with bottles and on my left a guy jumped out from between the cars and pointed a sawed-off shotgun at us. He fired from between the parked cars across the street on my left and the glass came down on me. I was already stomping the gas pedal trying to get us out of danger. A few blocks away we checked and everybody was okay other than being sprayed with glass no one was hurt. I was in a rage I drove like a madman with only one thing in mind and that is to back to the neighborhood for the sole purpose of grabbing a gun than heading back to Bridgeport for some paybacks. Halfway back to the neighborhood a squad car popped up behind me on Archer Street and Ashland Avenue I didn't stop and took the left turn and the chase was on. I kept heading to the neighborhood but on 39th and Ashland I decided because there was no way of getting away given that the streets were wet and the car being a two door with guys trapped in the back seat, they would be sitting ducks if I bailed out and ran. Plus, there were other squad cars who joined in the pursuit. I already knew I was going to jail; my driver license was suspended God only knew what else might pop up when they ran my name. I decided that I was going to jail for more than a suspended license that night, as the officers from the first squad car stepped out of their vehicle, I still had the car in gear, so I shifted the vehicle into reverse and stomped the gas pedal which caused the back tires to screech on the wet asphalt for a few seconds than we slammed into the front of the squad car. The cop ran up to my window with his gun out and was yelling "what the fuck is wrong with you, get the fuck out of the car". I played the victim card and explained to him that I just got shot at and was just nervous. That I intended to put the car in park but instead put it in reverse and my foot slipped off the brake and hit the gas pedal. If the police back in those days were anything like today's police than I may have had 12 bullet holes in me. He saw the broken glass all over the interior of the vehicle and bought my story about the whole thing being an accident. However, that story did not save me from going to jail and only did I go to jail but I received 12 traffic citations and had the pleasure of spending the night in the lock up of the 35th and low police station but was released the next day from traffic court. Life was different in those days for example I got caught driving on a suspended license under different circumstances in my neighborhood, I knew like most people did in those days that you can ask a cop if you could buy him lunch after being pulled over for a driving violation and 99.9% of the time he would accept the offer. The going rate at the time was $20 and with the reckless life I was living, what did I care about asking a police officer to take a bribe from me, what could I possibly lose so I asked and it worked. I paid off three cops in a few weeks period while driving in and around the neighborhood, on one occasion I paid a cop two time than on the third time I only had $14 so he took that and told me to go park the fucking car already. On another occasion, I was pulled over for speeding down Ashland Ave near Cermak street again I asked this cop if I could buy him lunch, he looked at me for a second then said "okay I'm going to walk to my car then when I come back have it folded real small and be ready to put it in my hand". He walked to his vehicle reach for something walked back to mine stuck his hand in my window and took the $20 bill and left. I was 16 or early 17 when I was paying off these cops and it was at the age of 17 that my luck seemed to be running out. I didn't drink much at all but one night I was drinking and got a bit buzzed and wondered off into Damen field which was at the westside of my neighborhood. I stumbled onto some Satan Disciples of 51st street but these guys I was cool with but among them were two Disciples I had confronted a few months back and one of them had denied being a member of the Disciples. I fronted him off in front of his boys and his boy who was with him at the time of the incident confirmed my story. After that I turned to talk to an SD I knew well and the guy I fronted off sucker punched me than we ended up having a drunken fight which did not last long. At the end of that fight he was informed by the other Satan Disciples that if he wanted to be a member, he had to kill a Latin King. A few months after our fight that Disciple walked up to the leader of the Bishops while pretending to want a light for his cigarette and when the Bishop stuck his hands in his pockets looking for a light the Disciple pulled out a sawed-off shotgun and blew the Bishops head off. Later that year I got a hold of an old style 32caliber revolver the kind you must push a button then pull the pin out of the front of the gun, so the cylinder can fall out to load and unload the gun which was a pain in the ass. One afternoon me and Problem picked up some 32 caliber shells for that gun, but we didn't load the gun. We were walking down 48th street as we got to the corner of 48th and Ada a 48th street boy turned that corner and ran right into us. We immediately went into action, we jumped him than I stepped back, and Problem stayed on him, I pulled the gun out and started working on loading it. I tried to release the pin, but I was having trouble pulling the it out because I was trying to do it too fast while looking back and forth from the gun to Problem and telling him to hold him and not let him go. Finally, the pin came out, but the cylinder slipped from my hand and hit the floor and the guy seen what I was doing. He knew his life depended on him breaking free from Problem and running for his life. He broke free and was now running for his life and by the time I got the gun back together he was almost at the corner. I took off after him, he turned the corner before me when I turned the corner, I took aim and fired but I missed. He was quick, he ran between the parked cars and this was all in broad daylight, so we had to disappear fast someone was bound to call the cops. Not long after that incident one of my older boys named Ed was visiting Big A's house and noticed I had the gun so, He gave me a bullshit story about some Mexican guy having a bunch of money and was always beating on his girlfriend. In short, he wanted my help in robbing and punishing this guy which I agreed to without hesitation. So that night we set out for 45th and Paulina where this Mexican guy lived in a house situated in the middle of the block on the west side of the street but before going there, we were walking through an ally a block away and we ran into an old white man. Ed tried robbing the poor old guy who turned to be broke but as the old man was walking away Ed whispered to me to give him the gun, so he could shoot the old. I refused to give him the gun, that should have been the Q for me to get the hell away from him and to get all about our plan, but I did not and would soon regret not walking away. The guy we were to rob lived in a back cottage, so we walked through the gangway and up to the door. Ed kicked it in then we rushed into the dark with hardly any light inside the cottage. I had the gun in my hands pointing it into the dark, we walked through the kitchen and as we entered a bedroom there was a figure to the left in bed. I was in front of Ed, in an instance the figure jumped at me and now was holding the gun with me and we were now fighting for the gun and there was no way I was going to let take it. He was doing his best to take the gun away from me, I yelled to Ed "grab him" but there was no the prick Ed was gone. Me and the guy fell on the bed and the gun was pointing in his direction, so I squeezed the trigger hoping to hit him. The gun fired, and the shot had to have just missed his head at which time he immediately let the gun go, I back away from him while pointing the gun in his direction and took off out of the cottage. I had no reason, nor did I want to shoot him especially after Ed ran out and left me there. From there I walked the neighborhood for a few minutes looking for that asshole Ed but instead run in too one of the older Saints who picked me up, I told him what had just happened. We drove around the neighborhood looking for Ed, but he was nowhere to be found. About an hour later I asked the older Saint to pull over at the laundry mat, so I could use the telephone to call Big A's house. I called Big A's house and was told that detectives were there looking for me. I got back into my boy's car and told him to drop me off at Big A's house and he did. When I walked in the house Big A handed me the card that was left behind by Chicago detectives who wanted to speak to me, I asked if the detectives said why they were looking for me, but he said no they never said why. It was no surprise that the Chicago police were looking for me, I thought to myself "there is no way they are looking for me because of what me and Ed did and where the fuck was that asshole Ed at anyway", but to my surprise I would soon find out how wrong I was. I called the detective and he came to Big A's house but when he arrived, he read me my rights than placing me under arrest. He transported me down to the 35th and low police station. I was booked and charged with home invasion, attempted murder, armed robbery and unlawful discharge of a firearm among other charges. I later found out that Ed was a coke head, (addicted to cocaine) in those days if you used hard drugs you hid it from your friend who did not use it. After running out on me this stupid fuck received a little cut on his side which was probably from jumping fences while trying to get away than he had someone drive him to the hospital claiming to be a stabbing victim. As usual the hospital informed the police that they have a stabbing victim, so the police arrived to obtain a statement from the him to make a police report. When the police showed up, he panicked and started to tell them about what had happened at the guy's house, in short, he spilled the beans but was blaming me for everything. There you have it all this was going on while me and the older Saint were driving around looking for his stupid ass. I was charged as an adult since I was now 17 years old and the next day I was bonded out by my family. I went home to face my father who didn't say much this time which made going home easier to deal with. The very next day two more detectives from Chicago Homicide Division showed up at my family store, they said they wanted to talk to me, but it had to be done at the station. I could have refused to go with them, but at this point it really did not matter because I could care less what was on the mind of these cops, there simply was no way on God's green earth I was going to confess to any murder. They took me to 3900 S. California which was the station that dealt with homicide cases. At the police station, they asked me what I knew about this dead guy who was shot and killed in an abandoned building on 46th St. and Paulina which was down the street from the guy's house we broke into the night before. I now knew this was some bull shit and these mother fucking detectives were going to try and pin this murder on me. I told them I didn't know anything about it or had anything to do with it, that I was done talking with them and if they were going to charge me to go ahead and do it. When they heard what I had to say the younger detective took out his handcuffs and put one cuff on my right wrist and the other part of the cuff on a ring in the wall. He then told me that I was going to jail for the rest of my life for killing that guy because they had information that implicated me in that murder. I just stared at the wall not saying anything which frustrated the shit out of him so he grabbed me by my collar with his left hand and with his right hand he picked up a plastic spoon off the table then put it up against my throat and said "do you know what the niggers are going to do to you in jail "he had me shoved against the wall. I looked at him smiled and started to bang my head against the wall as hard as I could while yelling at him "you think that scares me I will kill any mother fucker who tries fucking with me, you don't have shit on me because I did not kill that guy" he now had a shocked look on his face and released my shirt. They walked out of the room and about 5 minutes later They came back uncuffed me and told me to call my father, so he could pick me up. I later found out that these bastard cops knew I had nothing to do with this murder because they I was arrested about 9 PM and the guy was killed at about 2 AM that night while I was in lock up at the police station. After all this mess my father got me a job from one of his friends at a Submarine sandwich joint on 79th and Ashland in a black neighborhood and that neighborhood belonged to the Gangster Disciples. I worked the night shift behind bulletproof glass I took the bus to work and I had no problem walking through a black neighborhood especially if the neighborhood belonged to Folks because I knew how to deal with them. Hell, I leaned towards Folks but most of all there was nothing to fear I was looking death in the face daily anyway. The only thing that job did for me was to introduce me to the other side of the Folks (Black Folks). I met people like Shelby, Beaver and this character named King Lavelle and developed a good relationship with them. I also met a Cook County Sheriff who sold me small caliber guns like

22's and 25 caliber nothing big. While working there a one of those young GDs did something that hit every news channel in Chicago he shot and killed an up and coming basketball player from Simeon high school named who was destined for the NBA. The news media's version was that basketball player had no gang affiliation which according to what I heard from the GDs on 79th street that was bullshit. According to many the basketball star was a member of the Black P Stones and it was he who was trying to front off the young GD in front of other students. Well the young GD happened to be carrying a gun and saw fit to pull it out and point it at the basketball star. The star instead of backing down started to disrespect and antagonize the young GD even more saying things like "you ain't gonna use that shit" repeatedly until the young GD shot once which I am sure was not meant to kill him but unfortunately, he died. I am in no way justifying his killing, it was a senseless killing but so was the killing of any other gang member in the city of Chicago who do not receive much attention if any at all! I worked at the Mr. Submarine restaurant for a few months and then got another job at an auto body shop as a porter. The manager at the shop named Rudy was a cool guy who treated me like I was his son. The body men and painters working at the shop were white, so I had to earn their respect there immediately. They behaved like I was beneath them because I was a porter who washed cars and sweeping floors and they tried treated me as such. After being there for a few days a body man named Jeff said something to me in a disrespectful manner about something not being clean. I noticed a short 2 x 4 a few feet away from where me and Jeff stood, so I walked over and picked it up than walked back to where he was washing his hands and told him if he ever spoke that to me ever again, I was going to bust his fucking head. He had a shocked look on his face as I was yelling at him with the 2x4 in my hand. Rudy came out of the office and seen me holding the 2 x 4 so he called me into the office and asked me what happened but there was no way I was going to cry to him and I kept quiet. He proceeded to tell me how my family got me the job there to try and straighten me out but here I was trying to hit Jeff with a 2 x 4. He asked me not to do that again and if there was ever a problem to let him know and he would take care of it. Telling him or anyone else to handle my troubles was not going to happen, in my world that was out of the question because it was a snitches way of handling things. After that incident, I never had any problems out of anyone at the shop! While working there I learned how to peel a steering column on a car (stealing cars). After learning how to steal cars I was doing it to make extra money, taking cars for parts like rims and tires, stereo systems and body parts. Working did not mean we stop gang banging I was still banging after work and any other time I could even when I ran errands for the shop. I had also started hanging out with a guy from the neighborhood called Green Eyes who lived on the next block behind my house. We basically hung out at night if we did not have any money, we would somehow scrape up a few dollars for gas and weed. We would drive around in his father's car doing dirt like Jack rolling (robbing) drunks coming out of bars late at night on 47th street. I was still going to court for the case with Ed it was one continuance after another, but I was still living my life as if I did not have any legal troubles. I was also piling on more legal troubles, one afternoon while driving a friend's car I drove into the Latin Souls neighborhood and noticed two guys walking down 49th and Hermitage. I recognize one of them who known by the nickname KitKat from the Latin souls and the other turned out to be his cousin Bookie from the 22 boys, they didn't notice me creeping up behind them. I drove up the curb and was now driving on the side walk going at them from behind and they did not hear me until I stomped the gas pedal. They heard the roar of the car's engine, they looked back and saw the car coming at them, so they immediately dropped their school bags and took off running through the gangways. They were lucky because I would have run them over without giving it a second thought. I stop the car on the sidewalk where they dropped their bags then got out and picked up the bags, talking them with me as souvenirs. I made my way back to the neighborhood than went through their school bags and found all their gang drawings on their folders. A day or two later Gang Crime Unit from 51st and Wentworth street were looking for me. They found me a week later and arrested me for trying to run over those two guys, the charge was attempted murder attempted assault or something of that nature. This was 1984 and things were starting to change, for example what these so-called gangsters did calling the cops on me and pressing charges, it was a hard pill to swallow for me. The rule was and always should be that we don't involve the police in our affairs no matter what. They both were students at Currie high school and I knew KitKat from the eighth grade at Seward school. I had a friend who was a girl named Mamma G who went to school with them and she also knew KitKat from Seward school. Mamma G is Slay's from the Saints sister, so I asked her to take a message to KitKat for me telling him why he was snitching and pressing charges against me. I told her to tell him that he needs to make things right by dropping the charges against me that this was not the way the game is played. She came back and told me that KitKat said it wasn't him who was pressing charges, that it was his cousin Bookie and that Bookie was not going to drop the charges against me. I didn't know Bookie but now I knew he was a mother fucking RAT who was refusing to drop charges against me. This was something new for a gangbanger to be doing it out in the open without any shame what so ever, I mean snitching has been around since the beginning of time but out in the open meant things were changing and not for the better. A month or so after that Bookie himself was arrested for a well-publicized Chicago case which was the shooting and killing a 9year old child on 47th and Marshfield while shooting at my boys. It was one of the first if not the first incidents in the city where an innocent child was gunned down by gang gun fire. My court date was coming up for Bookie's case against me and when that day came, I went into court for my first hearing. My case was called, I walked up to the judge's bench and the states attorney stepped up then said, "your honor the people of Illinois would like to drop and dismiss this case against this defendant because the victim in this case is now in custody of the Cook County Jail for killing a child". I was thinking to myself as I stood there in front of the judge "good for that rat mother fucker". During the years 1984 and early 1985 more bad things were happening to some of my boys who I was really close with. One early morning two Saints that I was very close to, one called Malo and his brother Henio were drinking by their uncle's house on 43rd and Honore street. They were very drunk by the time they left their uncle's house and as they were walking out of the front door, they ran into a Latin King called Mustang who was from 26 Street and happen to be on the block visiting a girlfriend he knew. The two brothers started fighting with Mustang and as soon as Mustang broke free from them he ran into the girl's house retrieved a butcher's knife. Mustang was back out on to the street where he proceeded to stab both brothers, he sliced Malo's arm first then jumped on Jinio stabbing him a total of 47 times killing him. That morning I heard the tragic news about Malo and his brother and was very upset wishing I could have a chance at killing Mustang myself. Not long after that, one evening the Latin Souls came into the neighborhood looking to kill a Saint but instead killed an innocent guy named Gennaro who was a Thee Boy and wounded another Thee Boy. Gennaro was a real good guy from the neighborhood who had nothing at all to do with gang banging. After shooting the Thee Boyz the Latin Souls ran into my boy Stoney down the block who in turn shot the driver and the two shooters in vehicle ran off on foot. After that day, Stoney was on the run for shooting the Latin Soul who was the driver of that vehicle. A few weeks after that incident some of the boys drove into a Latin Soul's neighborhood armed with guns to get some payback for them coming into our neighborhood and shooting the two Thee Boyz. They went there in a van and Stoney was with them, while the others exited the van and proceeded on foot Stoney stayed in the van. The van was parked under the viaduct on 49th and Hermitage street and was left running. Stony was seated in the middle seat behind the driver sits, then out of nowhere a detective car pulled up and well known and much hated gang crime detective exited the police car. Stoney could see them and I sure they couldn't see into the van, so he jumped into the driver seat of the van and drove off heading straight for the hated detective. The detective jumped out of the way and opened fire at the van with his gun as it past near him by out and he emptied his magazine into the van trying to hit Stony. By the time the detectives got back in their police vehicle Stony had turned the next corner and was out of sight. Shortly after that they found the van running in an alley behind a taco joint on 47th St. but Stony was nowhere to be found. That detective along with other detectives were out looking for Stony daily because they didn't take it lightly that a gang banger would try and run over a decorated gang crime detective. One night I was getting dropped off at my girlfriend's house on 45th and Hermitage by Big A. As I got out of the Van, I heard someone calling me by Little Problem's real name, "AL, AL come here" from across the street. The streetlights in these old gang infested neighborhoods was shit most of the time half the lights did not work. I didn't respond and continued to walk while looking back in the direction of where the voice was coming from than a figure stepped out of the gangway and into whatever little light there was. It was that hated gang crime detective, he instructed me to go over to him which I did. He asked me where Stony was and I told him I had no idea that I hadn't seen him in a long time, of course he knew I was lying. He called me a liar and said, "you let him know that I'm carrying an extra gun for him so when I kill him, I'm going to put it on him" he pulled a small revolver and showed it to me. He turned and proceeded to walk down the street and I did the same and I headed back across the street to my girlfriend's house. I was again arrested along with Big A and Little Problem a few blocks away from where we were attempting to steal a vehicle near Kelly High School. We tried to steal this vehicle when something spooked us, so we left the vehicle alone and took off walking and we were about two blocks away when an unmarked police vehicle with two detectives in it pulled to the curb next to us and approached us. They ordered us to put our hands on the wall then they proceeded to search us and while they searched us, they were making comments about us trying to steal a vehicle down the street. We said nothing, they handcuffed us both and placed us in the backseat of their vehicle. When they got in the vehicle the detective on the passenger side lunged over the seat and proceeded to hit us with his radio in the rib cage area and shoulders, we just took it and said nothing! When we arrived at the police station on 35th and Lowe street they took us upstairs to the second floor and left us handcuffed behind our backs instead of to the rings on the wall. Then they sat us down next to each other on a small bench and they had also arrested Big A, they apprehended him in his van a block away from where they picked us up. Both officers sat down at their desk and proceeded to fill out the arrest reports. The officers were both white the one with the darker hair who I thought may have been Italian asked my name and after telling him my name he asked me,

Detective; "Where are you from"?

Me; "Jerusalem, I'm a Palestinian".

Detective; "Holy shit let me ask you something, how does it feel to be a bastard without a country".

When I heard him say that everything around me turned red, I started yelling profanities at him. He got up and grabbed me by the shirt then started punched me in the face multiple times, but I felt nothing and was still yelling at him. I was saying "you hit like a little girl mother fucker, little boys in my neighborhood punch harder than you". He really got angry and he put me in the headlock and proceeded to punch me in the rib cage, but I kept repeating the same thing and was even laughing at him now. He stopped and let go of me then he backed up a couple of feet and was looking down at me like a wounded dog because his pride was hurt then he sat back down and said,

Detective; "Your mother has VD"

and without any hesitation I answered him back,

Me; "She does have VD, because my father fucked your wife who had VD and then went home and gave it to my mom, you mother fucker".

And I kept on talking shit to him, at that point I did not give a fuck what he did. To my surprise he turned into a totally different person now pretending to be the victim, asking me why I was being an ass hole with him and that made me talk more shit to him. A few minutes later a bum looking uniformed Chicago police officer, a wannabe detective I am sure, appeared in the door way while I was talking shit to the detective. The uniformed cop looked around the room and said, "what the fuck is this asshole's problem". I answered him with a "Fuck you too Asshole" he then walked into the room and grabbed me by the collar pulled me up of the bench and proceeded to beat me back and forth across the face with his fist until he broke the lens on his watch on my face, I saw a piece glass from his lens fly to the left and it seemed to be moving in slow motion. He then threw me on the floor and stepped on my neck and punched me a few times then picked me up and pushed me back on the bench. I didn't spare him either he received enough profanities for him to choke on. I was eventually taken to lock up fingerprinted but this time no mugshots were taken because my face was all bruised up. The next day we got out and met at Big A's house, I walked over to the mirror to inspect the injuries on my face and the bruises were still visible and there was also scuff marks on my chest and rib cage area, but they didn't look fresh enough to me. All I could think about at that time was to give those coppers some of their own medicine. I told Little Problem to grab a towel wrap it around his fist and punch me in the same bruised up areas on my face in order to make them look fresh again. He was reluctant to do it but I insisted and kept pressing him hard enough until he eventually agreed and did what I asked him to do. After doing so I asked Big A to drive me to the 5700 block of South Wood street where there was a small hospital called Central Community Hospital. I went to the ER and a nice white nurse tended to me and asked,

Nurse; "What happened to you"?

Me; "a police officer arrested me last night and beat me, he was just doing his job"?

Nurse; "what? That's not his job he is not supposed to be doing that, where did this happen"?

Me; "35th and low, I didn't know he couldn't do this to me"?

I was playing the role of a naïve teenager because I felt they deserved that and more, it didn't matter that I had Little Problem punch me in the face to make the bruises fresh because we just replaced what had healed from the night before and we did not do anything extra. The nurse walked off and made some calls and about 20 minutes later as I was sitting behind a curtain on a stretcher with my shirt off, a white shirt (Lieut.) or a captain I cannot remember which, walked in and with him was a blue shirt carrying a briefcase, the white shirt asked,

White shirt.; "what happened son, a police officer slapped you a couple times"?

Me; "slapped me a couple of times? it wasn't your neck being stepped on or your face and rib cage being punched repeatedly, does my face and body look like I been slapped a few times"?

The white shirt took down the information and told me they're going to investigate and that I would be hearing back from someone soon. About a week after that incident I happened to be standing on 45th and Hermitage and it was just starting to get dark outside. A silver four-door Oldsmobile Cutlass with tinted windows pulled up in front of Slay's house where I was standing. I must admit I was snoozing, not paying attention to my surroundings and got snuck up on. The driver's door opened than the driver came out and put his hand over the roof of the car pointing a gun at me and fired what sounded like a 22 caliber. I bolted heading south and he fired again but missed, I didn't notice the three other cars behind the him which meant I ran the wrong way. Guys were getting out of those cars and coming at me from in between parked cars. Finally, one of them kicked me in my side and I lost my balance which caused me to fall against a building as I was falling, I noticed a heavyset guy carrying a baseball bat coming at me. He hit me with the bat on the top of my head a few times dazing me, now everybody was on me kicking me while the guy with the bat was getting in a hit here and there. I covered my head the best that I could with my arms, so my arms and legs were taking most of the hits from the baseball bat. I then heard one of them saying "drag him in the street and run him over" someone grabbed me by my ankles and started to drag me but my baby blue converse All-Stars slipped off my feet in his hands because we never tied our leases. Suddenly they stopped because they heard police sirens a few blocks away, the guys let go of me and jumped in their cars then took off. I got up off the ground and stumbled a few doors down to my boy's house. I open the door and stepped into the hallway grabbing my left thumb which was swollen from the baseball bat hit. Also, my left and right arms near the elbows had knots as if the bones were trying to rip out of my skin. My boy's mother happened to be standing in the hallway talking to one of her friends. She looked down at me from the top of the stairs and seeing that I was all beat up with no shoes on she kept asking me "what happened Imad"? as she was walking down the steps towards me. I couldn't really answer because I was now starting to feel the pain deep in my bones to the point of becoming breathless, kind of like when one falls on their knee and loses his breath or hitting the funny bone in your elbow. She took me into the house and rubbed some Vicks vapor rub on my arms and about 5 minutes later I heard someone calling my name from the front of her house. I looked out the window and it was Big A, so I came down the steps jumped into the van. He told me the cops had a car pulled over with a few guys in custody at Davis Sq., Park. We pulled up on the corner and there were cop cars and people everywhere, I walked through the crowd and sure enough it was the Cutlass with three guys standing with their hands on the trunk of the car then I heard someone say, "that's him, that's the guy they jumped". The cop turned looked at me and asked, "are these the guys who jumped you son"? I told him "I never seen these guys ever before" and that is the way things were supposed to be done. The guy that took the shot at me was standing there looking down, I took a good look at him to burn the image of his face into my mind. The cops never found the gun so they released them which suited me just fine. I found out that these guys who fucked up and tried killing me if the cops didn't show up and scare them off were Two Six and Ridgeway Lords and trust me a Two Six paid a heavy price within days for fucking me up. Without a doubt, there are things that I cannot ever talk about in detail such as the pay backs on the Two Six. My luck was getting worse, I had a very strong feeling that I was going to be killed soon which Obviously did not scare me because I was still doing the same stupid shit day in day out. Things were also winding down in the case I had going with Ed supposedly he was going to plead guilty to lesser charges and was expected to receive a 6-year sentence. I also had made up my mind that on my next court date which was coming up on April 18, 1985 that I was going to plead guilty, and to try and get the shortest sentence possible. I was ready and looking forward to going to prison as crazy as that may sound it's the truth. I went to court that day met my lawyer and informed him of my plans, he approached the prosecutor and the prosecutor told him that I would have to accept six years just like Ed. My attorney argued that this would be my first adult conviction and that I was only 17 when the crime was committed. He also argued that Ed had an extensive adult record was receiving a six years sentence that surely, I should receive a lighter sentence. The prosecutor took that into account and dropped down to four years but made it clear that he was not going any lower than that. My attorney informed me of the deal the state was offering, and I said, "take it" but my attorney tried arguing with me that I should give him more time to argue for a lighter sentence than the four years. I stopped him and said I was ready to go, just take it and let me go do my time. A few minutes later my case was called, I walked up in front of Judge and pled guilty to three lesser charges and was sentenced to four years on each count to be run concurrently which meant I would only serve half a of the four-year sentence. The judge scolded me, calling me a menace to society then handed down the sentence and remanded me to the custody of the Illinois Department of corrections.

The same gang graffiti which I did back in my day.
Some of My Saints brother of my era.
Crazy Horse, Lil Crazy Horse, Stony, Henio, Malo, Gato, Butcher, Lil Dirt Ball, Moses, Beto, Sir Player, Cochise, Chico, Mustang, Gringo, Andy, Fonso, Sly, Elvis, Santo, Fleabag, Lil Joe, Dago, Lefty, Puma.

My Time in State Prison.

I was taken into custody and processed through the Cook County jail on 26th and California then a day or two later I was placed on a bus and shipped out to Joliet state penitentiary. I arrived at Joliet and like all other prisoners was placed in the Annex building for orientation which was across the street from the main prison. I remained in the Annex for seven days of mainly 24hour lockdown without recreation, television or radio. At the Annex, we were medically and mentally examined evaluated then were processed into the Illinois Department of Corrections. On the day of those examinations we were placed in a big room and one person at a time was called in to see the doctor and other staff. On that day I met a few Latin Folks from the north side of Chicago mainly Maniac Latin Disciples and Imperial Gangsters and when they asked about my gang affiliation, I told them that I was a Saint from the south side and we plugged up with the folks in the joint. Some of the black guys in the room from the Gangster Disciples were eye balling a nice pair of gym shoes on the feet of a white kid which meant he was going to have to give them up very soon and sure enough within the next few minutes he gave them up without any abjections. After that week, we were moved over to the main prison and I was placed in cell 839 of the East house which was the last cell on the 8th gallery. When they called Chow, I went down to the chow hall and in the chow hall there were a few kitchen workers sitting on the end tables at the rear facing us as we walked in. These kitchen workers where there to try and figure out who was Folks and who was people. They did this by making a sign to the new inmates and if you were Folks you stacked your right fist over the left fist and if you were people you tapped the left side of your chest with your right fist and then made an open hand with five fingers open. From there the guy would approache you and questioned you about the area you were from and the gang you belonged too and thereafter you received a care package. But if they found out you were lying about your gang affiliation than you better be ready for one hell of an ass beating along with being extorted for the rest of your bit (sentence). I knew my boy Santo was in the Joliet at West house with the main population and he was riding Folks, so they didn't have to go too far to check me out. I gave the guy that approached me this information and he said he knew my boy and that he would speak to him then handed me my care package which consisted of body soap, deodorant, toothpaste, toothbrush, snacks and smokes if you smoked. I remained in Joliet for about a month like most people and was hoping that I they would keep me in Joliet with my boy and not transfer me to any other prisons. While there at Joliet I ran into Santo a few times, he told me to try and stay there with him and I told him that was my plan. I met a kid my age who was a Two Six from K town also known as Dark side. He was serving a 27year sentence for murder and attempted murder on Latin Kings. We became close friends he was a cool kid and a very likable individual and it was these types of friendships that later made me contemplate and realize that I couldn't possibly get out of jail and go back to the streets to fight people who were my good friends while we were in prison. I ran into the case manager who was handling my case and informed him that I wanted to stay in Joliet and he asked me why. I told him that it was close to home and one of my guys was there doing his time, so I wanted to stay there. He looked at me, smiled and said, "I'll tell you something, you are a young guy with a short sentence, I'm going to do you a favor and not let you stay I'll send you somewhere where you can learn a trade and get an education". That pissed me off and I tried my best to sway him to let me stay in Joliet other than do something stupid which did not guarantee that I would stay in Joliet anyway. They finally designated me to Sheridan correctional Center it was a prison for younger inmates with short sentences in those days. I arrived at Sheridan and like all new arrivals was placed in building C7 an orientation building and again at chow I went through the same process of are you Folks or People. The one from the folks turned out to be an Italian kid named Tee who was from our other branch in south Chicago on 87th and Houston. I didn't know Tee from the streets, but he knew about the Saints and that his branch originated from ours. Even though that branch was now known as only Spanish Gangster Disciples without the word Saint they were still using our symbol the halo over the six-point star. So, I thought I was covered as far as checking to see if I was really hooked up on the streets. They still had to check which was understandable because some fools thought they could walk in and say that they were hooked up, so they could receive the luxuries of being a gang member. I saw one case where an African American guy said he was a Gangster Disciple from some area on the southside of Chicago but was not. The Gangster Disciples found out he was lying, news came back that he was not a GD but was a neutron in his neighborhood. They gave him an ugly beating and made him wash dirty socks and underwear every day to humiliate him. I stayed in C7 for a week, during that week we were not allowed to go to the recreation yard or the gym for security reasons I'm sure. After C7 I was designated to building C6 I met with the Latin Folks who were in the unit and was informed that there would be a meeting the next day at the evening yard call so the new arrivals could meet all the other Latin folks within the prison. That night I sat down and wrote a long letter to Big A and his brothers, I mother fucked them in every way possible in it and I never heard from them. Once upon a time I felt that Big A and his brothers were my brothers but that was the furthest thing from the truth. At that point in my life I had a clear picture of Big A and his family and was glad they did not know of other crimes I committed by myself or with other stand up Saints who never opened their mouth to anyone about what we did because if they knew than the cops would have known. It was safe to say that the chapter of my life which included Big A and his family was over! The next day I went out to the yard for to meet everyone and be introduced to the other Latin Folks. I was looking for Tee from our other branch, but he was still at work in the kitchen and would not be released for another half hour. Some of the folks from the southside of Chicago such as the Two Six and Satan Disciples knew that us Saints were renegades on the street and they tried their best to stir up trouble for me. The Latin Folks who were talking to me about my affiliation had not talked to Tee yet, so they told me to give them a few minutes to talk amongst themselves. A few minutes later one of the Folks called Mousey approached me and wanted clarification on my nation (gang). I told him I was a Saint, so he said "Satan" I said no and by this time I was becoming agitated, so I spelled it out for him "S A I N T" he said okay and walked back to the meeting. A short time later he walked back to me and said, "look bro some of the folks are saying you guys are DK on the street". I explained to him that not only are we DK on the street but everything K (killer) that we are renegades but within the prison system we ride folks. I started to call of the names of Saints who were incarcerated throughout the prison system who were riding Folks. I told him that there was only one option for me and that is to ride Folks and if there was a problem then I would have to ride renegade just like the streets. There was no mother fucking way I would ever ride People (Latin King) I would simply rather die than do that. He seen how frustrated and angry I had become that he said, "Look bro be cool, there is no problem we'll straighten it out just give me a few" then he walked back over to the meeting. A few minutes after speaking to Mousey Tee showed up and walked up to me shook my hand then asked how I was doing and if I needed anything else. I thanked him and explained the situation to him about what was going with Folks. He looked over at the group in the meeting and said walk with me so we walked towards the meeting and when we got to them he asked a thousand pardons, a term of respect used when interrupt a meeting or a conversation when asking to be heard, then we stepped into the meeting and he basically told them that I was one of his and that my branch was renegade but his branch is Folks. He also let them know that if they had a problem accepting one of his then he is going to have to come off count with the Latin Folks and ride with me. The whole thing was settled and there was no more mention of it again. I started to investigate what type of educational programs the prison had to offer, and I found that you could either get your GED or take a vocational course. I decided to take a crack at getting my GED but when I started the GED class it became clear to me that there wasn't much learning going on hence it would be a waste of time. Guys just sat around chit chatting, so I knew that I would just sit there and waste my time because you are basically left to teach yourself. Shortly before I left the GED class, I signed up for something I liked in the vocational building which was auto body and Fender. My instructor's name was Bob who was a decent human being who treated all the inmates in his class with decency and respect. The prisons were wide open in those days there was extortion going on, inmates walked around the yard with cans of Coke mixed with Southern comfort and other walked the yard smoking weed and so on. Prison guards in those days tried to befriend inmates there was a lot of unity, respect and discipline among prisoners who were convicts and not inmates. I had my first trouble in no time with a white kid who was hanging out with the North siders, a group made up of white guys who were a part of the Latin Kings, who bumped into me and then mumbled something as if I was the one in the wrong. I turned around and gave him three cracks in the face before he could even blink an eye and I did that right in front of a prison guard. I was taken to segregation and spent a few weeks there before I was released back to general population. My vocational class was going great my instructor was impressed with my work and wanted me to stay on as an instructor's aid after the six-month course was over which I accepted. Within six months I had gained a spot (a position of authority) as committee man among the Latin Folks and was moving up the ranks. My mother and sisters would come to visit me every other weekend and to my surprise my father showed up a few times also my girlfriend would visit whenever she could. I had put in a request to move to one of the new units where living conditions were much better than where I was. In the newer units you could get buzzed in and out of your cell anytime you wanted by calling it into an intercom system and the cells were a bit bigger, cleaner and were all one-man cells unlike C6 which had all two-man cells. So, after a short stay in unit C6 I was transferred to C-17 and sure enough it was just I was told you just call your cell number and the officer in the control room hits a button and you're out of your cell. The units are made up of two sides, each side has two halls A and B on one side C and D on the other side. In state prison you could buy your own TV, hot pot, radio, fan, blue jeans and sweat clothes. One day one of the Gangster Disciples in my unit came to me and was complaining that his TV had stopped working. After hearing that, I thought for a minute and then an idea came to me. The guy who stayed in the cell across from me was a member of the Gaylord gang who were based on the north side of Chicago and they were predominantly white had the identical TV. I couldn't stand the guy or the Gaylords not to mention that they were partners with Latin Kings. The guy was only had a few months left on his sentence and would then be going home soon. I told the GD who worked in the barbershop if he could get his hands on a Phillips screwdriver and if so to bring it with him to the unit. The next day he showed up with the screwdriver and we waited until recreation was called that evening and crossed our fingers that the Gaylord would go out to the recreation yard. Sure, enough when they made the yard call the Gaylord went out to the yard, hell this guy was going home but the GD was serving a 40-year sentence, so he needed the TV more and that was the logic I used. The GD came down to my cell with his TV set and I walked out to the dayroom as if I was getting something to scope the situation and be 100% sure the coast was clear. I had left my cell door slightly open so when I came back down the hall, I called the Gaylord's cell number and the officer popped it open never giving it a second thought. I walked in and grabbed the Gaylord's TV and peaked out down the hall to see if the officer was looking and he wasn't, so I hurried to my cell with the TV. All we had to do was swap the back covers of both TV sets which was the only part that had the inmates prison number and we were home free. We put everything back together and returned the TV set back to the Gaylord's cell. That evening when the Gaylord returned from the recreation yard and tried turning his TV on, but it never came on which made him highly upset and I heard him say "Fuck my TV stopped working". The guy never suspected any foul play but reflecting back on what I did, I will admit it was a rotten thing to do but next to some of the other things I had been doing in my life you can look at it as a grain of sand in a vast desert. I am not proud of it but unfortunately that was the life I was living, and I saw nothing wrong in the things I did no matter how big or small. Being hooked up in a gang did not mean you wouldn't have to make your bones in prison and especially with the people you were hooked up with. For example, I had a problem with a GD because he was acting like I was supposed to fear him do to his size and when he seen that I was not, he made a statement about us handling business if I had a problem. What he meant by handling is to go toe to toe in a body punching match without any face hitting then at the end of it shake hands and hug without any hard feelings. I had no choice but to take him up on the offer no matter how big he was, so we went into the shower and took care of business and

I did the best that I could and held my own. I never folded and went all the way until we both stopped, his hits were hard because he was much bigger than I was but I gave back hits as hard as I could, at the end of it all he understood that I was not going to accept any disrespect from him even if it meant death. In C17 I met a Yugoslavian kid through a GD called Dog and on one Saturday morning as I was sitting with the pair in the Yugoslavian kid's cell just shooting the shit with them when the cell door opened, and the unit prison guard walked in and shut the door behind him. The guard was real cool guy, he sat down and joked around for a few minutes then stood up and put his hand in his pants and pulled out a bag of weed which looked like a few ounces and handed it the Yugoslavian kid. About a month later I was sent to the hole (segregation) for cursing and threatening the unit guard who was a well-known asshole. I spent a few weeks in the hole and was then released back into population but had to go back to the old buildings. I was placed in C2 which was like C6 all two-man cells and no buzzing in and out, it was all done the old way by keys. My cell mate was a white kid named Johnny who was a Simon City Royal an arch enemy on the streets to the Gaylords. Simon City Royals were Folks, but they were having problems in the prison system and in some prisons the Folks were either not carrying them or if they did, a tight leash was put on them and just like the Gaylord's the Simon City Royals were predominantly white. Me and Johnny kicked it off pretty good he was enrolled in one of the vocational classes I can't remember which but we would head to school together in the morning. One morning Johnny told me that the Gaylords were talking about smashing him (beating him up) when he went to the vocational building. The Gaylords also knew that the Royals were on shaky ground with the Latin Folks so they figured they had no backup. The leader of the Gaylords was this big corn fed looking white guy called Cowboy and that was the person who had threatened Johnny at the chow hall that morning. As usual me and Johnny headed out to school but this time, I told him to walk up in front of me and he did. As we got close to the vocational building, I saw Cowboy and about four other Gaylords coming from different directions towards Johnny I yelled for Johnny to hold up and I walked up to him than stood next to him. Cowboy approached and started to address Johnny, but I immediately cut him off with a question, "what's the problem" and he said;

Cowboy; "Devil we have no problems with you, our problem is with this guy"

Me; "how can that be if I am Folks and he's Folks, his problem is my problem and if you have a problem with me then you have a problem with every Gangster (folks) in this joint"

Cowboy; "I thought these dudes (Simon City Royals) weren't on count"?

Me; "well you thought wrong and I know that this is the reason you and your boys are trying to move on him. If he did something that was disrespectful to you in some way, I'll hear you out and go from there. If he's wrong, then he would be dealt with but that's not the case you just wanna fuck with him because you think he's got no backup".

Cowboy and his guys turned and walked off and that was the end of that. Other than shit like that prison life was smooth and majority of drama had to do with gambling, drugs or homosexuality. I was still in C2 when one of the news channels was having a special on the opening of Al Capone's safe in the Drake Hotel. That evening I decided to stay in the unit rather than go to the gym so I can watch the opening of the safe in the unit's dayroom TV with a few other guys. As I said the halls and cells in these old units had to be opened with a key so the officer would do a hall run every hour. When the officer did the hall run, I went into my cell put some water in my hot pot and left it on low heat than went back out to the dayroom and waited until the next hour. My plan was to make me a cup of coffee with a cigarette while watching the program. I put a chair in front of the dayroom TV so I can be close enough to see what they find inside the safe. When the next hour came, I walked to my cell and made the coffee then came back to find an older EX Latin King named Tommy had just come in from the gym and was sitting in the seat I had set up. I walked up to him with the coffee in my hand and respectfully said;

Me; "Excuse me bro that's my seat right there"

Tommy; "I don't see an ID, a cup or anything else on the seat saying it's yours".

For a second my mind was racing trying to figure out what was going through this guy's mind and now he was putting me in a position where I would have to do something to him. He was being trying to be cute and he was being funny, but he was playing with fire and just didn't know it. I was standing inches away from the left side of his body as he was seated in my chair and looking forward. I was really hoping he would get some sense in his head and just get up, so I tried again and said,

Me; "look bro stop playing that's my chair I set it up and that's all there is to it"

Tommy; "if you want the chair you know what to do"

And for a second the thought crossed my mind that I should just throw this smoking hot coffee in his face which would have burned the fuck out of his face but decided against it. I didn't need the coffee for this guy so I put the cup down which should have been a sign for him that something bad was about to happen but it didn't. I knew I was going to have to knock the fuck out of this guy, but I wanted to see where he wanted to go with this when he said, "you know what to do". I am sure the other convicts wanted to know what he meant also, so I chuckled and said,

Me, "Na bro I really don't know, so you tell me what it is you want me to do to get my chair"?

While smiling and still looking forward he answered me with this. "you can say, Tommy can I please have my chair"

I was on fire and my blood was boiling now, my body was so tense I didn't even have to cock my arm back to strike him with my fist which was only a few inches from his left jaw. When my fist connected with his jaw his head dropped between his knees. He then got up but was dazed confused and off balance he looked down then opened his mouth and spit out a few small pieces of his back tooth. A GD walked up to him and punched him on the right side of his head which dazed him even more. The guard who was the turnkey that evening walked into the dayroom and asked what was going on. The guard's name was Blast who was the kind of guard that played things the old fashion way, if two inmates had a beef and both agreed to go heads up, he would have no problem with allowing them to do so in the showers. I told Tommy in front of Blast if he wanted to go heads up that we could go in the shower and handle business. Officer Blast heard that and said if that's what you guys want to do that's fine with me. Tommy wanted no part of that but kept whining about how I sucker punched him and wouldn't shut his fucking mouth. I told Tommy that he left me no choice and that now talking was over, that he could get some get backs in a head up fight but he refused and that was the end of that. I always kept a close eye on him because he may try to stab me or hit me with a pipe or something like that, after all the guy was once upon a time a gang banger but he never tried anything stupid. Not long after that I was again moved to one of the new buildings C 19 this time. The shipment bus came every week like clockwork with it came new inmates among them were new Latin Folks one of them being Rocky from the Ambrose of 18 Street also P G who was also an Ambrose of 18 Street, that area is known as Pilsen. At the time of their arrival Niggs in Mousy were calling the shots in the joint for the Latin Folks and I had a position as a committee man. A few months after the arrival of Rocky and P G the Latin Folks wanted to hold elections for first C (first in command) and second C (second in command) because many of the Latin folks were not happy with Niggs and Mousy being in charge. I was nominated along with Rocky for the positions of first C and second C and a vote was taken to see which one would hold what position. After the votes were counted, I was chosen for the first C position and Rocky to hold the second C position. Once the results of the vote came out a meeting was held, and it was then that I informed everyone that I would be declining the first C position and would only accept the second C position. The reason was very simple, Rocky had a longer sentence to do and was older than me. So as far as I was concerned, Rocky was more qualified for the position of first C than me, everyone accepted. A month or two after the election we received a kite (letter) from Joliet prison informing us that an Ambrose had informed prison officials about Shanks (homemade knives) which belonged to Latin Folks. Because of this informant some of the Folks had lost a year of good time along with disciplinary transfers to another penitentiary. In this kite we had a prison picture of the informer, so we had a meeting and it was agreed that if this Rat showed up other Ambrose would handle that business. The Rat was from their organization and this was done for two reasons (1) out of respect for them to handle their own (2) to clean the blemish this guy put on their organization by informing. No one knew which prison this Rat was going to be sent so kits were sent to many prisons. After sometime the informant showed up to our prison and of course all the Latin Folks were instructed to pretend like we had no idea what he did in order to give the Ambrose time to formulate a plan to hit him and there was no need to attack him out in the open like fools and have people receive new charges. There were 3 Ambrose spread out throughout the prison and it was winter time, so the gym was used rather than the recreation yard and that made it harder for everyone to see each other. Another problem was, this Rat wasn't coming out of his unit other than to the chow hall and that was only sometimes and there were no Ambrose in his unit. A few days later I went to my auto body class and I saw him walking into the vocational building so that gave us an option. I watched him walk to the end of the hall where the carpentry class was located. My class was located in the center of the building directly in front of the entrance doors of the vocational building. We had a meeting and It was agreed that an Ambrose who was at the vocational building along with a Maniac Latin Disciple would take care of the Rat the next day. The next day I looked for the Ambrose who was to do the hit, but he was not in school. On the other hand, I did see the Maniac Latin Disciple who was waiting and ready. At lunch, I seen Rocky and asked what happened to the Ambrose who was to take care of the informant because he was not in the school. Rocky told me that the guy had run into some trouble that morning with the guard working his unit and was sent to the lieutenant's office than was sent back to the unit a few hours later. After hearing that I told Rocky that I along with the Maniac would take care of the Rat after lunch if he and P G would agree and they both agreed. I walked off in search of the Maniac and found him then filled him in on the new plan, so we made our way back to the school before the Rat did. It was not the norm that a second C would take care of that kind of business, but it was taking a bit longer than it should have. It was also my pleasure to serve this Rat because my boy Santos was also caught up when he informed on the Folks in Joliet. Me and the Maniac made it back to the school before most people, so made our way down the hall and waited for the Rat. I was on one side of the wall in the hall while the Maniac was on the other and by now guys were filling the hall. Finally, the Rat came down the hall and as soon as he passed us, we were on his ass like white on rice and the by the time we were done between our fists, the small pipe and our steal toe boots the Rat was left with a broken jaw a fucked-up nose and few fractured ribs among other injuries. They took him away and locked the school down so they could go from class to class inspecting hands and faces looking for cuts and bruises but came up with nothing. I went back to my unit and right after the institutional count the control officer in my unit called me to his station. I walked up there and he gave me a paper pass with instructions to go to the captain's office, I didn't ask why or for what because I already knew what it had to be about. I went down to the captain's office and was instructed to sit down in the hall way and wait for the captain to call me in. A few minutes later I was called in, there with the captain sat an officer who investigated incidents in the joint. The captain looked at me and asked,

Capt." what happened in the vocational building today"?

Me; "you mean the commotion in the hall"?

Capt." yes the commotion in the hall".

Me; "I have no idea, the only thing I heard was that there was a fight or something like that".

Capt." you know there are 200 people in that building and no one seems to know anything".

Me; "the only thing I know is what I told you".

Capt. "that's funny because I hear you were in the middle of it all".

Me; "How could that be when you just told me that there are 200 people in the school and yet no one knows anything, but now you're saying that you heard I was in the middle of it. I had nothing to do with it, I was not involved in whatever happened in any way".

Capt. "go back to your unit and be sure that we are going to get to the bottom of this".

I went back to my unit and continued doing my time which was flying by. I only had to give the state 24 months in total and if I received my 3months good time that would put me out the door at 21 months. I tried putting in for work release but was ultimately denied without a reason so I filed a grievance and my hearing was set about three weeks after I was called to the captain office. The hearing for my grievance was held in the same building as the hospital. I walked in the waiting area and was sitting there when low and behold the Rat Ambrose we fucked up was brought in by two prison guards with shackles around his waist. He looked bad he had a brace holding the right side of his jaw together, his eye sockets still showed some bruising and the white parts of his eyeballs still had red in them from trapped blood. He was brought in with another inmate from segregation so one officer placed the Rat in a room by himself and the other officer placed the other segregated inmate in the room with me. These rooms did not have bars but they had big glass windows so you can see clearly in the next room. I asked the inmate who was placed with me if he knew what happened to that guy's face in the next room. He told me that the guy was in protective custody, that he heard him tell the police on the way from segregation that he was jumped by the Latin Kings. I looked over at him and I knew he had no idea who I was because he never met me. He did not know that I was one of the people who caused all the damage to his body and face and how could he because he never got the chance to look at his attackers. A minute or two later I was called in for the hearing on my grievance and as expected they upheld the decision to deny me. In 1986 my uncle who was imprisoned by the Israelis was released after serving 18 years along with 99 other Palestinian political prisoners in exchange for an Israeli pilot who was shot down over Beirut in 1983. After his release my uncle was exiled to Syria where he lived in one of the Palestinian refugee camps. I was getting out in January 1987 and a month before getting out I met one of the new Latin Folks who just left cook county jail at the gym. When he found out that I was a Saint he gave me some pretty disturbing news, he informed me that two of my boys were riding People in Cook County jail the two being Cocomo and Little B. I am sure they were approached the same way I was and buckled under pressure instead of standing strong they ran to the Latin Kings. The news made me sick to my stomach and this was the reason I was hoping the Saints would unite with the folks on the street back then. I couldn't believe that those two gave in like that but they did and there was no turning back from that. Cocomo was incarcerated for killing one of the boys called little Dirt Ball, they both got into an argument. Cocomo pulled out a 410 sawed off shotgun and pointed it at Little Dirt Ball's chest. Little Dirt Ball pushed Cocomo and that caused the gun to go off which put a hole through little Dirt Ball's chest killing him instantly. I had a few run-ins with Little Dirt Ball myself in the past he would get drunk and act stupid not a summer would pass when I didn't have to knock his ass out. I am sure he got on Cocomo's nerves but there is no doubt Cocomo should have never pulled a gun on one of the boys to begin with. A few weeks before my release I was served with papers from the INS and in those papers, I was informed that the government would be looking to revoke my green card and deport me back to Jerusalem. On the day of my release which was Jan/16/1987 two INS agents picked me up at the gate and drove me to the Dirksen federal building in downtown Chicago. When we arrived at the federal building the agents went back and forth with me about my criminal history because the only record that came up was the case, I was incarcerated for the other stuff, but all juvenile troubles were not coming up. They kept asking if I was sure I did not have any other criminal history and I said no like I was going to give them information they don't have. Finally, one of the INS agents told me that they were going to release me then gave me a phone and to call my family to come pick me up. Before I close this chapter let me be fair to my father. One thing about my father, he loved Palestine and sacrificed a lot with his brother for it and he would never ever sell out even if it meant his death unlike many other Palestinians who have not sacrificed nor are they willing to so. He is an honorable Palestinian nationalist who is respected by many for that but unfortunately that did not make him a good husband nor a good father.

Me at the young age of 19 years old in state prison 1986.

1987 Life After State Prison

Now that I was free I had to get my driver's license and begin the process of trying to get my life together. Thank God for the trade school in prison which gave me the opportunity to become a certified auto body man and the chance to get a job in the auto body shop industry. I got my driver's license back and trust me it took some doing to get that mess straightened out. One lessons in life is that it is easy to screw things up and very hard to undo the mess you created from screwing up. I got my first job at a restoration body shop called B&J antiques on the north side of Chicago which is no longer in existence. As always, my mother was there through thick and thin and to my surprise my father seemed to have changed a bit. As for my best friends Big A, Problem and Little Problem well they were no longer welcomed in the neighborhood, as a matter of fact one of the saints had shot Problem but only wounding him. I also found out from my brothers and sisters that two suits from internal affairs had come to the store to speak with me about the incident of the cops beat me up. They ran into my father who told them "don't worry about it my son is a punk gang banger who more than likely had it coming". I myself never heard anything from them, it pisses me off that they never attempted to get in touch with me simply because I was in prison. If it was to indict me for another crime, they would have found me and would have drove however many miles to the prison just to serve me with the indictment. On my free time after work I was everywhere, I purchased a car and was basically having fun chasing girls spending a lot of time at the lakefront and staying out of trouble the best way I could. I ran into my boy Malo at Davis Sq., Park, I was happy to see him, and we talked for a while, but he wasn't the Malo I once knew.

He was still beating himself up about the night his brother Jinio was killed, he kept blaming himself for it. I tried telling him to let it go that he should stop blaming himself because it was not his fault, we talked a little bit more than parted ways, but I never thought that it would be the last time I would see Malo alive again. A few weeks later Malo would take his own life, he was drinking at his mother's house with a Saint called lucky and some of the other boys. I heard that Malo had been talking about killing himself when he was drunk because of what happened to his brother, but I never heard him say that myself say he was going to kill himself. Whenever he behaved like this whoever from the boys was with him would keep their eye on him and make sure he did not have a gun on him. That night he was with lucky and somehow Malo carried out what he had always said he was going to do, he shot himself in the eye and that was the end of my brother Malo. Years later I find out that Malo started up with his "I am going to kill myself" but this time he had a pig called Lucky with him who told him to shut the fuck up and do it already while laughing. Lucky challenging Malo to do it, gave Malo the encouragement he needed so he pulled a gun out and put it to his eye than squeezed the trigger killing himself. After leaving my job at the restoration body shop, I went to work for CDE body shop where my old manager friend Rudy was still employed but this time around, I was an auto body man and no longer a porter. In The 21 months I spent in state prison many things changed on the streets there were many new Saints as expected. The Latin souls' neighborhood had dwindled down to only a few city blocks. The 48th St. boys were now known as La Raza street gang and the unification of the Latin Folks was starting to fall apart and likewise with the People nation on the streets of Chicago. As for the Latin Folks It all started in late 1986 between the Ambrose of 63rd and the Two Six over an incident involving a girl. An Ambrose shot a Two Six and in retaliation the Two Six shot up a house party that belonged to the

Ambrose but instead of shooting Ambrose they shot SDs and 22 boys hence a bigger war was breaking out. Now the war spread from Two Six and Ambrose to Two Six and Satan Disciples including the 22 Boys. At that time, I mainly hung out with some of the older Saints at a neighborhood tavern even though I wasn't much of a drinker, so it was just a place to shoot the shit with the boys. Stony had been picked up some years back for the shooting of the Latin Soul and the incident with gang crime Detective Joromis. When Stony completed his prison sentence he was deported back to Mexico, but he made his way back to Chicago and was gang banging like he did years before. One night, Stoney asked if I would give him and lucky a ride to Lucky's house where they were going to spend the night. On the way to Lucky's house I tried putting a bug in Stoney's ear about slowing down and letting the younger boys in the hood take care of business. I told him that he should kick back and not get heavily involved especially that he was back in Chicago illegally. He was agreeing with me, but I had the feeling that my words were falling on deaf ears. A few days before giving him that ride, I heard that he was out gang banging and had beat a guy so bad that the guy fell into a coma. Stony was messing around with a girl called Ya Ya at the time. About a month after giving Stony a ride I received a call from Mo that Stony had been shot in the head the night before and was not expected to recover. The story of Stony's death went something like this, Stony was out looking for his girlfriend Ya Ya and someone told him that she was at a local nightclub called the Brass. Stony went there looking for her but she was not there so he turned around and was headed out the door but got into an argument and a fight with the bouncer at the entrance of the club. What Stony did not know was that someone in the club had recognized him and was planning his murder. While fighting with the bouncer whoever that person who was planning to kill him got his chance while Stony was on top of the bouncer. The guy walked up to Stony and tapped him on the head with the gun, Stony looked up and the guy fired a single shot into his head Stony, the bullet entered his forehead then exited behind his ear. When I went to see him at Mount Sinai hospital in the intensive care unit I immediately knew there was no way he was going to make it. He was on a life-support machine and that was the only thing keeping him alive. Every now and then I would have to put some work in for the neighborhood because circumstances left me with no choice. I still carried a gun here and there depending on where I was and how I felt. As for Stony he passed away a few days after I visited him and that was the end of a fearless warrior. One evening, having nothing to do I went to a Thee Boy and Party Boy party, while there I was having a conversation with a Thee Boy when Stony's name came up and from out of nowhere some guy who was visiting from out of town said, "fuck Stony". I immediately gave the guy a crack in the mouth and from there it turned into a brawl. It turns out the guy I cracked was related to one of the Thee Boyz and his cousin did not appreciate me giving his cousin a mouth shot. After cracking the first guy I cracked who ever came up in my face even if they were trying to break up the brawl. I was not trying to figure out the peacemaker from the foe as far as I was concerned, they were all foes at that point. Even after the situation was calm I was still fuming and I addressed all of the people at the party with these words "there is about 20 or 30 of you and only one of me so I'll be back with something that will even the odds" some of them tried to calm me down and talk me out of leaving but I was not hearing it. I jumped in my car then went to a Saint's house and retrieved a 38caliber pistol then went back to where the party was. By the time I got there almost everyone was gone except one vehicle which was pulling away a white Ford Escort. I jumped out of my car and fired a single shot at the car as it was driving past me fast, but I hit the driver's door right in the center. I knew the guy who was driving the car and the girl who owned the car. They never called the cops and just let it go, but most of all I thank God my shot was not a few inches higher because I may have killed the driver. My old friend Green Eyes who was broke like me before I went to prison was now dealing marijuana and cocaine and was making a lot of money at it. Unfortunately, he was not the same person I knew, he changed and had turned into this arrogant asshole. One day I was double parked and was sitting in my car on 45th and Hermitage when Green Eyes pulled up next to me and said, "snow cost more than gold" with a big smile on his face. What he did pissed me off to the point that I wanted to forget we were friends and bust his head because I knew he was acting like this purely out of arrogance. He had formed a new group of friends who were kissing his ass which along with money he was making was the cause of his arrogance. I put my car in gear and pulled it up a little further ahead of him and blocked the street. I got out of my car and stood in the middle of the street waiting for him to pull to where I was standing. He didn't see anything strange with me blocking the street, so he pulled his car close enough, he then put his car in park so we could talk but he never got out. I leaned towards his car window then asked him to repeat what he had said, and as soon as he started to utter it out of his mouth I reached into his car through the opened window. I grabbed him by his hair and yanked his head out the window and proceeded to punch the living fuck out of him and thought about grabbing a pipe out of the trunk of my car so I could bust his head, but I didn't want to let go of his hair because he would get away. He was already attempting to reach the shifter handle on center counsel with his right hand and stomping the gas pedal, but he couldn't reach the shifter to put the car in reverse. I tried opening his car door so I could pull him out of the car but was able to slip from my grip and put the car in reverse and stomped the gas pedal, the car went back about two car lengths and stopped. I was standing in the middle the street, he was eye balling as if he was thinking about charging me with his car to run me over. I was yelling at him daring him to do it "come on mother fucker if you got balls try and run me over" but instead he reversed to the corner and took off. It didn't take a rocket scientist to figure out what he was thinking and where he was headed, he was going back to his house to grab a gun, so I jumped in my car and drove to his house to make things easy for him and give him a reality check. I got to the front of his house and found the car he was driving parked half way up the sidewalk. As soon as I pulled up, he was already running out his house, so I jumped out of my car and started walking towards him daring him to pull out the gun he had. But he started to lecture me instead, on how wrong I was because we are friends and what I did was wrong. I was so heated and started yelling back at him, "That friend shit is been gone"! A guy we both knew named Abraham was standing in front of Green Eyes' house, he tried to cool things down between us but at that point I didn't give a fuck about cooling things down nor did I want to hear that shit. The last I wanted to hear was Abraham's peace-making bullshit, so I said, "shut the fuck up and mind your fucking own business". To be close friends when we had no money back and now that he is dealing and making money, he forgot all about our friendship. For the next few months it was a cat and mouse chase every time I seen him it was on but eventually, we talked and squashed the feud between us. He told me that I was wrong for thinking he changed, and he was the same guy but there was nothing he could say to make me believe I was wrong about him changing up. Let be clear, Green Eyes was no punk he could handle his own and was putting a hurting on many people whenever he had to, but he was running around arrogantly trying to throw shit in my face like me and him were in competition. From that day on we hung out together here and there, but he never conducted any of his cocaine dealing in front of me out of respect for me especially when I'm wasn't making a dime from nor did I want any part of it at the time. One evening I was carrying a gun while hanging out on 45th and Hermitage and I was talking to one of my boy's brother-in-law who just pulled up in his car. I was standing in the street talking to him when a car load of people was passing the intersection front us and I recognized the vehicle as one belonging to the La Raza street gang. I pulled out the gun and lit them up (shot up the car) as they crossed the intersection. The boy's brother-in law wasn't a gang member, so my action spoked the shit out of him and he took off in his car like a bat out of hell. Taking off like that didn't make him a coward, he did the right thing because he wanted no part of a murder in case someone got shot and killed. It was summer time and there was a lot of shit to do for fun in Chicago back in those days' things were different in the city, the lake front was open all night long, there were car races in the Stock Yards but most of all life was not as stressful as it has become these days. On one of those beautiful summer nights Green Eyes picked me up and we headed south on Hermitage to 47[th Street] while at the stop sign, I felt something to my left so I turn my head and glanced out of the side window behind Green Eyes and there it was a guy pointing a gun at my head from the car next to us. I ducked my head down and at the same time yelling at Green Eyes to take off because the guy next to us had a gun pointed at us. Green Eyes stepped on the gas pedal as hard as he could, and we sped off before and the guy never got a shot off. I told Green Eyes to go back to 45th and Hermitage where I retrieved a sawed-off 12gauge pump from one of the boy's house and hid in a gang way waiting for that car to come back but they never came back. I never knew who those guys were, but I was almost sure they were members of the La Raza gang. I was still working at the body shop Monday through Friday still living at home in my own apartment upstairs from my parents but as usual was not having much dealings with my father. I got invited like most of the Saints to one of my boys' wedding, he was marring my boy Santo's sister and the wedding was going to be held on 55th and wood street which was enemy territory. There was no way in hell I to going attend the wedding without a gun just to be on the safe side of things. As the old saying goes "I'd rather be caught with a gun than get caught without one" in that situation. When I got to the wedding, I noticed they had security at the door who was checking the guys, but the girls could walk in without being searched. I pulled this girl I knew to the side and asked her to sneak the gun in her purse for me and of course she agreed to do so. After we were both in the hall I retrieved the gun from her and stuck it in my waste. After everyone was in the hall and the back door of the hall which led to the alley was opened so I walked out into the alley to get some fresh air and while out there I decided to smoke a cigarette. As I was standing in the alley, I noticed a gangbanger looking kid walking towards me with his face looking twisted up as if he had a problem. I pulled out my gun and pointed it at him and just about that time one of the boys came out of the back door and seen what I was doing. As soon as he seen the gun in my hand he started yelling "wait, wait that's my cousin". I lowered my hand and put the gun in my waist then started to walk back with my boy following close behind me with his cousin. My boy was ranting while he was hyper ventilating, he was complaining to some of the boys that I had a gun and how I would have killed his cousin if he hadn't stopped me. One of my older boys called Mustang walked up to me and asked if I had a gun. I wasn't going to lie to him, shit he is one of my boys and I had no problem sharing that information with him. I told him that I did have a gun and he asked if I could please give it to him until after the wedding than he would give it back to me which I had no problem with. I gave the gun to Mustang and went about the business of enjoying myself. If my boy had not come out there that kid would have been dead, I had no problem pulling the trigger. For all I knew he could have been a Two Six, 22boy or a Latin Soul because that area was within their stomping grounds.

That night I left the wedding with a girl named Diana who would years later become my wife. I was starting to spend more and more time with Green Eyes by that time, I would page him, or he would come looking for me and we would hang out. I met most of his crew (guys who delivered his cocaine) and I already knew most from the neighborhood but not on a personal level. Green Eyes had already moved out of the neighborhood and was now living in the Marquette Park area on the block of 65th and Fairfield. He didn't feel safe in our neighborhood anymore a lot of the guys there didn't have much love for him not to mention the Chicago police from our area were hot on his trail. I don't know if it was paranoia or just because he could, but he started driving around with a custom-made bullet proof vest wrapped in black leather which from a distance looked like a plain old biker's vest. Speaking of bikes Green Eyes had a nice Harley Davidson and one night in September of 1989 he came by on his Harley Davidson and I took it for a ride in the neighborhood. I knew how to ride motorcycles from riding my mini dirt bike back in the day and I loved Harley Davidson motorcycles. In the early eighties one of our neighbors owned a Harley Davidson wide glide, I fell in love with the look and sound of the bike. I took off on the bike and rode around for a few minutes than I came down 43rd to Wood street and turned my head for one second but when I looked forward, I found the vehicle in front of me had come to a complete stop. I did my best to try and stop the bike but there was no way, so I decided to stuff the bike between the car in front of me and the parked cars next to it. There wasn't enough room for me to do that so the primary cover (clutch cover) on the left side of the engine got caught by the bumper of the car in front of me and that caused the bike to jerk and crush my left leg between the bike in the car's back bumper. My left leg snapped in three places below my knee and above my ankle than as the bike rolled from under me the sissy bar on the bike hit me in the back and throw me over two of the parked cars. I landed between the parked cars with my head missing the diamond plated back bumper of a parked pickup truck. There is no doubt in my mind that had my head hit the bumper of the pickup truck I would have possibly been dead. I landed and hit the pavement like a ragdoll, my body went underneath the pickup truck, but I was able to stop my body from going any further by grabbing the tailpipe of the pickup truck. As I pulled myself out my left leg felt like Jell-O below my knee, at that time I still was unaware that my leg was broken so I pulled myself out and tried to stand up, but my left leg buckled and bent to the left below my knee and shin bone popped out of my skin. I fell on my ass and just sat there because I knew at that point there wasn't anything that I could do but sit there and wait for an ambulance. The only things holding my foot to the rest of my leg was flesh and skin because both bones had clean breaks and were not attached. The accident happened in my neighborhood and word quickly spread causing people to flock to where I was. The ambulance arrived and took me to Holy Cross Hospital and a few of my older boys followed to the ER which always a good feeling knowing your boys cared about you. I later heard there was a rumor in the neighborhood that I must have been coked out (high on cocaine) because I was not bothered by the pain. Hearing about the rumor made me laugh because I have never touched the stuff my only bad habits were smoking cigarettes and later down the line smoking marijuana. I wasn't much of a drinker because I couldn't stand the smell or taste of alcohol let alone use hard drugs. I was operated on a few days after the accident and the doctor placed a rod, plate, screws, and pins in my leg to hold the bones together. I was released a few weeks later, I had to use crutches to get around so unable to work or do much of anything else for that matter. I went back to the hospital after a few weeks and the nurse determined that she was going to replace the cast because it was developing a foul odor from the dried blood in the cotton.

When she removed the cast, she looked over my leg and made a comment about my scars healing very well and then suggested that I wear a brace in order to let my skin breathe and told me to return in a week for the new cast. I left and never went back to the hospital for the new cast and just made do with the brace they gave me. When I ran into Green Eyes, he told me that my mother let him have it the night of the accident for giving me the motorcycle to ride and we both just laughed our asses off because that was exactly how my mother was, she was a very tough little lady. I went to visit Green Eyes on 65th and Fairfield and never went back to my apartment. Green eyes told me to stay there with him and I did, figuring I was done wasting my time being on the fence and was ready to jump into the drug dealing game. I was already going to be taking a hell of a chance being around him and his guys, even though there were no drugs in the house there was plenty of guns. At the time, Green Eyes was already fighting a case in Cook County Court for possession of a quarter pound of cocaine. I talked to my boys (Saints) about getting them into the game of dealing weed so they could make money for the nation rather than letting neutrons (non-gang members) make all the money in our neighborhood and they agreed. I obtained a few pounds of some top grade weed and gave It to them to bag up in small amounts and told them this would be on me but the next time they would have to pay up from the cash they made from the pounds I gave them. Unfortunately, those in charge of the pounds screwed it all up, by the time it was over there was no weed or money to account for so that was the end of that business venture, you can take the horse to the river, but you can't make him drink it. It was then that Green Eyes introduced me to a father and son whom I had known of since I was a young kid and had heard from back then about their alleged Mob ties. White senior and White junior owned a high-end auto repair shop dealing in vehicles such as Rolls-Royce, Mercedes-Benz, Porsches, Ferraris and other exotic cars. I was now living with Green Eyes along with my girlfriend who was pregnant at the time with our child. Me and the guys lived a life that was totally illegal, we dealt drugs, stole cars and carried guns. We had trap cars (low key vehicles used for illegal purposes) parked on the street with five, ten or fifteen kg in their trunks. One evening Lucky came to visit me at the house and a few minutes later Green Eyes showed up rambling on about the Two Six gang of 59th. He said that some of the Two Six boys of 59th St. had tried to get at him while he was driving through their neighborhood. I grabbed Lucky and one of the delivery guys called Biscuit and headed out to 59th St. we were armed with three semiautomatic pistols. We drove around the area for a few minutes but no one was in sight the area was a ghost town and the only thing we saw out there was a crew from the Chicago water department. Upon seeing them Biscuit said, "there's no one out here but these guys, I'll just shoot one of them". Up to that point I had done a lot of stupid shit in my life but there was no way in hell was I going to allow this fucking idiot to shoot one of these poor guys. I snapped on him "shut the fuck up we ain't doing no stupid shit like that" and that was the end of that, and we headed back to the house without incident. I thought to myself, here are these hard-working guys out here in the cold working to feed their families and this idiot with me is looking to end one of their lives because there wasn't any Two Six to shoot. By that time Green Eyes' case was winding down he decided to take it to trail and when he did, he was found guilty. The case carried a sentence of nine-years in prison to be served in the Illinois Department of corrections. The State wanted to take custody of him as soon as he was found guilty, but he had his attorney ask the Judge to allow him to go to the funeral of his cousin, who was really was his friend, called Bowtie. Bowtie was an older Latin Soul who was shot and killed a week before in front of Midway Airport. The argued that Green Eyes would turn himself in after the funeral and the Judge granted the request. Green Eyes

Green Eyes wanted time to think if he should stick around and do his time in prison or make a run for it to Mexico. He decided that he was going to make a run for it to Mexico the next day and when he failed to show up in court the judge sentenced him to nine years and put a fugitive warrant out for his arrest. Business went on as usual there were customers who had to be supplied and we went out and did what we had to get things done. At this point I was only helping in keeping things together and within a few days I gathered up a $128,000 along with pounds of weed and guns than me and one of the guys called Dicker moved them to one of their stash garages than placed everything in the trunk of one of the trap cars. A few weeks after leaving, Green Eyes started becoming paranoid about things like he was being cut out of the business. Green Eyes called from Mexico and got into an argument with Dicker threatening him, that he would be back in Chicago soon and that Dicker better have his gun ready. Being a neutral party, I tried defusing the situation Green Eyes was my friend and so was Dicker but of course me and Green Eyes had a much stronger history. Dicker and others argued that Green Eyes was way too greedy, estimating that at the time he had a few million dollars put up which they made together but were complaining that they had only received crumbs from him. As far as Dicker trying to cut him out, that was far from the truth because I was there handling things and would not let that happen. The money and the weed in the garage came up missing, the garage was no forced entry into it, so it was clear that whoever went into the garage and took the stuff had a key to the garage. The only one with keys to the garage amongst at the time was Dicker so the accusation was directed towards him. But According to Dicker there was another set of keys that was in the hands of Green Eyes' girlfriend and he continued to deny having anything to do with the theft. I spoke to Green Eyes before he came back, and I decided that I would go to a local Ford dealer and trade my cougar XR7 for a high-top conversion van. I traded the cougar and gave the car dealer the deference in cash for the van. Green Eyes was on his way to Chicago and on the night of his arrival he called me to say that he was coming to the house for a sit down. Dicker and another one of the guys were armed that night, no one was taking any chances and tensions were so thick in that house you could almost cut them with a knife. The doorbell rang, I told the guys to just be cool and relax than went to open the door, upon opening the door I told Green Eyes the same thing. Green Eyes came in and talked things over and thereafter everyone agreed that there was a lot of money to be made and there were bigger deals being planned out where everyone will have plenty of money at the end. It was back to business but there very little cocaine left, so the goal of the day was to go out and get one of the connects to supply us which was not going to be a problem. We picked up five kilograms and got them ready to be packaged up for resale which would be in quarter ounces, half ounces, ounces, quarter pounds, quarter kilos, half kilos and so on. It was a very hectic situation because Green Eyes was a wanted fugitive and it was no secret that the Ninth District detectives were out looking for him high and low. In the middle of all this madness my girlfriend was pregnant, so I had to take her to the Dr. for regular checkups. One afternoon I took her to her appointment and by the time we returned home which was in the early evening hours we were met by neighbors who informed me that the house had been raided by police and they had just left shortly before my arrival. The police knocked the front door off the hinges and captured Green Eyes and arrested Dicker and Biscuit who was another worker. The Puerto Rican family who lived across the street from us told me that as the police were leaving with the guys in handcuffs a teenage white girl who lived a few houses from our house approached the police and informed them that we owned cars that were parked up and down the street. When the police heard this news, they marched everybody back into the house and went about the business of retrieving all car keys in the house. The cops went back out to the street with a bunch of car keys in hand then the little white girl pointed out the cars she knew belonged to us which were the trap cars. The police proceeded to open and search the cars and in one they found four kilograms of cocaine and in the other they found five or six more guns. I entered the house and found Dicker's girlfriend in there and the house looked like a tornado had gone through it, shit thrown all over the place. I sealed the door off the best way I could and waited for the next day to see what was going to happen in court. In court, Green Eyes was held without bond since he was already a fugitive, Dicker was given a bond but Biscuit had some warrants so there was no bond for him either. I picked up Dicker that afternoon from the front of Cook County Jail on 26th and California. We discussed our situation and our options, so we agreed that we had one real option and that is to re-cop cocaine and start making money. We were basically just about broke at the time and a big part of coke the police seized was not paid for yet so that was going to make it hard to get anymore coke from that connect. The coke was fronted under Green Eyes name but even so we still had to pay for it if we wanted more from that connect. I collected whatever money was on the street and gave it to a Colombian girl who had gotten the kilos from a Colombian connect she knew. She paged me and we agreed to meet at a Mexican restaurant on Cermak Avenue in Berwyn Illinois. At the restaurant, she was crying telling me how the connect who gave her the cocaine was threatening to do bodily harm to her if she did not produce the money for the seized cocaine. She told me that even though the connect knew Green Eyes had been arrested and the cocaine was seized he still held her responsible for payment of the kilos. I collected as much money as I could and gave it to her then told that I will cover what Green Eyes owed if the connect would front me some more keys. She said that she was sure the connect would not have a problem with giving us a few kilos when his shipment came in. Unfortunately, a few days after meeting with the Colombian girl a drought hit Chicago it didn't matter whether it was cocaine or marijuana, it was virtually impossible to get anything from anyone at that time. If you found something at that time the prices were sky high and the quality was not very good. We tried with other connects but everyone was saying the same thing "We are waiting for our shipment to come in". We only had a few thousand dollars left to play with and the few connects who would front us kilo gram amounts were out also. We had no choice but to try and cop one or 2 ounces for cash, that is if we could find it. We reached out to everyone we knew who was in the business and finally came up with one guy who had a few ounces for sale. I am sure somebody had some, but it was very hard to find and cannot walk around asking random people if they had cocaine for sale. That is how we started in small amounts with lower level customers until we could get larger quantities to accommodate higher level customers. From the time of Green Eyes arrest I had a set of detectives from the Ninth District who would stalk me, and I pretended not to see them. We still lived in the house Green Eyes was arrested on 65th street so they were out of their District because we were in the Eight District. Only a fool would have anything in that hot house and just by the way these guys were acting I was positive they were doing this on their own in hopes of stumbling on to some money. One evening me and Lucky were at the house and when it came time to leave, I looked out to see if these two assholes were parked down the street and they were nowhere in sight so me and him got into the van and drove off with in a few minutes these assholes were behind us. After not seeing them I did not look in the rear mirrors, but I did after a few blocks and low and behold they were there a few cars behind me. I mentioned it to Lucky and played it cool, I had 4 thousand dollars on me, but I kept a deposit book on me that I had from my family business which I could use for cover for small money like that. The detectives followed me from 64th and California to 47th and California than I decided to pull into a Shell gas station, and they followed me in. I pulled up to the first pumps and within seconds they were at our doors. The one on my side opened my door and sarcastically asked if he could help me as if he was an attended. They searched us including the van and of course they found the cash then they pulled me to the side and we trying to question me about the location of a garage Artesian street that a few hundred thousand dollars in it. To be honest I had no idea what they were talking about and that was my answer to them so the one that came to my door got pissed and started with his insults. They said they were going keep the cash they found on me and started to walk away so I reminded them of the deposit book in the van, that the money they were talking belonged to my family business and sure they could take it but my family attorney will be coming down to the station to claim the money. They looked at me with evil eyes than gave the money back but not without a bunch of threats about how they were going one day catch me with something and lock me up for it. A friend of mine named Mike Quintero from the Bridgeport neighborhood who dealt only in marijuana came to me with a deal about me and him partnering up on pounds of marijuana, but we would have to travel to San Antonio Texas to get them. I really didn't like the part about having to go get them ourselves but that was the only choice we had at that time because to make any real money on the marijuana we would have to go get it from there but the risk of getting caught before getting back to Chicago was great as fuck. I had to try and make a move to fill in the gap to make some money until the drought was over. Me and my friend flew down to Texas to check out the marijuana and make the deal. He was right the weed was of high quality and at a great price, so we purchased it and stash it in a vehicle he had down there and started to make our way back to Chicago.

Our dream of making money out of this deal was short lived, we were stopped by a Texas state trooper near Texarkana who discovered the stash. I called the Dicker who wired us bond money and then we took the next flight back to Chicago. When me and my friend went back to Texas for our first court hearing my friend took full responsibility for the marijuana and the case was dropped against me. After that ordeal we stuck to buying ounces of cocaine from the same guy we purchased from the first time. When I broke my leg on Green Eyes' Harley, I was working at CDE body shop on 66th and Western Ave and my Snap-On toolbox was still there I had not picked it up but now that I had time me and Dicker picked it up and took it to the White's family repair shop. I started helping by doing auto body work and Dicker would deliver the Coke and recover the cash and eventually cocaine was starting to make a comeback. I would re-cop with majority of the money we had in order to get better quality and a better pricing. I spent most of my day at the repair shop helping White Junior unless I got a tip from a reliable source about the possibility that a connect had received his shipment of cocaine and of course sometimes it worked out and sometimes it didn't. In a short time, we went from copping ounce quantity to copping quarter pounds than all the way up to kilos. As time passed, I developed a pretty good relationship with White senior and his son Junior. White senior had his own legal troubles, the details of which I did not know nor did I try to find out because it was none of my business and if he wanted me to know he would tell me. I learned long before You just don't go around inquiring about things like that because it was bad street etiquettes and the less you know the better off you are! White Junior was one sharp guy, he could just about figure out how to fix anything broken even if he had to fabricate stuff to make it work. He knew Porsches like he knew the back of his hand and he never half assed anything he did. Hell, the auto theft division of the Chicago police had been after the father and son team since the late 60s early 70s but was never able to get them on anything. These guys knew all kinds of people and had all types of connections, they knew a guy who knew another guy who knew someone that could make things happen. I had heard long ago that they were hooked up with the Chicago mob during the days when chopping cars was a booming racket. There was always someone coming around who was involved in some shady shit whether it be a safe cracker, a guy selling furs, diamonds rings, pearls and whatever else. There were also big time African American dope dealer coming in and out of the shop with big dollar cars. I met this kid called Bit who was a professional car thief, this guy was one of the best in the business according to what I was told by White Junior. He would snatch (steal) a Porsche 911 Turbo with a factory alarm in seconds which was not an easy thing to do, he was also snatching Harley Davidson's from yuppies up North and in the downtown area in broad daylight, it was a walk in the park for this guy. But this guy Bit had one problem and that was he talked way too much out in the open and was reckless so if I saw him in the shop, I always kept my distance from him and did not allow him to get too close to me! He would try speaking to me, but I always kept it to the bare minimum and got away from him. I didn't have to worry about seeing him too much because he wasn't around for long, he was busted for something stupid and was locked up in Cook County jail. We were purchasing kilogram quantities from different connects and money was coming in left and right. Green Eyes, Dicker and Biscuit were now starting their criminal trial for the guns and the 4 kilos. The trial did not last long, and Green Eyes was found guilty, but Dicker and Biscuit were found not guilty. A blind man could see that someone really had it in for Green Eyes and the sentence he received confirmed it. Biscuit was not released because he had other legal troubles that were pending, he received a short sentence for that and was remanded to the custody of Illinois Department of corrections.

Meanwhile me and Dicker were still on the hustle we had a Puerto Rican friend named Nicky from 24th St. who was a middleman for getting kilos for us. One day Nicky disappeared and was nowhere to be found, I looked everywhere I thought he might be, but he was nowhere to be found. I went to his girl's house looking for him, but she said she had not seen him and was worried that something terrible might have happened to him. Eventually Nicky showed up at the repair shop looking for me about later. When I saw him, he looked dazed with his eyelids blinking in slow motion and when I asked where he had been. He told me that he had smoked water (a marijuana cigarette dipped in PCP) and was later caught by the police running down Cermak Avenue naked in freezing weather then they placed him in the nuthouse while the police tried figuring out who he was. He said it took him sometime to just remember who he was and to try and make sense of where he was. Me and the Dicker had already moved from 65th and Fairfield and each got low-key apartments in a quiet neighborhood. I was now living on 55th St and Lawndale, and Dicker was living on 59th St and Lawndale. I eventually paid my mother a visit at her store and it was wonderful to see her especially seeing her without having to see my father who was running a store he owned in Downtown Chicago and of course she was so happy to see me because it had been months since we saw each other. She was full of questions, she wanted to know what I was doing and of course I lied to her about what I was doing. I told her that I bought and sold vehicles for a living and that I was making really good money at it. She looked over at me and said "I wish I could say the same for your dad" she said he was deep in debt and his business was sinking fast. I got off the subject of my father and concentrated on her and how she was doing, I stayed with her for a few hours then gave her my pager number and told her to page me any time she needed anything then hugged kissed her and left. I went to a neighborhood tavern and was talking to a few of the older boys (Saints) when an older Mexican guy I've known for years came up to me, he shook my hand and asked how I was doing. We had Smalltalk for a few minutes, then he pulled me to the side and said, "I heard you are in the business and doing really well at it". I had nothing to fear from him he's been around the neighborhood and us Saints for a long time, so I told him I wasn't doing too bad. He asked what I was copping (buying), so I told him kilogram quantities, and his response was "how much per kilo"? I told him what I was paying which was $19,500 a kilo. He didn't hesitate and said, "I'll give you each kilo for $18,000 and I guarantee you it's better than anything you're getting now". He surprised the shit out of me when he said that because I've known this guy for years and had no idea he was involved or would ever be involved in this type of business. This was a great example for the old saying "never judge a book by its cover". He was so low-key, it was hard to believe because he drove an old beat up car, he lived very modest life style and never displayed anything that would indicate that he was in the game. It was great now because the connect was right in my neighborhood, so I didn't have to worry about him with the quality and he didn't have to worry about me robbing him, shorting him on the money or ratting him out which was something you had to worry about when dealing with strangers. So, the relationship started, and we were now purchasing our cocaine from him and he was right about the quality of his cocaine it was better than anything we got from any other supplier and all our customers loved it. A few weeks after visiting my mother she paged me and when I called back, she asked me to come by and visit her. I went to see her the same day, I asked her if everything was ok, but she seemed a bit reluctant at first to tell me what was on her mind and she ultimately told me. She wanted me to partner up with my father in his business or at least if I could help him out financially. I told her that I wanted no parts of being partners with him, but I promised to bring her 100K or more in a few days or so. When she heard me say that she went silent for a few seconds and gave me a very concerned look then ask me if I was doing anything wrong and how could I get my hands on that kind of money. I denied doing anything wrong and assured her that I was making my money from purchasing wrecked cars at a cheap price then fixing them and making high profits when I sold them. What was I to do, tell her "Mom I am a drug dealer who sells cocaine"! I had to lie to her, because there was no way she would have ever accepted the money from me. As I promised I handed her $100,000 a few days later. When my mother gave him the money, he suddenly acquired a new-found love for me which was as real as a three-dollar bill. I didn't care I pretended like I never had any hard feelings towards him because I was doing it for my mom! In no time the hundred thousand dollars turned into over 500 thousand dollars. My father went on to open a supermarket in a black neighborhood fully equipped and stocked and the business was doing great. A few months after I started dealing with the Old Mexican (my neighborhood connect) I went into his tavern for the purpose of re-copping. I spoke to the Old Mexican briefly then he informed me that a friend of his who was also in the same business wanted to speak to me. He nodded towards a guy younger than him who was always shooting pool in the tavern. The Old Mexican stepped away to take care of a customer down at the other end of the bar, as the old man walked off the younger Mexican came and sat on the stool next to me and in a Mexican accent said, "you are Emay"? I said, "yes, Emad" he then said, "I am Ricky, you buy your stuff from my friend" which was not a question but a statement. I just looked at him while he spoke, then he told me that he was the main guy and from now on he is going to take care of me. He went on to say that I don't worry about the Old Mexican because he knew what he was talking to me about. He said he liked the way I handled myself and the reputation I had in the neighborhood of being a standup guy. He already knew what I was paying per kilo, so he said you are only going to pay $14,000 a kilo now then he smiled at me and gave me his pager number. It took a minute to digest that number because I was sure nobody in Chicago was paying that kind of money. A few months after that he dropped the price to $13,500 and if I wanted, he would front me as much as I wanted because he knew he could trust me. Whenever a new shipment of cocaine came in, he would page and when I returned the call, he instructed me to go see his worker Chico and pick out what I wanted. The meeting place would always be in some apartment, garage, or attic in my neighborhood and there would be hundreds of kilograms of cocaine stacked in boxes, that is how much he trusted me. I would grab my stuff then I would page the Dicker who would come by and pick up the coke then get some ready for resale and stash the rest. My connect would always try and get me to take more merchandise than I was taking but I wouldn't, I only took what I wanted and no more. I was making great money with the clientele I had, and there was no need to expand I wasn't trying to be any bigger than I was which was big enough as far as I was concerned. At $13,500 a kilogram and unlimited supply I could have been much bigger but that meant much more attention which was something I wanted no part of. One afternoon Ricky paged me and asked me to stop by the Tavern because he wanted to show me something. In those days mobile telephones were not as they are these days plus most people were very careful and too smart to talk business on telephones, it was pagers and payphones and we always used different payphones. I went by the Tavern and he took me to the back room where he had a pyramid of white plastic pipes stacked a few feet high and as long as a pool table and each pipe was about a foot long that were capped on both sides. He called in his worker who came with a hacksaw and proceeded to saw off the end cap then when his worker was done, he grabbed it and showed me the contents on the inside which turned out to be marijuana. Each of these pipes had a pound of marijuana stuffed in it but I wasn't interested because marijuana was too bulky and had a strong order which makes it hard to hide, and I had to sell a lot of it to make the kind of money I was making with the cocaine. He also offered me kilos of Mexican tar (heroin) he said he had 25 kg and he needed to get rid of them but had no clientele for the stuff and frankly I wanted no part of heroin. The going price for these kilos of Mexican heroin on the street at the time was between 55 and $65,000 but he offered them to me for $35,000. He was pushing me to take them because he knew that I had African American friends who were hustlers and he knew it was they who had the clientele for heroin, but I thanked him and declined the offer. Ricky and his people had a hell of an operation, as for people who think that Mexicans from the motherland are stupid are themselves stupid, ignorant and know nothing about these people. Most of them are law abiding people and I myself have nothing but respect and admiration for Mexican nationalist because they are kind hard-working, the fact is this great nation would be in big trouble without them. I headed out one evening to meet Ricky so I can pay him some money which I owed him, and it was at this meeting that he suggestion for me to purchase a mid-80s Oldsmobile Cutlass or a Pontiac Grand Prix for the purpose of having his people build secret compartments in the vehicle. The next day I found and purchased a 1983 Grand Prix which looked very low key. After purchasing the vehicle, I paged Ricky and handed it over to him so his people could install the secret compartments. By this time Green Eyes was awaiting his second prison sentence which was going to be a very stiff sentence from the looks of it. By this time very few people were willing to do anything for him and if you ask me many of seemed to be somewhat satisfied to see him in the position he was in. I couldn't help but think that way because almost everyone I spoke to had nothing but bad things to say about

Green Eyes. Each person had his or her excuse for feeling that way about him and to most of them they felt that he got what he deserved. As for me I was still helping him out the best way I could, he wanted me to go out and purchase pairs of high-top Nike gym shoes and to give them to a girl we both knew. He also asked me if I would give her a half ounce of marijuana and quarter ounce of cocaine and I did. Each inmate at cook county jail was allowed a pair of gym shoes by a visitor once a month in those days. Out of curiosity I wanted to see how the shoes looked after the girl stitched them back together and I have to say it was a professional job you couldn't tell where she took them apart to stash the drugs. She would take the stitching out of the fluffy part at the top of the shoes and empty the factory stuffing then she would replace it with the marijuana and cocaine and stitch it back up. Her work was very impressive because there were no indications that the shoes had ever been looked like they were tampered with! This went on like clockwork while he was in Cook County jail, the girl would send other girls to visit other inmates who were on the same deck (floor) as Green Eyes. I retained a different attorney to see if he could do something with Green Eyes' appeal because he was very unhappy with the way the trail attorney preformed during his trial. The day of Green Eyes' sentencing came, and it was not good the judge handed him a 45-year sentence for the new case and since he had a prior drug conviction the 45 years was doubled which made it 90 years plus the nine years from the old case so now his sentence was 99 years. But that was not the end of it the judge tacked on four more years for the bond jumping on the first case which made it a grand total of 103 years. After the news of his long sentence hit the streets I was probably one of very few people who had any dealings with him. You can't get upset about people abandoning you and not wanting to deal with you after your incarceration because that is something you must expect from most people "out of site out of mind"! A day or two after giving Ricky the vehicle he paged me and told me that the vehicle with the secret compartments was ready for pick up. I had well over a $100,000 for him so I took his money with me when I went to picked up the vehicle. I placed the cash in a big Jewel paper shopping bag and had Dicker drop me off in front of the Tavern where Ricky was waiting inside of the Grand Prix on the passenger side. I jumped into the driver's seat of the car and placed the cash on the floor between me and Ricky. One would think that we would have used the secret compartments for moving the money that day, but I was only taking him a few blocks from where we were so without giving it a second thought, I put the car in gear and drove to where I was dropping him off with the cash. We were driving down Ashland and as soon as we crossed 47th St. an unmarked police car jumped behind me and put his police lights on. I turned into the Goodyear parking lot on 48th and Ashland and immediately shut the car off then took the keys out of the ignition. I got out of the car and met the detectives before they got close to the car. The detective asked me why I had repossession plates on the vehicle, so I started telling him that we owned a body shop/dealership, so these are just like dealer plates that we used when we repossessed vehicles from customers who stopped paying. Upon hearing that one of the detectives told me that he was looking for a vehicle for his wife and that was my cue. I invited them over to the vehicle and opened the trunk to show him the vehicle which showed them that I had nothing to hide. I told him that we just purchased this vehicle from the auction and asked him to look at how clean the car was. He looked in the trunk and agreed then I guided him to the front of the vehicle and opened the hood. I was basically letting him search the vehicle the way I wanted and to keep him from looking inside the where the bag of cash was in plain view. He asked where the repair shop, I gave him the information and told him whenever he was ready to let me know and I would keep an eye out for whatever vehicle his wife wanted. They got back into their car and drove off and as soon as I got into to the car, I looked at my connect who was still looking straight ahead with a blank look on his face. He slowly turned his head and looked at me then said, "cobron you crazy" than his face broke into a big smile. He showed me how the secret compartments worked then I dropped him off and off he went with his cash. I paged Dicker and told him to come pick up the vehicle and when he arrived I showed him how to operate the secret compartments which was simple, turn the ignition to the on position and turn the rear defroster button on then take an unfolded paper clip and insert it into a very tiny hole that was drilled in the thin black line between the wood grain of the dashboard. The paperclip had to be inserted on an angle to push the concealed button behind the dashboard which caused both secret compartments to pop open, each compartment held 4 to 5 kilograms. We were at the shop most days and every so often the Chicago police auto theft division would raid it and as always, they came up empty-handed. White junior was no dummy, nothing was done at the shop all the dirty work was done in residential garages scattered around the city. On one police raid, there was a red 928 Porsche in the shop right under the nose of the police, the original one was a total loss but the one in the shop was a steamer (stolen) and all the dirty work was done on that Porsche before it entered the repair shop. Auto theft detectives tore the shop apart looking for anything, they inspected every vehicle including that 928 but came up with nothing. Like I said that car thief Nit also brought hot Harley Davidsons not only high-end vehicles, but the Harleys had to be Baggers or Soft tails no Dyna Glides or sportsters. The Harleys were re-sold to a local guy who parted them out and sometimes made complete bikes out of the parts which were then sold to a group of Germans who came once a year for the purpose of purchasing Harleys from this guy. The Germans would purchase 20 or 30 bikes at a time than ship them back to Germany for resale in Europe. I was introduced to the guy who was the president of the Chicago outlaws motorcycle club during that time through White Junior. The outlaw president was a good guy, he was a good enough of a guy that I once allowed him to use my Harley for one of their big parties because the motor on his bike had blown on him. Most guys would never let another guy ride their Harley, but it did not bother me one bit. White Junior also introduced me to a nice old man called Wally the wire who was an old-time safe cracker who had just been released from Marion federal prison. I took a liking to Wally and actually felt sorry for him, he was a very likable old man whose skills were now outdated and ineffective for that day and time. I looked out for Wally whenever I seen him and he would talk to me about cracking safes, he would talk about the ultimate score he was going to pull off soon as if it was the old days. He was living a fantasy because even in the late 80s early 90s alarm system technologies were way too sophisticated for his old techniques. White junior would never touch any of the steamers (stolen vehicles) on the streets and why should he when he had people like us who did not mind doing the dirty work. We would help him out by moving the vehicles around the city to different stash spots where they would get chopped up. If Dicker and I were not around the shop, he would page us and whoever was closer would come and take it to one of the stash spots, but it was Dicker who handled that task most of the time. I would pick up Dicker after he stashed the steamer and take him back to his car. On one drizzly after noon White junior paged me and the Old Man and put 911 behind the page which meant it was urgent to call him back. Me and Dicker were together when we received the page, so we made our way to a payphone and called him. The only thing he said was get to the shop in a hurry that Bit had something (a stolen vehicle) that needed putting up. when we arrived at the shop he told us the steamer was a block away from the shop. We went to get it and when I saw it, I told Dicker that I was going to drive it to the stash spot, he asked if I was sure and I said yes. It was a beautiful blue Porsche 930 slant nose turbo with a convertible top. When I got into the car, I thought to myself "this is one bad ass Porsche". It had a custom two-tone blue and white leather interior, an all Alpine stereo system and even had high performance aftermarket exhaust system. I guessed the price tag would have been about $125,000 or more which a great deal of money for a car in those days. I drove it to a stash spot that White junior had in Bridgeport one block away from China town and that car was chopped up into pieces within a few days. Dicker and I were eye balling a brown colored Rolls-Royce on 47th street which was way out of place in that neighborhood so it must have belonged to one of the business owners. The Rolls-Royce seemed to be saying to us "come take me". We noticed it one day parked behind a hotdog stand on 47th and Paulina which was a great spot to take it from even in mid-day, so we decided this was going to be the day to snag it. I drove Dicker who already had the window popper to break the window and a screwdriver for the ignition switch. Within a few seconds he had the car started and we were on our way again to the garage in Bridgeport, we never did find out who the car belonged to nor did we care. We had the keys and alarm code to the body shop, so we came and went as we pleased but we never took any drugs there nor did we do any type of shady deals in there because the shop was off-limits for all illegal activities. Besides you never knew who from law enforcement was watching the place. The shop was almost a city block long full of Mercedes, Porsches, Rolls Royce, BMWs and other exotic cars. We also Kept our vehicles in there, newer convertible Corvettes one with a big money race motor, a motorhome, three or four Harley Davidsons, European style XJ6 Jaguar with Dayton's spoke rims with Pirelli tires and a mint 1969 Cadillac convertible which we called boss Hogg because it was identical to the vehicle boss Hogg had on the

TV series Dukes of Hazard's the only difference was the color. We also were able to use any vehicle we wanted to use if it belonged to the White family. We had at our disposal dealer plates that belonged to the White family to use on our own vehicles, so no one bothered us because the plates meant the vehicles belonged to a car dealer. As I said many of White Junior's clientele were black high rollers (big time drug dealers) some from the west side but most from South and Southeast side of Chicago. There was a group of young black guys who were from the Robert Taylor housing projects who came to the shop and every time they showed up it was as if you were watching a rap music video. They showed up with four or five cars, all big-money cars such as 500 SL convertibles or SELs those vehicles at the time were going for $100,000 or more and you can add another $20-$30,000 in accessories. When I bumped into these guys, they could tell we were into the same shit by a simple conversation between us. Many of them were my age and they would always attempt to pull me into an outright drug business conversation, they told me how much product they were moving in the buildings they controlled and so on. One of them once told me that their daily sales in those building were in the tens of thousands of dollars a day and in $10 and $20 bags of crack cocaine. He told me that the cookers would cook kilogram quantities at a time in vision ware bowls. He told me that he knew I was hostler and that we should do business together, but I always denied it and declined the offer. I wanted no part of doing business with them because they were always reckless and did give a fuck about letting it be known that they sold drugs, I mean look at all the shit he told me without really knowing me, plus they were way too flashy. I was at the shop one evening when I received a page from my mother so I called her and when she answered the phone she was crying because my father had been arrested, something about my youngest sister. I rushed over to my mother to comfort her and to assure her that I would do whatever I could to help out. I called an attorney friend of ours whom I had met through White Junior, this attorney was once to be a big shot Chicago detective with the auto theft division at 11th and state. This Ex- cop turned attorney was once the arch enemy of White senior and junior but after his retirement from the Chicago police he became an attorney and somehow became a close friend to the White family. We used him for many cases and recommended him to a lot of other people in order to support him. He got on the case immediately, I gave him the bond money to get my father out and that night I took my mom over to Cook County Court to pick up my father. I felt sorry for him when I saw him because he looked like he had been through hell. The reason for his arrest had to do with my youngest sister who alleged that he molested her or something of that nature. A few months before his arrest my father had planned on marrying my middle sister Fatimah to a Palestinian guy. The marriages are usually arranged in this manner, the guy's family approaches your family and ask for the daughter's hand. You than do some inquiring about the guy if you do not know anything about him, such as his character and what type of family he comes from. If everything checks out that he is a good guy for your daughter, then you bring it to your daughter and if she agrees then you move to the next step which is the engagement then the marriage. The guy checked out as a good person, so my parents informed my sister Fatimah and she seemed to be in full agreement with my parents but then a day or two later she disappeared. To save face my father came up with this great idea of trying to marry my youngest sister who was almost 18 years old to the guy. My youngest sister wanted no part of it but did not object when she was approached by my father. The next day she went to school and made some allegations to her teacher about being molested by our father. There was no doubt my father was a guy who beat his wife and children and a husband who cheated on his wife even to her face but a molester of his daughters he was not. Immediately after the allegations were made DCFS was called by the school and they took custody of my sister. We were not allowed to see or speak to her as if the whole family committed a crime, we wanted to talk to her so we could try and make sense of this madness. I mean we had a very good idea that it had to do with my father wanting her to marry the Palestinian guy. After some time, I was able to contact her, and we arranged to have launch together at a restaurant in downtown Chicago. At the meeting she told me that she was feeling bad about what she did, that she didn't know what else to do because she did not want to marry that guy. I told her that she could have come up with something other than what she did. She told me that after my father spoke to her about marrying the guy, she went to a neighbor's house who and confided in her what my father wanted her to do. The neighbor advised her to go to school the next day and make those allegations about my father so the next day she went to school and that. The lady told her that the school would call DCFS and all DCFS would do is remove her from the house and that would be the full extent of it. My sister was such a naïve teenager that she believed that was the only thing that would happen. Near the end of the meeting she told me that she planned on going into court and recant her story and tell the Judge the truth, that this big mistake was brought on by her fear of marrying someone she did not want to marry. On my father's first appearance in court my sister walked up in front of the Judge and told him what she told me. After the judge heard what she had to say he dismissed the case than her and my father walked out of court hugging each other. I could not understand how my father expected to marry his daughters off in the Arab traditional way when he himself did not behave like the Arab traditional male not to mention what the hell my mother went through being married the traditional way. Did he honestly expect my sisters to jump for joy at the thought of marrying someone they did not know after living with him and watching the way he beat and abused all of us and most of all our poor mother who always complained about her arranged marriage with him? I understand how he would his disappointment if he was living up to the middle eastern/Islamic cultural code, but he was not! I guess his philosophy was "do as I say but not as I do". I was driving through the Stock Yards and noticed a familiar face stepping out of a pickup truck, it took me a few seconds to place the face. Sure as shit it was Cow Boy the Gay Lord that I was locked up with in state prison so I pulled over and we talked for a little while and from there we exchanged pager numbers. I thought it wasn't that bad running into him because he wanted to start copping (buying) cocaine from me. We started out pretty good, I would front him cocaine and he would pay me down the line when he re-coped but as time passed, he started to come up short when it came time for him to re-cop. Finally, one day I went to to see him in the basement of his house as always but this time to let him know that he had to pay everything he owed before I would give him any more product. After hearing what I had to say he got upset and started to say stupid shit then attempted to charge at me with his fist clinched. That was a mistake on his part, he did not use his head to think that maybe I might be packing a piece (carrying a gun) which I was. I pulled out a stainless steel 357 magnum that I had in my waist and pointed it at his face and that scared the shit out of him so bad that he dove behind a couch and at the same time begging me not to shoot. He was lucky that day because his girlfriend and a few other people were upstairs in the house otherwise I may have shot him. I backed up slow to the stairs then climbed them up to the main floor walking past his people with a smile and a nod. I am sure Cow Boy was upset about me pulling a gun on him in his own house, but he should have been upset at himself for trying to charge me when he was clearly in the wrong hence the relationship was over, and I chalk up what he owed me as a loss. I was at the shop one evening when the shop phone rang so I answered it and it was a collect call from Cook County jail, I accepted the call without waiting to hear the full message thinking it was Green Eyes but instead it was that clown Bit the car thief. He told me he had been in jail for a few months and as was talking 100 miles an hour as usual and he asked me to give White Junior a message which was to send him some money because he did not have any. The day came for Biscuit to be released from prison so me and Dicker drove down to Pontiac State penitentiary to pick him up. Nothing changed with this guy, we picked him, and he was still the same clown who was clowning around, but he was now hooked up with the Latin King. I immediately told him to get off that shit we had more important things going on than gang banging. Biscuit clowned around a whole lot but honestly this kid was loyal and trustworthy as they come. I bought him a nice low-key four-door Cutlass and introduce him to a young hot girl from 35th St. which made him happy as shit. Sometime in the summer of 1990 the shop was raided, White senior along with a Chicano drug dealer from the Pilsen area were arrested for attempted sale of 1 kg of cocaine to an undercover. I was told that White senior introduced the Chicano to a black buyer who as I said turned out to be some undercover police. As for me and my guys we were still making plenty of money and were not making much noise staying as low key as we could. My connect Ricky paged me as usual to let me know that a shipment had come in, for me to go see his worker to pick out what I wanted and the reason for that was to say to me, Look how close we are I allow you to see everything because of all the trust there is between us. I went to see his worker in one of the buildings in my neighborhood, his worker led me to an attic. I entered the attic and noticed that it was filled with these 2' x 2' cube boxes. His worker ripped the tape off one of the boxes then pulled out this small box a little bigger than a big cologne bottle box wrapped professionally in plastic and it had a picture of an angel as if there was a statue of an angle in the box. He then took the plastic wrapper off the small box and opened it and wouldn't you know it each one of these Angel boxes held a quarter kilo gram of cocaine in it. These guys were unbelievably professional and like I said the attic was full of these boxes. I had his worker put my stuff to the side and told him to give it to my guys when they showed up down stairs. White Junior introduced me to an Italian guy named Tony through who lived in the Bridgeport neighborhood. Tony was also involved in the chop shop rackets back in the day and was still playing around with tagging cars but for himself or helping in chopping of cars but nothing big. His garage in the Brighton Park area was sometimes used to stash hot Harleys that were snatched from the yuppies up north. One part of his garage was taken up by an old Ford cargo van which was a junk. One day I asked Tony what he was doing with it, he told me that he was waiting for the right time to snatch (steal) a new conversion van and use the tags from the junk van to retag the new one. I thought he was pushing it way too far with that idea, but it wasn't my place to say anything, it was none of my business. Not long after our conversation I heard that Tony snatched a brand-new Ford conversion van from the lot of a Ford dealership. Tony chopped up the old van and tagged the new one. While driving through the Bridgeport neighborhood I ran into Tony as he was driving the new van and my first thought was "This mother fucker lost his mind" but I didn't say anything. The old van was a 1976 cargo van, but this van was a brand-new high-top conversion van with all the bells and whistles. A few weeks after seeing Tony his wife was pulled over while driving the van by Chicago police who were smart enough to know the difference between a 1976 work van and a 1990s conversion model. They police took the van to one of their garages for further inspection and would you believe Tony did everything up top (Vin number on the dashboard) on the van but never took care of the bottom half (engine,

Transmission and frame). They arrested his wife and after running her name they figured out who her husband was now knew who so they told her to call her husband and tell him he could come down and take her place. She called Tony who had no clue what she was going through but now he did so he went down to the police station and was placed under arrest and charged with auto theft. It was stupid on Tony's part to do such a sloppy job on the van, whether he was burned out or just got lazy and figured no one would bother looking past the Vin number. I heard about the arrest and the sloppy job he did which was a surprise to me because I knew he had a reputation for doing professional work. A plan was put together to try and snatch (steal) the van back from the parking lot of 11th and state police station where it was taken. There was always a police officer in the guard shake at the entrance of the gated parking lot. The plan was for one of the guys called Jets to be dropped off a block away from the station then walk into the lot and drive off with the van. Jets walked through the open gate waived hello to the police officer in the guard shack and the officer waved back at him. Jets found the van then popped the ignition and drove out of the police parking lot without incident. He drove the van straight to Wisconsin to a farm where the van was chopped into small pieces and disappeared. When the detectives found the van missing, they went ballistics but there was nothing they could do other than threaten Tony that he was still fucked even if they don't have the van. At the end of the day with the van gone there was physical evidence which made it harder to prosecute the case, I am not sure what happened with the case, but I know that Tony never any jail time for it. I met a gun dealer through Tony who was from Tennessee, this guy would drive up to Chicago for the purpose of trying to sell fully automatic machine guns equipped with silencers. When I met the guy, he showed a submachine guy with a silencer attached to it then asked if I was interested, I looked it over but declided that I wanted no part. I had no use for that kind of shit he was selling because I had access to plenty of guns in if I had any trouble came my way. I was making a lot of money dealing drugs so why would I be out in the streets playing with violence and attracting unnecessary attention to yourself. White Junior's mother Betty also worked at the repair shop as a receptionist, who was a sweet lady and as far as I knew was not involved in anything illegal. Everyone had enough common sense and respect to never ever discuss anything illegal in her presence. Green Eyes had already been transferred from Cook County Jail to Menard state penitentiary in southern Illinois to serve his sentence. Me and him talked regularly on the phone to shoot the shit and to also tell me what he needed whether is was money or anything else which was never a problem for me to do for him. Green Eyes had a girl from the Bridgeport neighborhood call me to give her a pound of marijuana at a time and she would deliver to someone who was able to get it into the prison. One popular thing in prison is taking picture with other prisoners so he sent me a picture one day of himself along with the head of all the Latin Kings (lord Gino) also in the picture was Mustang from the Latin Kings who had murdered my boy Jinio, so I throw the picture in the garbage. After seeing the picture I had no doubt that Green Eyes was giving the Latin Kings part of what he was getting from me and I had already heard that he hooked up (is a member) with the Latin Kings. I never talked to the girl I just instructed Dicker to meet her and give her what Green Eyes asked for. As for my relationship with my boys (the Saints) things weren't too good between me and most of them because they were starting to allow the Latin Kings to enter the neighborhood to hang out with them which was something I did not agree with. I was driving through the neighborhood one day looking for one of the younger Saints called G H because I was told that he tried breaking into my father's cargo van. As I search the neighborhood for him, I noticed a few of the younger Saints by the basketball courts at Davis Sq., Park.

I parked the van and walked into the street approaching them and when I got close enough, I asked them if they had seen G H and they said they had not. My boys were in the company of three other young gang bangers who I did not recognize and had never seen before in the neighborhood. I did not need to be a rocket scientist to figure out that these three other guys were Latin Kings. One of the younger Saints named Henny introduced me to them, "this is Devil, one of the boys". I looked at them then asked if they were Kings and they said yes, upon hearing that I refused to shake their hands. I told those Kings that I was folks and was not happy about them being in my neighborhood. They just looked at me without saying anything, I then turned and walked back to my van and drove off. Not long after that incident I ran into my boy Santo who had tattoos of pitchforks on his body indicating he was Latin Folks. I ridiculed him "what's up bro, are the Latin Kings going to make you take those pitchforks off your body" he really had nothing to say other than "come on bro". I have a lot of love for Santo he was my boy, so I was not hold it against him because I did not agree with him on that point. At this time Lucky was back in jail again and I never seen him again but while he was out I tried taking him under my wing. I fronted him an ounce of coke and would have given him a lot more, but it was hard getting him to take that let alone more. It didn't take long to see why he would not take more coke, shit a month later he still had the same ounce. I woke up one morning and was getting myself ready to head out for the day when the telephone rang, I picked it up and it was a Green Eyes who wanted me to approach White Junior and ask him to give me $375,000 he was holding for Green Eyes. I tried telling him that I didn't believe White Junior was not going to come up off the cash, but he insisted that I ask him anyway. I left the house and went to see White Junior at his shop, when I got there, I approached him and relayed Green Eyes' message to him. As I was giving him the message his face was turned red like a tomato then when I was done, he looked at me and said "Imad please don't get involved in this shit and don't be listening to Green Eyes, I'll deal with him when I he gets out". His answer was clear to me, he wasn't going to give up that money which I already knew. He knew that Green Eyes had just received a 103-year sentence so there was no way they were going to see each other any time soon if ever. I had my own money and I took care of Green Eyes from it so I didn't need his money to help him, but he should have thought hard before trusting White Junior his money. I guess he trust him more than his own people but never the less I had to leave the shit alone because that deal was between them. When Green Eyes called me a few days later, I told him what White Junior's answer which made him furious at him for not giving me the cash. I kept my big Snap On toolbox at white's repair shop where I would sometimes store cash from the daily cocaine sales. Dicker would leave the money in the box for me then the next day I would collect it and move it. We were making so much money that it was getting hard to figure out where to put the it, you start running out of people who can be trusted, and this was not the movies where you can take all this cash to the bank There was money everywhere and it got to the point where a person loses track of how much money one had put up. The crazy thing about making illegal cash especially drug money, speaking for myself, I never felt like the money truly belonged to me because I knew we could be arrested at any time and law enforcement would come in and take everything under drug forfeiture laws. When they came, they would take homes, cars, motorcycles, cash and whatever else you. There was the envy and jealousy of people who were supposed to be on your side but, they were hoping and praying that you get arrested and or even killed. There were the people that we grew up with, who got paid to hold our stuff because they lived a very low-key life style which meant the police would never suspect them of being in possession of narcotics would betray you dipping into the coke. One such friend was called Tops who thought he could dip into one of the kilos without us noticing and for that he received the beating of his life for doing that. We were out there in the streets putting our lives and freedom on the line and this guy is stealing from us so he can feed some girl's habit so he could have fun with her. It was a stressful life to live always on the lookout, every time you went in and out of your house or anywhere else for that matter. I always kept my eyes on the rearview mirror looking for any sign that said law enforcement is on my ass, turning as many corners as I could before I headed to where I was supposed to go. On a few occasions the thought came across my mind about picking everything up and moving down south and forget all about the drug dealing business. There was enough money and toys, but greed always gets the best of all of us. I purchased a motorhome and we were getting ready to head down to Daytona Beach Florida for annual bike week gathering. On the evening of February 10, 1992, Dicker told me that White Junior said he needed his help the next day with some deal he had with Bit the car thief, something about a car he stole which contained a few kilos of cocaine in the trunk. I asked Dicker why White Junior would be talking to that fucking idiot about drugs since he has not been involved in the drug game not to mention his father's legal troubles. White Junior had a great business going at the repair shop making money and having fun at it. I told Dicker that I wanted no part of that deal and if he Dicker wanted to help white Junior then he was more than free to do so but not to expect for me to get involved, moving a hot car was one thing but with this, he was asking for too much!

Busted by The Feds
February 11, 1992

On the morning of Feb 11, 1992, I met Dicker as I usually did and we both drove out to a Harley Davidson repair shop in the southwest suburbs to pick up a gas tank for one of the bikes we had which was damaged by the mechanics while playing darts at the bike shop. The dart board was mounted on the overhead door and someone accidentally opened it causing the dart board to fall off and land on the gas tank. The owner of the Harley shop got me another gas tank which was different in color so I went to pick it up and was bringing it back to the shop so I could paint it the correct color. Me and the owner of the Harley shop were becoming close and we talked about me becoming a partner with him in his shop. After our discussion and a verbal agreement I took him $20,000 in hundred-dollar bills for starters a month prior. While at the Harley repair shop the Dicker received a page from white Junior and he went to the office of the Harley shop to use the telephone then after a few minutes came back to tell me that White Junior said the Bit was on his way to the shop so Dicker should start heading to the shop. I told Dicker to go ahead, that I was going to stay at the Harley shop, and he could pick me up when he was done but Dicker kept insisting that I leave with him so he would not have to come all the way back to pick me up. I told him again I wanted no part of that deal with White Junior neither should he because my gut was telling something was wrong with this whole thing. Dicker said you nothing to do with it just take the gas tank to the shop and start on it and I will handle the deal with White Junior. I told him there was no need for us to get involved in this stupid deal with White Junior and this loud mouth creep the Nit. I eventually gave in and agreed to go with Dicker, so I grabbed the gas tank and left the Harley shop and within 15 minutes we were at White's shop. Even though I knew that white Junior was doing a deal with the Bit and he was getting help from Dicker, I myself had nothing to do with this stupid deal. When we arrived, I grabbed the gas tank and walked to the front door of the shop and was buzzed in by white Junior's mother. I bumped into the Bit who tried speaking to me, but I ignored him giving him the usual get the fuck away from me look and kept walking without speaking to him at all. I walked out of the office area and entered the body shop area where I put the tank down than walked through the second set of doors which led to the mechanic shop area. A few minutes later I heard glass breaking and within seconds the door I had just walked through popped open and there appeared a guy dressed in black with a mask over his head, his jacket had three white letters printed on it which read DEA. He was pointing an M16 style machine-gun at me and telling me to get down on the floor. I just stood there for a few seconds staring at him looking him up and down and thinking to myself "White Junior, you are a stupid mother fucker". Again, he ordered me to get down on the floor but this time his voice was more forceful "get on the floor mother fucker" I got down and laid on the floor and as I laid there something inside me said "this is the end of the road". What I didn't know was that Dicker had slipped back out of the building and was not present in the shop during the raid. The place was swarming with agents they rounded everybody up in the front shop area and an agent called out my name, so I answered because I felt that I had nothing to do with this shit and there was no use in pretending I was not there. They searched the whole place and found nothing until they came to my tool box and when they opened it they found $50,000 in cash they kept searching and found nothing else no drugs, no guns or anything illegal. One of the agents asked me what kind of vehicle I owned, my everyday car was a 1984 Ford LTD station wagon which was in the mechanic shop due to transmission problems. I pointed at the car, he took one look at it and wanted nothing to do with it. He was hoping I would have pointed to one of the many expensive vehicles in the shop so they could confiscate it. After a few hours, the DEA grabbed me, and White Junior then put us into an unmarked Chevy minivan. On the way to the van one of the agents thought he was cute putting his arm around my shoulder and saying, "me and you are going to be good friends, amigo" thinking I was Hispanic. I gave him a go fuck yourself look then jerked my shoulder away from his arm. As we took off in the van, I heard the agent driving say on the phone to someone "we got that mother fucker" I knew he had to be referring to White Junior. After a 10minute drive we arrived at the federal Dirksen building in downtown Chicago where they took us to one of the floors and placed us into separate holding cells. After a few minutes my cell door opened, I was sitting on a small bench then I looked at the open door and there were four agents standing there. One of the agents at the door spoke to me and said, "some of the agents want to know if you want to talk to them"? I gave a simple answer "NO" and turned my head, they stood there for a few seconds as if they were hoping I would somehow change mind but eventually closed the door and left. After a few hours we were transported a few blocks away to the Metropolitan Correctional Center (MCC located on 71 W. Van Buren) and turned over to the authority of the Federal Bureau of Prisons. Our street clothing was taken away and we were given jail uniforms which were blue jumpsuits. We were on the fifth floor which is R&D (receiving and departure) for a few hours and from there we were taken to the 13th floor which is one of the floors of general population. We walked into the main floor and the officer instructed us to sit down at one of the tables. As I was sitting there an older Hispanic man walked up to me and said, "do not talk to any of the inmates here, most of them are snitches" and I thought for a minute than said to myself "this old man is nuts"! The officer assigned us to our cells and gave us a small bar of soap, toothbrush and a small tube of toothpaste. I ran into my connect Ricky's worker on the 13th floor who I used to meet to get my merchandise. When he saw me, he looked like he had just seen a ghost I could see the fear on his face never the less he came and greeted me with a smile and a hand shake. He had been arrested a few months before me for delivering a kilo gram of cocaine to guy who turned out to be a government informant. I'm sure he feared that if I was to flip and become a government informant than he may not ever gain his freedom. At the time he was only facing 5 years at most for the one kilo delivery. Fortunately for him I was not one of those people, I knew what I was getting myself into when I started dealing drugs that there would be a heavy price to pay if I was caught and still did it so now it was time to man up and take my medicine and not sell my manhood to get a lighter sentence. White Junior did not know who Ricky's worker was and I did not tell him who he was when he saw us conversing. We chitchatted the best way we could since his English was so fucking bad, it wasn't like I could ask another guy to translate for me. Even though I had lived among Mexicans for a good period of my life, I never learned to speak Spanish at all. By the end of our mumbo-jumbo conversation he seemed to be more relaxed because I assured him in every way possible that I would never open my mouth about him or anyone else. I mean Ricky knew better but this guy did not know me personally he just did what he was told. The next day we were taken back to the Dirksen Federal Building to court for a bond hearing. The bond hearing was held in front of a federal magistrate and let me tell you that was one hell of a circus because the agents made up all types of shit against us in order to prove that we were a danger to the community and a flight risk. As expected, and not a surprising we were denied a band because it was found that we were both a flight risk and a danger to the community. A Couple of weeks it became clear and comical to me that most of the inmates who were gang members and drug dealers there had this idea that they were still thugs and gangsters even after becoming informers, they walked around without any shame joking, laughing and still talking tough shit. How can that be when you sell your honor and manhood by snitching on others for fear of going to jail for your own criminal acts yet still think you are a gangster. Getting back to the bond hearing, it was then that we found out the government's case against you. We found out that the DEA had recorded all the phone conversations between the Bit and White Junior on February 10 and the 11th. We also found out that the Bit was carrying a recording device when he entered the shop on February 11 and supposedly there was an incriminating conversation between me and Bit on that tape. Our friend the retired police officer who was an attorney came in on our behalf as the attorney of record for that day. The statement of the old Hispanic man about so many inmates being informants was the absolute truth and that may have been an understatement. The MCC was like a big soap opera, co-defendants were informing on each other and people were breaking their necks to snitch first so they can get the better deal from the prosecutor's office. Some informants were even allowed out at night to set up their friends and drug dealing associates for the DEA. The government was arresting 20 or 25 gang members on a drug conspiracy, and within a week 18 out of the 20 would start cooperating with the government against the last two or three guys. It really didn't matter whether they were GD's, vice Lords, or Latin gang bangers it was about the same. I had the displeasure of meeting two Palestinian brothers who I thought were locked up for passing bad checks but instead turned out to be locked for a drug case and were two of the biggest RATS in the MCC at that time who even ratted on their first cousins. I immediately stopped speaking to them and even spit on the older brother when he tried speaking to me after I found out the truth about him and his brother. These two mother fuckers were ashamed of their race going around lying to other prisoners about their race pretending to be Turkish. It was as if I had entered the twilight zone, living in a world filled with spineless men. Not all was lost for the real gangster image, on the opposite side of the coin I met some good stand up mother fuckers who never folded and took their medicine like real men should. After a few weeks, our case was assigned to a federal Judge and right after that we had a hearing in front of him. It was at that time the assistant United States Attorney threatened our attorney friend in front of the judge saying that our friend was walking a very thin line for defending us I am guessing. We weren't planning on using him as an attorney, he was just trying to help us out until we retained our own attorneys who were familiar with federal law. I retained an attorney from Edward Gensin's office, who represented high profile figures such as R&B singer R Kelly, Gov. Rod Blagojevich and others. White Junior retained a well-known female attorney who would in the future represent GD (Gangster Disciples) leader Larry Hoover. After retaining my attorney, he came to visit me at the MCC to discuss the case with me and during this first meeting he inform me that the government was claiming to have incriminating conversations between me and their informant on a tape. I told my attorney that they were full of shit, that I was confident there was no such recording because I never had a conversation with the informant about any drug deal. My attorney than said, "if that's true than let's hope they don't erase or distort the tape claiming that it had malfunctioned and is inaudible". After my attorney said my gut feeling said was the government was going to tamper with the tape and claim the tape had malfunctioned. For my attorney to say that to me means that he knew this to be common practice in these situations and I knew for a fact that I was not on any tape recordings. A week or so later my attorney came back to visit me, and wouldn't you know it the tape supposedly malfunctioned. Now the government's position was that, even though the tape recording malfunctioned they were going to use the government to witness Bit testify as to what was supposed to have been on the tape hence the railroading begins. The only evidence pertaining to me about this crime of

February the 11th is going to hinge the word of their informant alone. Prior to February 11 the informant never mentioned my name not even one time and the government stated that I was in no way a target of their investigation. There were no tape recordings of me and no mention of me prior to that day by anyone in those recorded conversations. The government didn't have any witnesses to say I sold them drugs or that I purchased drugs from them. White Junior was called to an attorney visit one morning and when he came back he looked pale and his eyes were watery and bloodshot red. I asked him what was wrong with him and he told me that the government was threatening to indict his mother if he insisted on not cooperating with them. A week or two later he came to my cell looking like a broke man and told me the government had indeed indicted his mother and included her in the case with us as a co-defendant. They made up a story that on Feb 11 she went out of the shop to do counter surveillance (making sure there were no police in the area) but any logical person would have to ask if they are saying that now then they obviously knew that on the day of our arrest then why was she not arrested along with us on that day? The answer to that question is simple she never did any such thing, or she would have been arrested and taken into custody with us on that day. The DEA did almost everything in their power to break White Junior, another example of their madness was when he put a childhood friend on his visiting list. His friend was a civil attorney for a big law firm in Chicago but that meant nothing to the DEA they showed up at the poor guy's condominium early one morning and broke his door down while he was in the shower then gave him a sheet to wrap himself with then made him stand in the cold. They trashed his condominium ripping and breaking his furniture apart then threatening him the with an indictment if he didn't give them incriminating information about White Junior. He told them he could not help them because he did not know anything so they decided to visit the law firm where he worked and insisted that the firm open the office safe clamming he stashed millions of dollars from drug proceeds in their for his drug dealing friend White Junior and if they refused to open the safe then the DEA would obtain a search warrant to get it opened. After that kind of pressure, the bosses at the law firm opened the safe which only contained some petty cash and legal documents. When white Junior's friend showed up to work that day, he was humiliated then they terminated him. This is how the government (DEA) behaved when they didn't get their way. No one in our case was cooperating with the government so they resented that and were now going to do everything in their power including the destruction of other people's lives to pressure one of us into cooperating. We court one day during that first month and as we waited in R&D to be transported to court with other inmates from different floors who also had court on the same day among them were Mob Boss Rocky InFelice and two of his co-defendants. One of them, who I'll call B B, looked over at White Junior and said, "Hey Junior, how you doing and how is your father"? They obviously knew each other from the streets a confirmation that White senior and White Junior at onetime had mob connections so for me the rumor was confirmed. We were finally given a property bond along with electronic monitors for house arrest everything my family owned along with my brother-in-law's property was put up as collateral for my release. While on bond I was living with my girlfriend and our child who was about a year old. Now that I had been arrested and was on house arrest my father figured I was of no more use to him so he stop answering my calls whenever I called the store which came as no surprise to me. Keep in mind that he was in the middle east at the time of my arrest on vacation ejoying the 24 k that I gave him as spending money. I paid a visit to the owner of the Harley repair shop and asked him to start giving money to my girlfriend every month until he paid me back the $20.000 and he agreed to do so. The terms of my bond were that I go to work with my mother from

8 AM and had to be back home by 4 PM which gave me the opportunity to get out of the house and was also allowed to visit with my attorney at his office when we needed meet. A few days after my release on bond my telephone at home rang and when I answered it a voice on the other end said, "Hey big guy" I didn't recognize the voice, so I asked, "Who is this"? The voice on the other side said, "Joe Tina's brother" Tina is Dicker's girlfriend. Never in my life did I ever speak to her brother so at the time I couldn't figure out how he got my telephone number. I went off on him screaming "How the fuck did you get my number, I don't know you for you to be calling my house" immediately he said "Sorry" and hung the phone up. I later found out that he (Joe) was living in Dicker's apartment while Dicker was on the run. The DEA had raided that apartment looking for Dicker and found Joe staying there. Now it all made sense, the DEA could easily get my telephone number and they made Joe call me to engage me in a recorded conversation that would incriminate me. Joe's statement "Hey big guy" wasn't about my size since I am only 5'4" and if I would have taken the bait they would have used it in court to say "See he answers to being the big guy (the boss)" as they would later allege in federal court they would use Joe as a witness against since they did not have much against me. I am sure if he knew any information about the where a bouts of Dicker, he told them, as for me I had no idea where Dicker was nor had I heard from him after my release. Dicker was featured on America's most show wanted which airs on national television and had described him as being armed and dangerous. The government kept sending me messages with my attorneys asking me to cooperate with the offer of immunity if I did cooperate on White Junior, but my answer was always the same "No". On a few occasions they even mentioned to my attorney that I had a small child and should think about him, that my best bet would be to cooperate with them against White Junior. Our trial started in late June 1992 the main witness was informant/RAT Bit, the tape

recordings they had between him and white Junior and the $50.000 they found in my tool box. At the trial the government focused on me because there was no real evidence to implicate me in this crime. They painted me as this ruthless leader of a drug organization who ran it with an iron fist. The government's case should have been about the circumstances surrounding the days of February 10 and the 11th but instead they talked about the two years prior to those two days when it came to me. Since there weren't any recorded conversations between me and the informant and no real witnesses to testify that I sold them drugs or purchased drugs from them, the government decided to make up stories about me to pretty up their case against me. The informant Bit testified that he had met me in the summer of 1990 and from that day on to the day of my arrest he would see me on a daily basis. He also testified that me and him had many incriminating conversations about my drug dealing operation. He testified that I told him that my drugs came from Florida and the reason for getting them from Florida was because it was cheaper than Chicago. Here is an example of how stupid his testimony was, He testified that I told him the price for a kilogram in Chicago was $17,000 and the price of a kilogram in Florida was $27,000. Since when did 17 become a bigger number than 27 and this is how ridiculous his testimony was. Believe me if there was any justice in that court room the case would have been thrown out after hearing this idiot's testimony. Agents testified that they saw me walk into the shop with a paper bag insinuating that I had brought the money in that bag which was a fucking lie. The money which was found in my tool box had been there from the night before from drug sales of the day prior. I walked in with the Harley Davidson gas tank that I brought from the Harley mechanic shop as I mention before. On cross-examination by my attorney, the informant Bit was questioned about the time period in which he observed and conversed with me and it was narrowed down to the summer of 1990 spring the spring of 1991. My attorney pressed the informant Bit on this point, he asked him if he was positive about his testimony and he insisted that he was sure about this time period. He said it was during that time period when he observed me directing drug deals and had these incriminating conversations with me. He said, one day during this time period he observed me sitting behind a desk in the shop and I had stacks of money that were so high it was almost hard to see me behind those stacks of money. It was at that time that my attorney produced a time custody sheet from Cook County jail. He informed the court that he was going to introduce into the record exhibit 1 and the judge allowed him to do so. My attorney asked the judge if he could approach the witness to give him a copy of the document to look over it. The judge not knowing at the time what the document was allowed my attorney to do so and my attorney gave the document to the witness to look over it and then asked the informant,

My attorney; "do you recognize the person who is depicted in the lower right-hand corner of that document"?

Prosecutor; "objection Your Honor"

Judge; "the objection is sustained ask another question consular move on to another area and ask something you have not asked"

My attorney; "your honor this goes to the credibility of the witness, this witness just testified to observations and conversations he had of and with my client".

My attorney was cut off by the judge and instructed to go into another area which was ridiculous these were the first questions relating to that subject, this witness had been testifying to supposed observations and conversations with me between the summer of 1990 in the spring of 1991 and this document was clear proof that he was in the custody of the Cook County Sheriff at Cook County jail from June 1990 to July 1991. So his testimony about that time period was a lie he did not conversed with me nor did he observed me doing anything because he was in custody at the Cook County jail. The judge's behavior towards my attorney during cross examination was a clear signal to the jury that these lies were not important. My attorney was finally able to get the questions asked and to get an answer from the informant.

My attorney; "That is you in that picture is it not sir"?

Informant; "Yes sir"

Prosecutor; "Objection Your Honor he has already asked that question"

Judge; "Sustained moved to another area ask another question"

My attorney; "So you never did see my client, nor did you converse with him as you had testified to the other day because you were in jail were you not sir"

Informant; "No Sir not at that time no Sir but I mean after that, after that I did"

Prosecutor; "objection"

Judge; "sustained move on"

My attorney; "no further questions your honor"

The informant was now lost, confused and stuttering but was helped and saved by the prosecutor and the judge. My attorney walked back to the defense table then bent down next to me and whispered in my ear "this judge is railroading you son". What my attorney said was the obvious, the only witness just got caught lying about a large part of his testimony and nothing happened other than a continuous attack on my attorney to stop him from exposing the lies of this informant which were sanctioned by the US Attorney's office because they knew this while preparing him to testify before the trial. During one of the breaks my attorney made a comment directed at the prosecutor's table ridiculing them for indicting White Junior's mother. The prosecutor turned around with a big smile on his face and said, "We don't just indict their mothers, we indict their grandmothers, grandfathers and even their babies". During cross-examination of an agent, my attorney asked him if our case was made up by the DEA and the agent's response was

"Yes this case was fabricated by the DEA" key word here is "FABRICATED". Our case is what is called a reverse sting which was described as entrapment and illegal once upon a time in this great nation but unfortunately now it is legal to entice people into committing crimes and then arresting and charging them for crimes created by government agents. The informer Bit was busted trying to steal a car in Schaumburg and after his arrest he informed the Schaumburg police that he could set up a drug dealer in return for leniency. Upon hearing that the Schaumburg police contacted the DEA and informed them of what the Bit offered to do. So, a plot was planned and put together to set up White Junior and the plot was that Bit stole an M3 BMW vehicle and found 5 kg of cocaine in the trunk. Supposedly this plan would work because Bit informed the DEA that he had done this in the past with White Junior sometime in 1987 where he stole a vehicle and found 3 kg of cocaine in the trunk then sold them to White Junior for $10,000 a kilogram. You can clearly hear on the tapes Bit trying to talk White Junior into the drug sale, but White Junior was not showing too much interest in the drugs and kept telling Bit that he needed him to do something else which I am sure concerned the theft of a vehicle that White Junior needed. But Bit kept badgering White Junior, as directed by the DEA, to help him sell the 5 kg of cocaine and eventually White Junior gave in and said he would help him. In reality, there wasn't any cocaine at all and according to the testimony of the agents it was only sham cocaine. As far as I was concerned why would I even bother getting involved in such a risky deal such. For me to take such a high risk for these kilos at $10,000 when I was getting mine for $13,500 would have been very stupid! The stuff I was getting was top quality and I could get as many kilos as I wanted without upfront money and risk free to save $3,500 just made no sense to be involved in this stupid deal. According to the government They had never heard of me, their informant never mentions me nor was I ever mentioned in any of their DEA 6s (investigation reports) prior to my arrest. I was never mentioned in any of the recorded conversations between the informant and White Junior neither person ever brought up my name. On July 1, 1992, right before the court went into session the prosecutor turned towards the defense table looking very elated and said, "Just so you guys know the Dicker was captured on the border of Mexico this morning" he had a big silly looking grin on his face. On the morning of July 2, 1992, the case was turned over to the jury for deliberations we stepped out into the waiting areas. From the waiting area you can see into downtown Chicago out of the big glass windows and out of nowhere the day turned to night then a big storm hit the city of Chicago that day and a small tornado hit the taste of Chicago and destroyed it. A short time after the storm touched down, we were told that the jury had reached a verdict so headed back into the courtroom and deep down inside I knew it was going to be bad news for us. I based that feeling on what I had seen in the courtroom which was the judge's attacks on my attorney during cross-examination and seeing one of the jurors, an older white lady who was always making smiley faces, winking and waving at the head DEA agent who sat directly in front of the jury at the prosecutor's table than for the icing on the cake was how quickly the jury came back with the verdict. How fair is it that the government gets to sit right in front of the jury, not only were they sitting directly in front of them but they were facing them so they can make faces at each other. As for us we were way across the court room facing the Judge without a chance in the world of winning! The court was ordered into session and the judge asked the jury foreman "Has the Jury reached a verdict"? The foreman answered, "Yes we did your honor". The verdict was read and as expected it was guilty on the one and only count which was conspiracy to possess with intent to distribute cocaine. My attorney asked that the jury be polled so the judge instructed the jury that they will be polled. Polling the jury means that every juror will be called by name and that juror must answer with a simple YES or NO only! The clerk proceeded to poll the jury by calling the first jurors name;

Clerk; "Mr. G V was this your verdict then and now guilty"?

The courtroom was silent and there was no answer to the clerk's question, now everybody in the courtroom was looking at each other with a puzzled look. The judge instructed the clerk to ask again.

Clerk; "G V was this your verdict then and now guilty"?

Again, there was no answer. I started to count the jury to see if one of them was missing but then I noticed a lady trying to whisper to an older guy sitting to her left. She said, "they are asking you for your verdict" but that did no good the old man still did not answer. She then elbowed him and got his attention and again said "they are asking you for your verdict" but this time he answered, "not guilty". The judge had him brought out of the jury box and put right in front of the clerk than instructed him to listen to the question carefully and answer yes or no.

Clerk; "Was this your verdict then and now guilty"?

Juror G V; Holding his hand next to his ear he said, "I can't I don't understand you"

Clerk; "Was this your verdict then and now guilty"

Juror G V; "O my verdict? My verdict is here not guilty" he noticed the reaction of the clerk, the judge and all the noise being made in the courtroom, he then said, "I mean guilty I can't I don't understand you".

The Judge sent the juror back to the jury box and went on to poll the rest of the jury which were all guilty. No one said anything about the deaf juror, it was as if nothing had happened. I later learned that my attorneys should have asked the Judge for a mistrial immediately after we found that the juror had trouble hearing. Of course, we said nothing either because we put our trust in the attorneys who are supposed to know the law to protect our constitutional rights. If I could bring time back, I would have stood up in that fucking courtroom and argued the point myself than asked for a mistrial myself. Our bond was revoked than we were immediately taken into custody and a few hours later we were transported to the MCC. At the MCC we stayed on the fifth floor until one or two in the morning which was unusual, we should have been sent up to our assigned floors hours before. After that long wait an officer showed up and escorted us to the 11th floor which happens to be the hole (segregation). We had no idea why, but I knew enough about jails as to not waste my time discussing these types of issues with a prison guard because there isn't anything they could do about it. It wasn't hard to figure out why they placed us there, we were now convicted felons who were property of the US government as the put it and this was also part of our punishment for not cooperating with the government. A few days later a counselor came up to my cell door and informed me that the prosecuting attorney had sent a memo to the MCC on the day of our conviction telling them to place us under administrative detention (segregation). That memo stated that we were a threat to the running and orderly of the institution and a danger to others and including ourselves. It was the same thing every day wake up eat your breakfast which was delivered to you through an opening in the cell door, then sit around in a 6' x 8' cell until noontime when the lunch tray was delivered then sit around again looking at the walls waiting for your dinner to be delivered. Night time came and it was time for sleeping so you could wake up in the morning to repeat the same process again day in and day out. There was no television or radio and if you're lucky you may find a book worth reading on the book rack that they rolled past your cell every now and then. Inmates were held in the hole for many different reasons, there was always someone screaming, yelling at the guards and kicking his cell door. There was the occasional person who broke the fire sprinkler in his cell and flood the whole with oily nasty smelling water. Once a week you were escorted to the shower in handcuffs but the rest of the time you had to wash up in your sink with a wash cloth which is known as a bird bath. Anytime you were taken out of your cell it was in a set of handcuffs and this went on for almost a year. While in segregation I met a kid named Paul who told me that he knew who the informant (Bit) on my case was and he knew that he had lied on me in trial because he bragged about it to him. Paul said he was in the bullpen with my informant during my trail and he (informant Bit) would come back to the bullpen laughing and joking about all the lies he was telling in court. I asked if he would meet with my attorney and give him a statement which he agreed to do but it did me no good. My attorney never did anything with it he only came to see Paul because I insisted that he do so. Not long after talking to Paul I found out that he himself was a government informant who testified in many federal trails for the government. I pressed my attorney to try to do something with Paul's statement because he was a government informant who testified on many defendants in federal court. My attorney paid me a visit while I was in the hole to discuss my presentence investigation report and informed me that he seen the prosecutor who told him that he was going to ask the Judge to give me a life sentence to teach me a lesson that next time when the government says cooperate than I must cooperate and he also informed that nothing could be done with Paul's statement because no one would believe him ! When he finished speaking, I looked over at him and asked, "What does it mean when someone is sentenced to life in prison"? He looked at me for a few seconds than said "It means you spend the rest of your life in prison". I than said what was the purpose of telling me what he said since there is not going to be a next time for me to learn anything. He looked at me and said I felt that I had to mention it to you, a thought came to my mind and that was "Fuck these attorney's because they are full of shit who take an oath that they will not uphold"! He was right about one thing and that is the government would say Paul should not be believed and that is because they a bunch of fucking hypocrites who use witnesses like Paul as truthful people who have no reason to lie when they testify for them but when it comes time for a defendant to use one of these witnesses than they are no longer credible and should not be believed. I found out that my informant was placed on the 19th floor of the MCC who was always breaking the rules if the institution and in trouble with authorities. Sometime in 1993 while in the hole a correctional officer showed up at my cell door and instructed me to pack up my things because I was being released from administrative detention. He said I was being moved to the 15th floor of general population so I packed my things up and was then escorted to the 15th floor where Dicker was being held. They decided to final release me and White Junior from administrative detention because they had enough of our informant Bit who was busted breaking into the vending machines on the 19th floor. He would usually lean the vending machine forward so the candy fell out of the trays but this time he lost his grip and the machine fell breaking the front glass and that was the straw that broke the camel's back for him. Our informant Bit was placed in segregation and we were released into general population instead. In general population the cell doors were open at 6 AM so you could watch one of the four televisions or use the telephone then you're locked in your cell for the 4 PM stand up count for about half an hour. After the count the cell doors are opened again until 10 PM, from that time you were then locked in your cell until the next morning. Now that I was allowed out of my cell most of the day, I spent it playing one of two card games and those were spades or casino. There was a nice size window in one of the rooms where card games were played so I would stare out that window at the city watching people in their cars going about their daily business. I could just about see my neighborhood from it and would think to myself "I wondered if I will ever drive through it again and if so than how long before that time comes" shit wasn't looking good for me getting out any time soon. Staring out of that window at freedom gave me time to reflect on my situation, how I was blind and did not take heed and stop fucking around because I knew that this is exactly where you are going to be one day if I kept living the life I was living. Anytime you had a warning sign you immediately able to cover it up with deceptive thoughts of confidence which told you that you have nothing to worry because you were too smart to get caught. I watched inmates come into the MCC after their arrest and immediately grab a religious book and become holy rollers. They held prayer circles where some would cry while others gave them comfort and then there were those who pretend to have received the Holy Ghost. These hypocrites thought that somehow, they were going to fool God so he would save them from the trouble they were in or by some strange miracle the front doors of MCC would open and they would go home and live life happily ever after. Many of them pretended to be repenting and used religion as an excuse to become Rats and cooperate with the government on family and friends but all they were doing was saving their own ass by Ratting to avoid a long prison sentence. Not me I was not going to get down on my knees for anyone or anything because I had to look myself in the mirror and did not want to see a Rat looking back at me. On the 15th floor I had to see the two Palestinian brother who were pretending to be Turkish and I hated the mere sight these two Rats. Instead of being ashamed of their ethnicity they should have been ashamed of being Rats. While on the 15th floor I became acquainted with alleged mob figure J M "little J" and his cellmate alleged mob boss Sammy "wings" Carlisi. When I was housed in segregation, I learned from one of my many cellmates who came and went throughout my time there how to cut hair with a small pair of scissors that was sold at the commissary. I visited Sam and little J in their cell and would cut their hair whenever they needed it, the pair liked me because they knew I was a standup guy and not a Rat. Sammy was a very nice old man and little J was younger and therefore the caretaker of Sammy. Me and Dicker would chitchat about our days on the streets and how White Junior fucked everything up with his stupid deal. Dicker decided not go to trial and he pled guilty after hearing how things went at our trial. I remember him saying to me "Imad people like us get no justice in these courts, I'm not going to waste my time by going to trial". I told him that the government was asking the Judge to give me a life sentence in my presentence investigation report. He said he had a plea agreement with the government for 10-year sentence granted he pleads guilty and does not go to trial. Dicker told me about the day he took a beating from US marshals because he was on the same bus which was transporting the infamous bank robber Jeffrey Erickson who somehow came out of his hand cuffs and took a US marshal's gun. Jeffrey Erickson got into a shootout in which he killed a Marshall and an ex-Chicago police officer who worked security at the federal building, but Erickson did not get far because he was wounded so he put the gun to his head and took his own life on the outside ramp which leads to the street from beneath the federal court house. Dicker said that federal authorities interrogated all the inmates on the bus and accused them of giving Jeffrey Erickson the key for the handcuffs so he could free himself. The Feds knew that accusation was bullshit which was based on anger and frustration. Jeffrey Erickson was an inmate and the marshals were going to take their anger out on other inmates for what Erickson did. While awaiting sentencing I called home to talk to my mother and found out that the Chicago Police had raided my mother's house because my two rocket scientist brothers decided to start dealing cocaine and were stashing their drugs in my mother's house. I had no idea what would possess them to do such a thing after seeing what I was going through. The only answer to that question is "GREED" the same sickness that caused all of us to get involved in dealing drugs. My youngest brother was arrested and during the raid one of the lady officers was continuously insulting my mother by calling her a bitch. I would never have taken any drugs anywhere around my mother's house not in a million years. I told my mother to call my attorney friend the Ex-copper for help and guidance. I was sitting at a table on the main floor one afternoon when the floor officer called me for a visit. I thought it may have been an attorney visit because that was not my scheduled visiting day. When I got to the visiting room there were two people suits waiting for me who turned out to be from the INS, they informed me that upon completing my sentence the U S government intended on deporting me back to Jerusalem. To be honest at that time this was the least of my worries but that told me that I was going to have to do this sentence walking on egg shells because I was not going to give the government an excuse to keep me in prison after finishing my sentence as they were doing to the Cubans and others. I was going to have to stay out of any and all trouble for that day when I would have to face the immigration judge because Jerusalem was under occupation of the Israelis so they (Israelis) will not allow me to return. The US government may want to hold me in prison way past my out date so if I was getting into shit while in prison, they would use that to hold me and not release me hence I had to be on my best behavior. Mail call in prison is always after the 4 o'clock stand up count and hearing your name called out for mail was the high light of the day. I received a letter at mail call, I looked at the name of the sender and it was a girl whose name did not ring a bell but once I opened the envelope, I realized the letter inside was from Green Eyes. In the letter Green Eyes said that one of my boys (Lucky) had told him while they were together in Cook County jail that I was planning on killing him (Green Eyes) before his arrest and that his life was saved by the arrest. Lucky was a chump for telling Green Eyes this bullshit which showed me that Lucky was a lying spineless piece of shit of an individual. I was so pissed off that I immediately wrote Green Eyes back telling him that actions speak louder than words that I was always a good loyal friend and for him not to bother sending me anymore letters. I proved my friendship to him on many occasions and if he now chose to believe what a spineless scumbag like Lucky then he was more than free to do so. On July 1, 1993 me, White Junior, his mother and Dicker appeared in front of our trail Judge for sentencing. At the sentencing, the prosecutor was now asking for over 20 years for me rather than the life sentence that they initially were trying for asked in my presentence investigation report. The government was asking the same as me for white Junior and his mother but were only asking 10-years for Dicker even though he was charged with the same crime. The Judge stopped the prosecutor from rambling on about the 20-year sentence and asked him what the mandatory minimum sentence for 5 kg of cocaine is. The prosecutor went on arguing about other crimes and actually stated that I had come to this country for the sole purpose of committing crime. I heard that and was thinking to myself how in the fuck can this moron say that, I just turned 12 years old when I entered this country. The judge stopped him again and said, "I am asking you to give me the mandatory minimum for 5 kg of cocaine and that is it" than admonished him by saying "you want to give this guy, pointing at Dicker 10-years for the same crime? The judge continued, "you and I know why you want to give the other three defendants a much higher sentence, just tell me what the mandatory minimum sentence is and that's all I want to hear". The prosecutor's face turned red than he answered the judge, "level 32 your honor which is a mandatory minimum of 10-years". The judge sentenced White Junior to 10 years and enhanced his sentence by two points for being a leader and organizer on Feb 10th and 11th which brought him up to a 15-year sentence, his mother received a 10-year sentence, Dicker received 10-years and I was sentenced to 10-years but at the second category because of my past conviction which brought me up to 13-years. Under federal sentencing guidelines we were expected to serve 87% of our sentence. After receiving our sentences, we were no longer pretrial inmates which meant we were definitely and unequivocally the legitimate property of the federal Bureau of prisons and within a few weeks we were moved to the 21st floor. The 21st and 23rd floors are where sentenced inmates are held while awaiting designation to different prisons throughout the country. I had 13 years to do which was a hard pill to swallow if you considered the injustice that occurred during my kangaroo trial, but I accepted it, shit it wasn't like I had a choice in the matter. I saw other inmates receiving 30, 40 years and natural life sentences which made me thankful for my 13- year sentence even if it was for a fabricated crime. Some people could not deal with being locked up even if they had a short sentence, one such example was at the MCC is when a young Polish kid called Bones hung himself over his girlfriend leaving him. Bones was in his early 20s who only had a 3-year sentence so there wasn't much sympathy for the kid. While at the MCC I had the opportunity to meet an individual named J K and we kicked it off pretty good, he advised me that I should ask to be transferred to FCI Oxford in Wisconsin where he was doing his time. I followed his advice and asked the unit team at the time of my evaluation to be transferred to FCI Oxford. Being a federal inmate, you could ship you out to a prison in California, Texas or Florida. Being from Chicago held no bearing on what prison you were shipped to. I received my designation and it was to the Federal correctional institution Oxford in Wisconsin which was a relief, so I thought.

FCI Oxford Wisconsin

I arrived at FCI Oxford in the summer of 1993, the prison is situated in the middle of the woods and away from most of human life. It didn't take me long to start despising the place because it was infested with two legged Rats (snitches) and majority of the inmates were weak and disunited nothing like the old days of state prison. The staff showed no respect to the inmates and most of the staff were a bunch of miserable people made of husbands and wives who cheated on each other with other staff members which was common knowledge. They seem to drown their problems away with alcohol and thrived on trying to make inmate's lives miserable. When I say the inmates were weak I'm not speaking of physical weakness, no not at all, but they were willing to fight each other and even kill each other at the drop of a dime yet they would not stand together for basic rights such as being treated with respect from staff. How could they not be weak when majority of them had betrayed family and friends in their criminal cases by informing to save their own skin. I will say this, it was better than being at the MCC Chicago where I had lost a lot of weight, I went down to 125 pounds not to mention how pale I became due to the time I spent in segregation. There was a move every hour on the hour where you could go to either the gym, the recreation yard or the library. Federal prison was a bit hard to deal with at first because of the time I had spent in state prison which was totally different. New arrivals at Oxford are placed in a unit called Woodhouse for a few weeks and then you're transferred out to other units throughout the institution. J K was now back at Oxford, he had been at Oxford for some years, so he spoke to his case manager and counselor in his unit to get me moved there. The units in the institution were described in two ways, one set of units were up the hill and the other set of units were down the hill and the difference between the two sets was, up the hill units had more freedom and no locked doors at night where, down the hill units had a little less freedom and the cell doors were locked at night. In the late 80s J K made the headlines in Chicago for allegedly running a small drug organization in the Southwest suburbs of Chicago. J K and I were hanging out in his cell one evening conversing about the Harley Davidson motorcycles we owned before our arrest. The discussion turned to who the mechanic was that did the motor work on his Harley and would you believe it was the same guy who did the motor work on my Harley. It was the very same guy who I had given $20.000 for partnership in his business. The kick in the ass for me came when J K told me that the mechanic was a witness against him who testified against him for the government during his federal court. I knew then that I would never see a penny of that $20,000 and just chalked it up as a loss. I had already asked him to give monthly payments to my girlfriend and two years had already passed without my girlfriend seeing anything from that money. I thought to myself here is a so-called biker who I thought was a stand-up guy but instead turns out to be just another Rat. Years later I heard that the owner of that Harley shop went a little crazy because his daughter died in a fire at their place of residence while he was standing outside watching. I read J K's presentence investigation report and realized that most of what the news media said about his case was bullshit, it was a prime example of the MSM stretching the hell out of the truth. The money and drug amounts that were alleged in his case were nowhere near the media hype. As far as J K was concerned, I can truly say he was a good guy who did his best to help me out and I will always be thankful to him for that. While at Woodhouse I was assigned to the kitchen for work, my shift started at about 4 AM. In the kitchen my job assignment was the dish washing room feeding trays, plastic dishes and sliver ware through a big wash machine and I could not get out of the kitchen job until I served a month there. A lot of my free time was spent at the law library reading law books to get an understanding of the law and to see if I could in some way help my attorney on my appeal by trying to find similar cases that had favorable rulings in the seventh circuit Court of Appeals. And trust me when I say that it was not an easy task because it is a very conservative circuit and very pro-government, but so are most of the other circuits in the country are the other than the Ninth Circuit Court of Appeals. I was eventually moved to Dane unit up the hill where J K was and there after he introduced me to the head unit orderly who promised to try and get me a job as a unit orderly which was a gravy job. It was summertime now and the weather was beautiful, it reminded of Wisconsin Dells which was only a few miles from this miserable prison. It brought me back to memories of Wisconsin that were joyful, some of the few good times I could remember with my father. This trip to Wisconsin was nothing like the trips I had as a teenager, this one was a nightmare not because I was in prison but because of the individuals I was incarcerated with. It was 1993 and thought to myself "Fuck, I have almost two years in but 11 more to go before I can think about being free and be away from these Rats". I had been railroaded in court but something inside of me said that I was not going to get any relief on my appeal, so I was prepared myself to do the whole sentence. I had no faith in the justice system and how can I after the experience I had in court during my trail. My negative opinion about not getting relief from the appellate court was not baseless, I was basing it off what I had been reading in the appeals books from the opinions of judges in the Seventh Circuit. Every now and then the court would throw somebody a bone to try and show that they were fair and followed the Constitution cases were few and very far in between. I was eventually assigned as a unit orderly as a trash guy, I would put the bags on a cart and run them to the compactor by the kitchen. Federal prison is much different from state prison because you are incarcerated with people from all walks of life, I met people from almost every part of the world there. By 1994 the so-called conservatives along with pro-incarceration politician creeps were screaming about wanting to eliminate education and exercise equipment within the prison system. Their logic was the most ridiculous thing I had ever heard especially the part about eliminating education for prisoners. I decided to sign up for the GED class which turned out to be a mistake because the class was a joke. They placed us in this big open room than threw a book at us expecting us to teach ourselves. Most of the inmates in the class spent their time discussing sentencing laws and dreaming about the day the government was going to change the law from inmates serving 87% of their sentence to 50%. After spending 60 days in the GED class we could drop out of the class in those days which I did as soon as I gave them 60 days. After that I spent most of my free time either working out, kicking the soccer ball and regularly visiting the law library. I met alleged mob hitman Harry Aleman who was living in the same unit as me and who spent a lot of his time painting and playing pinochle with other alleged outfit guys from Chicago. Harry also liked watching TV at night and would sometimes do so with a character named M K who I had met at the MCC in Chicago. I didn't like M K from the first time I met him, it was something about him that gave me the creeps. When it came to me participating in religious services, I was not involved in any but African-Americans Muslims at the prison would always approach after hearing my name and ask where I was from and if I was a Muslim. When they found out that I was a Muslim they wanted to know why I never attended Jumma prayer (Friday service) and that annoyed the shit out of me. I was arrogant and thought to myself "who in the fuck do these guys think they are asking me this shit, I was born a Muslim from Jerusalem and here these converts are acting like they own my religion". That is how arrogant and stupid I was thinking I was better that

I had more right to Islam than they did because I was born into it, yet I did not know anything about it. When I was first arrested and placed in the MCC it was during Ramadan the month of fasting and I there was an older Palestinian guy locked up with me for buying a trailer full of hot merchandise from another Palestinian who turned out to be Rat/informant. This Older guy approached me while I was smoking a cigarette on the deck when he approached me than asked why I was not fasting. The old guy was a real nice who meant no harm by saying what he said, but I had to explain to him how I felt, that I was not going to run to God and pretend to be a religious person because I am now locked up. I sarcastically asked him to fast for me and continued smoking my cigarette like I did not have a worry in the world. Fasting in the month of Ramadan for what, hell I didn't have any religious beliefs at that point in my life. I had stopped believing in anything that had to do with God or religion long ago not to mention the fact that I knew nothing about the religion I was born into. During my incarceration I called my mother almost every day even if it was for just a minute or two so I could hear her beautiful voice and know she was doing okay. The only two people I would call was my mother and girlfriend but by the time I got to FCI Oxford me and my girlfriend were already drifting apart as to be expected in most relationships under these circumstances. I did not call anyone else nor did I have the desire to call any other people because I wanted to deal with doing my sentence on my own and not have many attachments to the free world. I had to condition myself to forget about the outside world and to concentrate on doing my time. Most of the things I had when I was out, materialistic things such as, the motorhome, Harley Davidson motorcycles, Corvettes and even the cash were already disappearing and that was fine by me. Hundreds of thousands of dollars were coming up missing and no one seemed to know how or who took what. I had a few hundred grand stashed with my mother and there was the half a million invested in the store and of course I had cashed stashed with a few other people and as cash started to come missing I didn't let it affect me when I found out because I was not going to allow anything to make my time in prison hard. Even before I got to FCI Oxford my father had decided to abandon my mother, he sold the supermarket which was worth half million or more for $135,000 to be paid in payments to my brother-in-law who turned out to be a thief and a shyster to say the least. My father was back together with his old sweetheart, the one he almost killed me for recording over the taped love message she sent him. My father was now living in Baraboo Wisconsin which is next to FCI Oxford where I was incarcerated. He told my mother before abandoning her that he had to go live his life that my mother didn't know how to live life. I also found out that he had told my mother after my arrest that he was going to testify against me in court to make sure I received a life sentence, but It didn't surprise me one bit when my mother told me what he said. I was called for a visit one day and When I got to the visiting room the visitor turned out to be my father. We talked for a while then he told me he wanted to bring his girlfriend so she could meet me on the next visit. I asked him not to bring her that I was not interested in meeting her plus there was no way I was going to let him bring that lady to visit me because it would have been blatant disrespect to my mother. I am guessing he didn't like what I had to say because I never heard from him after that and he was also harassed my mother to give him back the $135 he once sent me. My mother sent him the $135 and told him, "as long as I am alive my son does not need money from you or anyone else so don't ever send him anymore money" and he never did. I called my girlfriend one evening to check on my son and learned that my attorney asked her to let me know that he wanted me to call him as soon as possible. The next day I called my attorney and found out that the informant Bit had reached out to him and wanted to give my attorney an affidavit to clear me of the charges leveled against by the government. The informant gave my attorney a statement over the telephone which was typed into an affidavit and given to a private investigator who went to visit the informant at the Cook County jail. On that visit the informant repeated what was in the statement to the PI and signed it. In the statement he stated that his testimony against me and White Junior's mother was totally coerced by government agents. He said me and White Junior's mother did not do anything wrong, but government agents kept saying to him "couldn't he have said this, couldn't he have done that" referring to me and the same for White Junior's mother. My attorneys never followed up with the informant to get the statement notarized so it could become an affidavit, so it remained as a statement and not a legal document. Notarizing the statement and turning it into an affidavit would have been the correct thing to do because it would have blown the lid off the case and would have gotten prosecutors and DEA agents alike in big trouble. The informant was allegations constituted a crime, coercing a witness to commit perjury is outrageous government misconduct. Our attorneys filed a motion in court on our behalf under newly discovered and exculpatory evidence. One part of me said this is it I'm going home maybe not today but soon, but the other part said the opposite especially because my attorney did not get the statement notarized. I had a strong feeling that the government was going to go around this by getting to the informant and threatening him before we got to court. I had no faith in the justice system, so I felt that there was no way the court was going to allow our motion to succeed. Here was an informant exposing in detail how a prosecutor and DEA agents coached him into lying on the stand in federal court. A week or so later I asked my attorney, "now that the witness recanted his testimony and has exposed government agents for breaking the law, who will protect him from government agents who will threaten him to recant in their favor, after all they are the government who have all the tools and power to get to him? My attorney had no answer to that question and had no answer as to why he did not get the statement notarized. It was than that I started to understand that most attorneys are full of shit and are themselves working with the government otherwise why would they not get the statement notarized and ask the court to protect the witness. We obviously couldn't protect him from the government after he recanted so that made chances of success for our motion very slim. After a month or two I was transported back to the MCC in Chicago for a hearing on that motion. While at the MCC I ran into a Palestinian guy who used to visit our neighborhood store in the early 80s. I thought highly of this guy until this meeting when he suggested that I should cooperate with the government in order to get a lesser sentence. After hearing him say that I told him there was no way on God's green earth that I would inform on my friends needless to say that was the last time I spoke to him. The day came for the hearing, so we were transported from the MCC to the Dirksen federal building. The hearing was held in front of a magistrate judge rather than the trial judge who had heard the case and knew the main evidence against me, and this woman was this witness. They brought the informant into court looking scared to death the prosecutor asked him if what he said in the statement was a lie and the informant's answer was that it was. They made up a silly story about the informant being intimidated by someone in state prison, so the magistrate denied our motion. Later my attorney had the audacity to say to me that he expected the magistrate to deny our motion because he is a company man that he spent most of his life in the US Navy then became a federal magistrate. There was a similar situation about newly discovered evidence in a case a year or so before our motion was filed. But In that case, there was mass media coverage and that was the case of the El Rukin gang who were in segregation with me during my stay there. Unfortunately for us, there was no media coverage and if there was then I am sure things would have turned out much different for us. This witness' testimony of our alleged involvement on February 11 was recanted, then it was recanted again in favor of the government. Than let me remind you of his testimony about incriminating conversations and observations which we proved was a lie during the trail because he was in custody at the Cook County jail. Then the fact that there was no testimony of witnesses saying they purchased cocaine from me or sold me any, now combine all of that with the deaf juror. It sickens me when I watch TV shows that portray criminals getting off by a technicality or because their constitutional rights being violated, those shows are pure bull shit and their sole purpose is to brainwash the public into giving up our constitutional rights and to support law enforcement even when they break the law. A week or two after the shame hearing I went back to FCI Oxford and from there I went back to the life I was living before I went back to court and that was working out and spending as much time as I could in the law library. I read a lot cases including Supreme Court cases from the 50s 60s and 70s dealing with perjured testimony, and those opinions that court stated "when a witness provides perjured testimony it is like pouring a small vial of poison into a pond therefore the whole pond becomes poisoned" but these were different times you had a Fifth Amendment right against self-incrimination, a fourth amendment right against illegal searches and seizure but now things were different the Constitution was being stepped all over in courts across this nation. I also spent some of my free time playing a little soccer, one day as I kicked the soccer ball a European-American guy walked up to me and asked if we could kick the ball to each other. I said sure, we kicked the ball for about 20 minutes then we decided walked the track and shot the shit. He introduced himself as Randy, and I also introduced myself but when he heard my name he asked where I was from. I told him I was from Jerusalem he immediately stopped for a second and looked at me than asked if I was Jewish. I said no that I was a Palestinian, He gave a sight of relief and we started walking again than said, "that's good your people are the only people on earth fighting the antichrist". What he said surprised at what he said but I had no idea what he was talking about, the usual reaction from people after finding out that I was a Palestinian would have been "Palestinian, man you guys are terrorists" even if it was said in a friendly manner that was the usual reaction. I really had no idea what he meant, whether he was talking about Palestinian Christians, Muslims or both as a single people. He directed me to find and read a few books such as the "Thirteenth Tribe" which exposed the identity of today's Jewish people and whose author is a Jewish guy. The other book was "Pawns in the Game" written by a Canadian Adm. named William Carr. I read Mr. Carr's book which was very informative and I am sure the 13th tribe would have been a good read but I never read it. Randy was part of a movement called identity Christian and was serving a 90year sentence in a militia type case with multiple defendants. I believe they were accused of killing a radio talk show host in Denver Colorado, there is a movie about the killing of the talk show host who happened to be Jewish. My attorney was working on my appeal brief but I was not counting on getting any relief from it even with the strong issues we were going to argue. Some might say that I was being negative that I should be thinking positive but after what I experienced in court and what I had been reading in recent court opinions I could not help but feel that way. I was tired of having mother constantly worry about me, so I wanted to at least try and make her happy, so I decided to start making a complete change in the way of my thinking and living to become a better person. I did my best to maneuver myself around trouble because I was incarcerated in a den of snitches who reported everything to prison officials and did not have any shame or care who knew it because there were so many of them. But while at Oxford I had an incident with a Latin King from the north side who was a government Rat on his case. The king was in the door way of my cell talking to my cell mate and for some reason we exchanged words and as I turned to walk away he reached around my cell mate and sucker punched me in the head. Immediately my cellmate and another friend from Chicago named Jim got between us and separated us and that was the end of it for that moment. I was planning to do something horrible to that Rat such as putting cans of soda in my pillow case and sneak into his cell while he was sleeping and but his fucking head in, but I had to use my head on how to get him. If the prison was filed with standup convicts than I would have had no choice but to do something immediately but that was not the case and had I done that I would have been charged with another case. Like I said most of the inmates in federal prison were government informers looking for anything to snitch about so I was not worried about what a bunch of Rats would think. I would have to get him on my terms when the time was right. Some of the Latin Folks that were there who knew me came to my unit wanting to do something to the Rat King, but I told them to stay out of it, that I would handle it my way when the time was right even if I had to wait a year to do it. After that incident the Rat King just about broke his neck to be as nice as he could to me, he would cook food and always bring me a plate which I accepted but threw it out as soon as he was out of the door. A few weeks after the incident with the Rat King I was standing in the hallway waiting for chow call when I heard a younger African-American Muslim asking an older African-American Muslim, who in the past asked me why I was not participating in Muslim services, if he heard about the incident between me and the Rat King. The older Muslim's answer to the younger one was "as long as he (meaning me) stays away from worshiping the creator then he will always have problems". They didn't know I was standing a few feet from them and when I heard that I felt like shit, I felt real shame and that statement stuck in my head. To give an example of how pathetic the inmates were, there was a staff member who worked in the kitchen at FCI Oxford named Peterson who was a fat ass racist redneck with a heavy southern drool who hated inmates especially black ones yet black inmates who worked in the kitchen under him were always playing and joking with this racist asshole. I happened to overhear a conversation between Peterson and a group of those black inmates who worked under him which went something like this "Mr. Peterson whatsha do when you be at home for fun" they asked and his response was, "I shoot cans all day long". They were lost and had no idea what he meant so they asked him, "you mean pop cans"? He looked at them and started laughing then said, "Na, you stupid mother Fuckers Puerto Ri CANS, Mexi CANS and Afri CANS". O, those stupid mothers fuckers thought it was so funny that they looked like they were about to pass out from laughter. I couldn't help but think to myself, "what a bunch of weak retarded mother fuckers". If an inmate had said something like that, they would have jumped all over his ass for saying it. These same inmates would be the same guys who would possibly kill another inmate for changing the TV or for accidentally bumping into them but were cowards when it came to a staff member. My attorney came to visit me at Oxford to discuss my appeal and during that visit he asked me if I knew alleged mob hitman Harry Aleman. I told him that Harry stayed in my unit so he asked me to give Harry a message that he should stay away from M K. I told my attorney that he is a little late because M K was scooped off the compound a few days before his visit. The government was planning to prosecute Harry Aleman for a murder case which he was acquitted of by a Cook County Judge. It was the case of a union representative who was murdered in a shooting and the allegated gunmen was supposed to have been Harry Aleman. My attorney who was representing Harry and their argument was that Harry should not be tried a second time for the same case because he was acquitted in the first trial so to try him again would constitute a double jeopardy. The government on the other hand was arguing that Harry was never put in jeopardy in the first trial because the judge was paid $10,000 to acquit him hence, he was never in jeopardy. According to a Chicago attorney who cooperated with the government and brought down corrupt judges and attorneys in what was called the Gray Lord corruption case. That attorney alleged that he had delivered $10,000 in cash to cook county Judge Wilson who was the presiding judge to acquit Harry. It was clear now why M K was scooped off the compound, he was going to testify that Harry had confessed to him or something like that. When I got back to the unit, I found Harry and pulled him to the side than gave him the message, when I gave him the message, he stared into the distance than cracked smiled and thanked me. After that we stood around and talked for a few minutes about whether the state could possibly re-try him. I honestly believed the state would not be able to re-indict and try him but Unfortunately, a few weeks after that conversation the court ruled in favor of the state and the green light was given to re-indict and prosecute Harry for the murder. One of the Chicago newspapers ran a big article about Harry's case and in it there was mention of the state using M K to testify against Harry. M K's testimony would be that Harry confided in him that he did in fact have the judge paid off to acquit him. M K was full of shit because Harry would never talk about anything illegal or ever admit something like that to anyone so yes, he was a lying fucking Rat! M K was looking for a way out of jail which was hard to understand given he was almost done with his 5year sentence so maybe he was looking fame, but I was sure than that he was already a Rat and people did not know it. Harry was tried, convicted and was than sentenced to life in state prison without the possibility of parole. The time came when something inside me said "it is time for you to start going to Friday Muslim prayer" plus the statement of the older African-American Muslim had a strong effect on me that it was pushing to want to find out what Islam was about. I wanted to know what drove these African Americans to love the religion I was born into I myself knew nothing about. I thought it was an Arab thing I had no clue that Arabs were the minority in Islam. I had no clue there were millions of Eastern European Muslims or that Indonesia has the largest Muslim population of the world. To be fully honest I also wanted to go out of my pride being hurt by what the older African American Muslim said. I felt I had more of a right to Islam than he did because I was born into it and he was not, so I was going to claim what was rightfully mine by going there. I didn't even know how to perform the traditional Muslim prayer which something Muslim children know how to perform. It was now mid1994 and there was rumor circulating around Oxford that a new federal prison was being built in Illinois near Peoria. At my six-month team meeting my case manager mentioned it to me and asked if I was interested in being transferred to the new prison in Pekin Illinois which was music to my ears because as I said I hated being at Oxford. Without any hesitation, I told my case manager that I was very interested and would like to be transferred to the new institution.

FCI Pekin in Illinois

In October 1994, I was transferred to FCI Pekin in Illinois and was the first prisoner to set foot in that prison that day, there were about 40 other prisoners along with me. We had the prison to ourselves and that was such a stress-free period having only 40 inmates when you had to deal with 1300 inmates or more in other prisons. Most of the staff were local people who knew nothing about prisons, I don't mean they were stupid or lax on security, but they were rather nice and treated us like human beings because they were not poisoned by veteran prison guards yet. The food was unbelievably good for prison, they also took their time filling up the prison which meant we had a cell to ourselves. There weren't any long lines at the commissary, recreation yard or the chow hall all of it making life easy. I signed up for the GED class because it was going to be a class setting where there is an actual teacher teaching the class. I was the first student to get the student of the month award and not long after that I passed the GED with a cap and gown graduation. When we were preparing for the GED test, we were going to be taking the state of Illinois GED test which required that we also take the US Constitution test but right before we were to take the test the administration changed it to the Iowa State test which excluded taking the US Constitution test. At the time, I did not see anything wrong with their decision to change it and neither did any other inmate. But as time passed, I began to read and understand that this so-called war on drugs was a war on our freedoms and it was being used to trample all over our constitutional rights. It is being used as a tool for mass incarceration to accommodate the massive prison expansion which was now becoming a private industry. so why would they want to educate inmates about the US Constitution. That was a slick calculated move on the part of the government but to us prisoners we took it as a blessing that the Constitution was excluded from the test. If all the inmates learned what the constitution said than we would realize that our constitutional rights were stepped all over from the time of our arrest to the day we received our prison sentences and beyond. That is the only logical explanation that I could come up with as to why they would change the test. I changed prisons but it was still the same game plan which is, spending a lot of my time in the law library reading new case law trying to get my attorney any new case law that I thought might be helpful to my case. My first job assignment FCI Pekin was at the wood shop in mechanical services. I just sat around on a bench doing nothing from 8 am to 3 pm but I also had another job as photographer in the visiting room taking pictures of inmates and their families, I was also assigned to take pictures of inmates at the recreational center. Whenever my family visited me, I always discourage them from coming to visit me because I did not want them to endure the mental anguish from the atmosphere of the prison visiting room which tends to drain all the positive energy out of you. That was the way I felt about visits but other inmates spent as much time as they could in the visiting room with family and friends and enjoyed the hell out of it. I had friends who sent me letters asking me to put them on the visiting list so they could come visit me, but I refused and told them that it would make me happier if they went out and spent the day with their family rather than being stuck in a prison visiting room with me. To keep myself busy I also participated in the ceramic program which is part of hobby craft making vases and chess sets and I also helped loading and unload the kilns. As for my religious participation at the time which was late 1994 and very early 1995 well there weren't many Muslims at that time, but I did go to Friday service and ran into a group who I thought were Muslims. This group was the Morris science Temple of America, but I would soon find out that it was basically a Black nationalist movement and had nothing to do with the religion of Islam at all. As I said at the time I had no idea what the true Islamic teachings were so I thought that these guys were actually Muslims. I even stood up with them Holding my hands up with seven fingers pointing up. Another Black nationalist movement which has nothing to do with Islam is the Nation of Islam both organizations were created here in the United States and have nothing to do orthodox/Sunni Islam. Personally, I don't care what a person's beliefs are nor do I care what race or color a person is because I have met good and bad people from every race and religion. My mother would always ask me if I heard anything from the attorney hoping I had some good news for her, and it broke my heart having to tell her no. It is a fact that prisons are big business and the commodity is human beings so it would make no sense for the government and the courts who are on the same team to release people. It did not matter if a thousand people had issues which constituted reversal on their appeals only one or two were going to get relief and likewise for congress, they were not going to change the sentencing laws or give out more good time anytime soon in those days. I dreaded the thought of having to one day tell her that I lost my appeal which I was sure by than was more than likely going to happen in case. My attorney sent a private investigator to interview the juror who could not hear during the polling of the jurors. The investigator met the juror and asked him if he remembered the case, the juror answered in the affirmative and he went on to tell the investigator that he remembered the case very well. He said the case was about a "CHOP SHOP" and that all the defendants were guilty of the crime. There was mention of a chop shop at the beginning of the case very early on and that would mean that he only heard that part of the case yet found us guilty of a drug conspiracy. Oral arguments were heard in my case in front of a three-judge panel in the seventh circuit Court of Appeals and not long after that the appellate court affirmed our conviction which means we lost our appeal. The judges made lightly of the perjured testimony and as far as the deaf juror was concerned, they blamed the trial attorneys for not speaking out the minute they found that the juror could not hear. The court's opinion made it clear that the attorneys were to blame hence they were (our attorneys) ineffective by not doing anything about immediately. The court further stated that filing a post-trial motion was not the correct avenue in dealing with the deaf juror issue which what our attorneys did, we suffered the consequences for our attorneys' fuck up. After the loss of the appeal at the Seventh Circuit   our attorneys prepared briefs for the United States Supreme Court and of course chances of getting your case heard by the Supreme Court are two, slim and none. I never kept my mother in the dark about my case I was honest with her and assured her that no matter what, I was doing well and for her not to worry about me at all. I called home one day and was given some very horrifying news about my middle brother's infant boy. My nephew who was in the care of my mother had fallen off her couch and bumped his head on the floor then went into a crying fit for a minute or two and went silent. My youngest brother came downstairs to my mother's apartment after my mother started yelling out to him for help. for him and found the child to be non-responsive. My brother called the ambulance immediately but unfortunately the ambulance was taking too long to arrive, so my brother decided to carry the baby and ran down the street to the firehouse which was two blocks away. When I received this news I was crushed, I was a walking zombie who could not help my family in their time of need. I mean it killed me to know that I had to sit there helplessly not being to help in anyway not even be able to hug and comfort my poor mother, brothers or sister in law. The baby was put on life support for a shot time but eventually passed away, not only did we have to deal with the passing of a beautiful child but now the state was trying to put the blame on my poor mother and youngest brother. Again, I told my mother to call my friend attorney the EX police officer and he was there for my family not just as an attorney but also as a friend. A week or so after two detectives came to my mother's house and said they wanted to take my mother to the police station for some questioning, so my mother did not object and went with them. At the police station, the two detectives started harassing my mother and blaming her for my nephew's death telling her she was going to jail for killing him. My brother called my attorney friend and he promptly made his way to the police station, when he arrived at the station he looked over at my mother who looked dreadfully beat so he walked over to her and gave her a hug then turned his attention to the two detectives ,who he knew from his days of being a police officer, and scolded them for the way they were treating her. He told them if they were planning on charging her with a crime than do it and if not, he was taking her home. The detectives told him to take her home and apologized then said they were only doing their job. The attorney helped my mother up and walked her out of the police station then drove her home. It was like living in hell doing time while trying to deal with the death of my nephew and thinking about what my family was going through. I couldn't eat, think or sleep much it was the most helpless feeling I had ever felt in my life and the only thing I could do was to pray that God helps my family pull through this mess. As time passed, we were all able to deal with this mess as the old saying goes "What does not kill you will only make you stronger" but one thing for sure, it will scare the fuck out of you on the inside. I had already explained to my girlfriend that she had to move on with her life, to go and find herself a good person to be with so there wasn't much dealing with her at that point in my life even though we were together since our early teens. The Rat Latin King who sucker punched me at FCI Oxford was now with me in FCI Pekin, but he didn't last too long because he got fucked up bad enough that he was taken to the hospital and was never to be seen again at FCI Pekin. I don't know what happened to him, but I do know that shit comes back to bite you in the ass when you do wrong. I became friends with a quite guy who turned out to be from Queens New York name Tommy Mickens AKA Tony Montana. Me and Tommy had something in common we did not have too much dealings with many people in the joint (prison) but him even more so than me. We hung out together, worked out together and ate together at the chow hall so I guess one could say we were more like blood brothers now rather than just friends. Tommy is well known in New York City, among NBA players, is mentioned in LL Cool J's book and is even mentioned in one of 50 cent's songs. I was the only inmate Tommy would hang with so some inmates thought I must have been from New York. Mob figure Little J M was also serving his sentence at FCI Pekin with me so we would sometimes walk the track at the recreation yard. Little JM introduced me to a friend of his who was also an alleged mob figure and the brother of Frank Calabrese from the Bridgeport area in Chicago. Another guy I became acquainted with a pretty tough old man named Junior who was an alleged mobster from Philly and a co-defendant of Nicky Scarfo. For some reason Junior didn't like Little J M and had no problem making it known to me even though he knew that I was friends with Little J M. Junior knew me for a sometime now and knew how I carried myself that I hated Rats hence I would never say anything to Little J M. Junior's cellmate was Frank Calabrese's brother, one day as I was talking with Junior at the recreation yard he told me that Frank Calabrese's brother is a Rat. He said Calabrese's brother was having nightmares which caused him to do a lot of talking in his sleep and he would shout profanities at his brother Frank accusing him of taking all the money. I couldn't Junior said he was a Rat because that was a heavy jacket to put on somebody especially when You had no proof. I thought Junior was losing his mind for saying that because I knew for a fact Little J M would not be walking around with him and if he really was a Mob Rat he would never be on the compound! Generally, mob Rats were placed in the witness protection program or tucked away in a very low security prison under fake names where they would be safe. One day as I was standing on the walk in the center of the prison compound talking to Junior, Little J M happened to pass not far from where we were standing. Junior looked at Little JM than turned to me and said, "I hate that mother fucker, he killed my friends, two brothers who were great guys". I acted like I did not hear what he said and never responded gave a response to what he said because that was the correct thing to do on my part. I knew if he thought I wasn't a standup guy he would have never said that to me. I never opened my mouth about what Junior said to me until now because it is now public record after the mob "family secrets" criminal trial but junior made that comment to me sometime in 1996 or 1997. I knew who Junior was talking about when he said, "two brothers", as a young kid growing up in Chicago, I remember hearing on the news about the murder of two brothers who were allegedly part of the Chicago mob (the Spilotro brothers). I now wonder if Junior was intimidating Frank Calabrese's brother in the cell and making him talk about things he should not have been talking about and that is why he called him a Rat. As I expected the United States Supreme Court refused to hear my case, but I still had one more avenue to try and get some relief and that was back in the District Court in front of the original trial judge. Specifically on the issue of ineffective assistance of council when they did not address the deaf juror issue immediately when it was discovered. With the help of friend who was a good jailhouse attorney we prepared a habeas corpus 2255 and mailed it to the District Court so now I had to wait to see how the judge was going to deal with the issue since the appellate judges clearly laid the blame on my trail attorneys. My friend Tommy had put in for a transfer to the East Coast so he could be closer to home something he had been trying to do for some time now. Right before Tommy got transferred out to the East Coast, me and him were leaving the chow hall after eating when two rookie officers stationed at the exit doors picked us for a random shake down. I never had any problems with being shook down because that was life in prison so the younger of the two white officers took me and for some reason thought he could try to manhandle me. I asked the officer to calm down and do his job without and to stop trying to manhandle me. He let go of my jacket then said "Stop talking or I am going to peel the clothes off my body" meaning he will strip search me. I turned around to face him than said, "You can strip search me all you want but you are not going to manhandle me, I don't care if you put me on top of a table while the chow is full of inmates and strip search me that way but I am not going to allow you shove me around"! By the time of this incident I had been in prison for six or seven years and like most inmates had been strip searched a hundred times or more, so it made no difference to me to get strip searched one more time. He and the other officer walked me over to the restroom in the chow hall with Tommy following behind. Me and the two officers went into the restroom and they stripped searched me but after the search I am positive the officer understood that him trying to humiliate me with threats of a strip searching did not work. I never used any profanity with him because that is exactly what he wanted so he could have reason to right me a ticket then place me in segregation. I had learned long ago that you could demand and receive your respect from prison staff by being respectful yourself. Using profanity and threats towards staff is an idiot's way of doing things, taking that route gave them exactly what they wanted which only made doing your time hard. After that day, that young white rookie did his best to be nice to me and treated me like a human being and I in return treated him with the same respect. He also became my boss down the line while I was a compound worker (walking around the compound picking up trash for one hour a day) so he gave me a job to move a trash cart one time a week. That job took 15 minutes to do and should have been given to someone who had more seniority than me. That officer understood that I wasn't one of those coward/rat inmates who was scared to stand up for himself. Tommy was eventually transferred to FCI fort Dix a lower security institution in New Jersey. That was truly a sad for me I had lost a brother and chances were that I would never see him again but nevertheless I was glad for him to be closer to his family and friends. My cellmate was also getting a transfer to a lower security institution which meant I had to look for another cellmate to live with. It was very important to find the right cellmate and for me he had to be a standup guy not a Rat, good hygiene, not a drug addict or a homosexual. Some inmates in prison live in denial, I am talking about inmates who think it is ok to mess with homosexual but think of they themselves are not homosexuals so those are also excluded from being picked as a cellmate. There is nothing homophobic about this because I am entitled to believe and feel as I choose just as you have the right. Three important things one should stay the fuck away from if you want to do your time as peaceful as possible and those three are staying away from gambling, drugs and homosexuality. I did matter to me what race or religion was when looking for a cellmate if we are compatible so we could do our time as smoothly and peaceful as possible without causing each any grief. Every person has a right to do and believe as he pleases but I also have the same right to choose who I want to live with and who I don't want to live with, it was nothing personal. A guy I respected recommended a young African-American kid named Bee from an Iowa town bordering Illinois. I already knew the kid stayed clear of homosexuality and drugs from seeing him around the unit, but I had no idea if he was a Rat, so I asked the guy recommending him if the kid was a Rat and the guy vouch for him and I had to move fast before the unit councilor just put anyone with me.

The kid moved in the next day but the same day he moved into my cell, I was approached by another African-American inmate who informed me that this kid was indeed a Rat. I waited until the 4 o'clock lock down count and confronted the kid but he denied the allegation which was expected. I did explain to him that he had two choices (1) to produce paperwork showing he was not a snitch or (2) not produce any paperwork but he would have to move out of my cell. He took option number (1) and said he would be getting his paper work the next day from the case manager. I gave him a day to come up with the paperwork or start the process with the unit counselor to move to another cell. The next day the 4 O'clock came without having said anything to me and he was walking around as if we never had an agreement for him to produce his paper work. Evening time right before locking down for the night he walked into the cell closed the door, I immediately asked where the paperwork was. He said he is unable to get it which I knew was bullshit so I told him that it was fine but now we could no longer live in the same cell. He looked at me and said, "Where are you going to go" insinuating he was not going to move out, that I was the one who would have to go. I put my steel toe boots on then started to prepare a strong cup of coffee and while doing that I advised him that he may want to do the same because we were not going to sleep in peace in that cell after lockdown. I walked down to the microwave made my coffee and came back up to the cell and sat down at the little table. He had not moved an inch and was thinking hard while staring at the wall than a minute or two later he looked at me and said, "Man, I ain't trying to have no problems with you, tomorrow I'll talk to the counselor and move to another cell". I was truly relieved to hear that, because I was not trying to go there with this kid but sometimes you are put in a position where there is no left or right but to take these situations head on. While this was going on with my new cellmate another inmate came to visit me in my cell and told me that someone in the unit was talking about busting my head after my cellmate produced his paperwork and proved that he was not a Rat. I asked him to tell me who was making these threats against me, but he was reluctant to tell me. I insisted that he tell me, and he eventually did but he asked me not to confront the guy. He was hoping I wouldn't confront the guy, but he knew I had to confront the guy immediately. The main thing was finding out who the guy was because I would know if he was a real threat or just a harmless shit talker and then I would know how to deal with him. When I heard who the guy was, it surprised the shit out of me because he was always breaking his neck to say what's up to me. He was an African-American kid from Detroit Michigan called Tone who I knew was going to be no trouble at all. I walked over to his cell and on the way there I asked a GD from Chicago to watch Tone's cell door for me. I walked into Tone's cell and he was talking to two other inmates, so I asked him about the threat he made against me. He denied ever saying it then just as he was denying it there was a knock on the cell door and it was the kid who told me what Tone said. I waved for the kid to come in, he entered the cell then I asked him to repeat what he told me to Tone's face. As he was saying it Tone's demeanor changed because he knew he could not deny it anymore, so he looked at me said, "And what if I said it". I didn't hesitate and immediately gave him two cracks in the face, and he fell backwards on his bed and covered his head and didn't attempt to fight back which is exactly what I expected from him. Unfortunately, the GD who was watching the door opened it and lunged at Tone and gave him one crack in the head before I could stop him. Inmates in federal prison are very geographical they click with each other based on what city and state they are from so if two inmates are from the same city, they would call each other "homeboy". I knew the inmates from Detroit were going to turn it into, two guys from Chicago jumped on a guy from Detroit and make a big stink about it which exactly what they tried to do. The next morning inmates from Detroit Michigan were flocking to my unit making it their business by getting into my business. An inmate came to me and said for me to go out to the recreation yard on the 9 am move so me and Tone could go heads up (fight) in the outside restrooms. At 9 am I made my way to the recreation yard and found about 10 to 15 Detroit inmates huddled up around Tone pushing him to fight me. After a few minutes one of the Detroit guys called H who was trying to hype Tone to fight walked up and said, "Forget it man Tone is a mother fuckin coward, he ain't tryin to fight you" and that was the end of that. Not long after filling my 2255 petition I received a decision from the district judge in which he denied me any relief. In his opinion the judge wrote that the attorneys were not ineffective because they had filed a post-trial motion addressing the deaf juror issue. The district Judge contradicted the three-judge appellate panel stated in their opinion. During oral argument the judges hearing my appeal clearly stated that a post-trial motion was not the correct avenue for dealing with the deaf juror issue and now my trial judge is saying it was the correct avenue. These people that hold all the power bend and break all the rules any way they want without any repercussions! By this time, I was spending a lot of my time reading books that dealt with religion and history. I had made up my mind that if I was going to believe in a religion then it would have to pass the test of appealing to my sense of logic. I also could not understand but wanted to understand the logic behind three religions which caused confusion, hate and plenty of killings between the masses so I wanted to know which religion was the correct, was it Judaism, Christianity or Islam. I decided studied the teachings of the three faiths Judaism, Christianity, and Islam and everything I read was based on historical fact and not someone's opinion. It did not take long for me to find out that all three Abrahamic faiths were really one in the same and it was people who created the divide by naming some of those faiths after human beings and this was done after those who delivered the message were long gone. For example, Moses may the peace and blessings of Allah/God be upon him never told his people the message he was bringing to them is called Judaism and the name comes from Judah the father of the tribe of Judea. Likewise with Christianity which is named after Jesus, may the peace and blessings Allah/God be upon him, never called himself a Christian nor did call his teachings Christianity during his time on earth. It was clear to me when I studied the teachings of Moses and Jesus (PBUT) that they preached that Allah/God and they commanded their followers to worship him by submitting themselves physically and spiritually which happens to be the same message that Prophet Mohammed, may the peace and blessings of God be upon him, preached to his followers. The word Islam merely means submission to the one God who created the heavens, and everything else. Islam is the only religion out of the three faiths that is not named after a human being so the point I am making is that the message of both Moses and Jesus, peace be upon them, was Islam and nothing else. If you doubt what I say, then I would suggest a great book you to read which is "What Did Jesus Really Say"? by Misha 'al ibn Abdullah. Read for yourself and investigative to understand and you will find that the three faiths are connected to each other who were sent from the same source which is Allah (God)! Studying the three faiths helped me to become a better person and taught me to respect and accept people from the other two faiths and to try and diallage with those people rather than debate with them. I saw a lot of inmates who did some studying into their own faith than became holier than thou start to condemn other people's faith without cause. I myself did have a problem with the Nation of Islam because they claimed to be Muslims but were only a black nationalist movement. I had no problem with them being black nationalists, but they distorted Islam and I constantly found myself having to explain to European Americans inmates that Islam was not a black religion, nor do we preach or believe that the white man is the devil because those were the statements made by the so-called Nation of Islam. Another area that I chose to stay clear of were the TV rooms which are a big thing in federal prisons. If you are a guy who enjoys watching television you are going to have sit in the TV room with a bunch of guys who watch nothing but nonsense and are going to talk most of the time and chances are you are just going to aggravate yourself by going in there so I made it my business to stay away from there. I observed inmates who worked in the prison slave factory come running into the unit on their lunch break to watch soap opera shows such as All my Children and One Life to Live. Some of these inmates had 30-year sentences for nonviolent drug crimes who had children at home. They gave up trying to fight in the courts to at least try and get their time cut down but were willing to spend the next two or three decades in federal prison without a fight. Another type of inmate that truly got beneath my skin were the hypocrites who bragged about how much they loved their race as in the case of some African American inmates who always proclaimed that black men and women are kings and queens. There was one individual talking that black power stuff who beat an older African American man with the cloth iron for changing the TV while he was watching a show. If he really loved his race so much than Instead of beating the old man with an iron, he should have been trying to help these two young African-American who were Crips from Los Angeles and could not have been older than 21 years of age. The only thing these two wanted was to try and talk a young white kid from Oregon into letting them fuck him. They would lay in wait for him hoping to catch him going to the shower so they could get a glimpse of his ass. Ever since the movie colors I had always wondered what the word Crips meant so I asked these two young Crips gang, and to my surprise they just looked me and shrugged their shoulders because had no clue what the word meant. Not long after asking them I stumbled onto an article about the Black Panther party and in that article, there was an explanation for what the word Crips meant (community revolution in progress) which started out as a positive movement to help the African American Community. When I ran into the two Crips, I decided to educate them on what their gang's name meant and how it came to be, but it just flew right over their heads and again they shrugged their shoulders and said, "shit homie we ain't know that shit". I had the pleasure of meeting a white kid who was doing a 13-year sentence for getting drunk and acting like an idiot on flight from Wisconsin to Florida who was always trying to figure a way to get high, tuning BIC pens into syringes to use them for shooting up heroin. There was the Cubans of the Mariel boatlift who were kept in federal prison for 13, 14 years or more without charges after completing their prison sentences without any real hope of being released anytime soon. Many of these Cubans were suffering from mental illness and many of them would lash out against himself with a razor slashing their arms and legs. Meanwhile Back in Chicago the feds were indicting high profile gang leaders who were already serving long prison terms in state penitentiaries, such as Larry Hoover the alleged leader of the Gangster Disciples. The writing was on the wall and the time was ripe for the government to crush the hierarchy of most Chicago street gangs. It did not help Larry Hoover that one of guys from his organization was running for a political office as an Alderman in the City of Chicago. Larry was truly trying to do right by transforming his organization from the Gangster Disciples street gang into a legitimate organization called Growth and Development. There is no doubt Larry was working very hard to give life to this vision of Growth and Development but there was no way the government was going to allow that idea to succeed. The government was going to do everything in its power to crush that vision and they ultimately indicted and convicted Larry along with some of his right-hand guys then placed him in a super max underground federal prison in Florence Colorado. They also picked up lord Gino from Menard state penitentiary on his out date after he served over 25 years and handed him an indictment, so he never hit the streets but was taken into federal custody. Most of the witnesses if not all against these two leaders were members from their own organizations, a bunch of so called thugs snitching on their own leaders to get a light sentence. When I heard about these indictments on the Chicago news, I thought to myself "these guys (gang leaders) are in for a hell of a surprise" because they lived like kings in state penitentiaries but now that was all over. Their status and power will no longer mean anything, they were going to be like any other inmate. One late afternoon as I was cooking something in the to eat in my unit after the 4 o'clock count when the PA system started announcing a lockdown of the institution over and over which is an indication that something big was going down. I looked out of the window towards the compound and seen an inmate who was a member of a Texas gang running through the compound stabbing his archrivals the Surenos (Southerners) a South California gang. As always, after a big incident like that the institution is lockdown for days and inmates are pulled out of their cells in handcuffs and taken to offices throughout the unit to be interviewed. I was handcuffed and taken to the officer's station where a white woman was sitting behind the officer's desk, so I sat across from her and she started the interview. She asked me where I was at the time of the incident and wanted to know if I knew or seen anything. I told her I was in the unit at the time making something to eat, that I knew nothing and seen nothing. Then she asks me another question, "Well, if you knew anything would you tell me"? I gave her a simple answer "No I would not". My answer seemed to surprise her and catch her off guard, so she gave me a look that said, "how dare you say that to me". I had to explain to her that my only obligation is to do my time and mind my business that if I was going to inform on people than

I should have done it in court where I would have been home with my family and not sitting in front of her today. The Taxes gang member who did the stabbing was about to be released in six months, you would think that he is the last person to commit such an act because that meant another indictment and a new long prison sentence for him. One would assume that you had to worry about someone with a long sentence doing something like that because he had nothing to lose. That is not the case these Texas and California gang bangers, they don't give a fuck about catching another case for their cause. I was walking around the recreation center one evening when one of the Latin folk who was a member of the Imperial Gangsters, a gang from the northside of Chicago, approach me and told me that a Board Member (a guy with a high position) of the GD's had arrived at the institution and wanted to meet all the Latin folks in the joint. I didn't have to think twice about telling the I G that I was not interested in being at this meeting regardless of who the person was that was calling the meeting. After a short discussion with the I G I agreed to go meet with the guy, but I told him that I was not going to do anymore of these meetings. We walked out of the recreation center and into the indoor basketball court to meet the Board Member who was talking as if we were in state prison. He told me that Larry was one (Top Man) and he was two (Second in Command) which really didn't matter to me what his rank was. I just wanted to get done with this meeting and get away from that whole seen before some of the Rats spotted us and made a big deal out of this meeting! I tried explaining to him that federal prison was not like the state joint (prison) and the best thing he could for himself was to fly under the radar. Nothing prepared me for his next statement, "Na shorty G this place ain't no mother fuckin different than Statesville penitentiary" which made me feel like this guy had just arrived in federal prison system and just did not know any better. I was wrong it turned out that he had been in the federal system for about eight or nine years and had just been transferred from Lewisburg penitentiary in Pennsylvania. After the short meeting was over, I pulled the I G to the side and asked him to never call me to another meeting with this guy or anyone who had the same mentality. I also bet the I G that the Board Member was is not going to last a month on the compound because the Rats were going to have a field day ratting him out. He told me that he wanted all the GD's in the prison to produce their presentence investigation report in order to weed out the rats which was comical to me because I am sure many of them were government informers. It was estimated in those days that close to 80% of federal inmates had in some way cooperated with the government. As I predicted within a month the prison administration snatched the Board Member up and placed him in segregation then transferred him to another institution far from home. I word was that well over a hundred and fifty Rats from the GD's dropped kites (snitch letters to the lieutenant's office) on the Board Member to get him remove off the compound. This was a prime example of someone being out of touch with the times and he wasn't the only one. I was cool with a stand-up cool kid from the other side of the fence (Black P Stone) who was living in a fantasy world just like the GD Board Member. That person was Jeff Fort 's (alleged leader of the El Rukin gang) son Anthony Fort aka "little A" who was always a very respectful. Little A was caught up on the way things used to be and for some reason refused to accept the fact that things had changed, that loyalty and honor among thieves did not exist anymore. Little A was a Muslim like myself so he would come visit me in my cell and was always saying off the wall shit, like his brothers (gang members) were waiting for him to come home from prison to lead them. He was always talking about things that meant something once upon a time, things that meant something when there was respect, love and loyalty for the leaders of Chicago's street gangs. I tried my best to convince him to forget about that shit because the things he was saying no longer existed, he would nod and tell me that I was right but a few minutes later he was back saying the same bullshit. On a few occasions I told Little A without sugar coating it that if he went out to the streets with the mentality that he was going to be a leader of his gang then he was going to be dead within a month after hitting the streets. Things changed and had been changing for some time with Chicago street gangs especially after the big boom in the drug trade in the mid-80s a lot of fake gangsters were allowed into Chicago street gangs because of their connections to those who had large amounts of drugs and were considered good providers and in many cases the guys with the big money were even given positions of authority in the gangs. By the early 2000s most Chicago Street gangs were loaded with members who behaved as chiefs and none wanted to be Indians. The writing was on the wall and I didn't have to be on the streets or in state prison to know how things were unfolding. The concept of unity on the street of the two organizations (Folks and People) had already disappeared and most if not all the gangs of Chicago were fighting each other. There are no doubts street gangs still have some very tough guys but being tough is not enough without discipline, loyalty, respect and above all not Ratting on other people which happens to be an epidemic these days. Just before Little A was set to be released, I was on the telephone talking with my mother and next to me on another telephone was a guy who was a Black P Stone from the 100s (far south Chicago). Little A walked up behind the Black Stone who was on the phone and the guy said to the person he was talking to on the other "Hey here, someone wants to talk to you". Little A got on the phone and the Black stone walked off and a short time later he came back and took the telephone back from Little A. When Little walked off, I heard the Black Stone ask the guy he was talking to "what he say" he then chuckled and said, "yeah you ain't tryin to hear that shit huh" then chuckled again.

The phones are an inch or two apart and you are almost shoulder to shoulder with the guy on the telephone next to you at FCI Pekin, so it is impossible not to hear what is being said by the person next to you. Little A went home but unfortunately within a month he was kidnapped from his house, tortured, shot multiple times and killed than he was thrown into a small lake on the borders of Illinois and Indiana. Rumor was that Little was kidnapped and murdered by the guy he was introduced to by the Black Stone the day we were next to each other on the telephone. The Black Stone who introduced Little A to the guy on the street had nothing to do with the harm that came to little A. It was now 1998 and my security level was getting lower, so I had to put in for a transfer to a lower security institution and I chose an old prison in Milan Michigan. I was hoping to go there because an old institution still had weights and a lot of other programs unlike all the new institutions that had nothing for inmates except concrete, steal, glass and a slave factory. As I said Everything was taken away a few years back such as weights and the most ridiculous of all was to do away with educational programs. Anyway, it was time to leave FCI Pekin because they were already tightening up on everything and had turned some of the two-man cells into three-man cells and trust me when I say the fucking cells were bursting at the seams. We were now in 1998 and as I was waiting to hear back about my transfer, I almost fucked everything up out sheer stupidity. I went to the chow hall, grabbed my food tray then sat down at my table when a guy in the next table stood up and started yelling across my table to his friend. This was another example about respect disappearing from so-called thugs/convicts, once upon a time you just didn't reach or scream over people and therefore, I use the term inmates repeatedly because there is a big difference between a convict and an inmate! That was something you just did not do, it's an act of disrespect anywhere but especially in prison to scream and yell are nerve wrecking in place filled with madness hence everyone is already on edge without that type of bullshit. Right after he screamed, I lost my appetite and started mad dogging (giving him hard looks) the guy but I knew the guy he was called C; a Crip from Houston Texas and he also knew me. We were cool and never had a problem but this day for some reason I was agitated to the point that I did not care about what this would lead to or the what the consequences could be. He looked at me and asked if I was all right which was like pouring gas on the fire for some reason, but I didn't respond and kept mad dogging him than I picked up my tray of food and threw it in the garbage. I left the chow hall and walked straight back to my cell house to dig up a small home-made shank then turned back around and went back to the front of the chow hall to wait for C. While I was waiting for him to come out a kid called Bean who was sitting at C's table came out of the chow hall after seeing me standing out there through the big windows of the chow hall. Bean approached me and asked if I was cool then immediately tried diffusing the situation by telling me that C was a standup kid and there are a lot of worse people than him on the compound to beef with. As Bean was talking a friend of mine who was a GD happened to walk out of the chow hall, he noticed me and came up to speak to me than heard Bean trying to calm me down, so he put his arm around my shoulder and walked me back to the unit. I put the shank back in the spot where I got it from and later thought long and hard about how stupid my actions were to put myself in a position like that over some stupid shit like that. I thank God for sending these two people to intervene and stop me from making the mistake of a lifetime and if they had not than there was the possibility of me stabbing C and spending the rest of life in prison. It's that demonic feeling that takes over and blinds you from seeing and understanding anything logical and all you want to do is be destructive than within seconds or minutes your world is turned upside down for something meaningless. One evening as I was returning to my unit from the recreation yard, I ran into alleged mob hitman Harry Aleman, Little J M and Frank Calabrese's brother. I shook their hands and told Harry who I had not seen since my transfer from FCI Oxford that I was sorry about how things turned out for him in his old murder case. I also told them that I was being transferred to Milan Michigan then wished them the best of luck. Frank Calabrese's brother asked me to look up his brother Frank who was at FCI Milan and tell him that he was trying to get transferred there so they can be together. My transfer papers came back that I was approved for Milan Michigan which was a great relief to know that I was going there instead of one of the new institutions. A few days after receiving the approval my unit officer told me to pack my things and take them up to R&D. On a Wednesday morning I was fitted with transfer clothing and at about 10 AM I boarded a federal Bureau of prisons transfer bus then headed out to MCC Chicago where I would be spending night. It had been about 5 years since I saw the city of Chicago and when the bus approached the city and I saw Downtown I realized how much I missed and loved Chicago. I had shut out of my memory the free world and most of all the city of Chicago to the point where if I was ever standing close to the I V room and the Chicago news came on, I would walk away in order not to see the picture of the Chicago skyline. I spent the night at the MCC and the next day I boarded the bus and looked back at the city as it faded behind me as the bus headed down Interstate 94 towards United States penitentiary Terre Haute in the State of Indiana. When I got to R&D at Terre Haute, the officers who were doing the strip search happened to be rednecks, but one was an asshole because he would strip search a person than would yell out "GIVE ME ANOTHER CRIMINAL" instead of just saying give me another one. He was obviously trying to get a negative reaction out of one of us so he could be a bigger asshole. I spent a week in segregation at Terre Haute not far from where Timothy McVeigh was being held on death row. In 1995 Timothy McVeigh Blow up the Murrah Federal Building in Oklahoma City and because of his terrorist act Congress and the Senate passed the antiterrorism bill of 1996 and in that so-bill, inmates lost a whole lot. Educational programs, exercise equipment, habeas corpus was reduced to a single filing even if new evidence proved that a person was in fact innocent. Immigration and deportation laws were changed so that a deportable alien had no chance to fight his deportation under any circumstance regardless of the situation if he was convicted of a felony. What did education in prison and immigration have to do with Timothy McVeigh's terrorist act? The answer to that question is "nothing" because he was never an inmate nor was he an immigrant, but politicians are good at sneaking want they want passed into big bills such as that antiterrorist bill. A European American who was in the US military not prison is the cause for prisoners and immigrants lost a lot do to the crime committed by this guy. After spending a week at Terre Haute I was transferred to FCI Milan in Michigan and when I got there, I was placed in the FDC (federal detention center) for screening which took about a week to do than I was moved over to the FCI.

FCI Milan

One side of FCI Milan is made up of old brown brick buildings and most are connected except for the three newer buildings set off to the side. The other side is surrounded by a double fence with guard towers overlooking the recreation yard. The staff at Milan were so much different than any of the other prison I had been in. In the other prisons most staff were miserable and acted as if they were at war with the inmates but at Milan, most of the staff treated us like human beings and very few acted like miserable assholes. Treating prisoners with respect and dignity does not mean they were breaking any laws or rules, they had a job to do and most did it in a professional manner without having to act superior and treating prisoners as inferior. One of the first things I did was to find Frank Calabrese and give him the message from his brother which I did as soon as I was able to find him. FCI Milan is a low security institution and most inmates there were like most inmates in federal prison, first time nonviolent drug offenders according to the federal government. Since FCI Milan was in Michigan and Michigan has the largest middle eastern community in the United States there were more Middle Easterners there than any other prison I had been to. They were from all over the Middle East Lebanese, Yemeni, Iraqi/ Chaldean/Assyrians, Jordanians and Palestinians some were Muslims (Sunnis) others were Shia or Christians. Milan was a very old prison so there was a lot of things for inmates to do and that kept inmates pre-occupied, which naturally kept tension and stress levels down. Prisons that are lacking in educational and recreational programs tend to have more disciplinary problems out of the inmate population. Inmate movement was restricted only from 8 AM to 4 PM Monday through Friday but after that it was open movement. Inmates could move from their units to the recreation yard or chapel freely until 9 PM and on the week-end it was free movement all day until 9 PM. The religious department had three chaplains, father Howard for the Catholics, Rev. Brooks for the Protestants and Imam Mukhtar Curtis for the Muslims and all were decent kind and caring people. I had heard about Imam Curtis long before I came to Milan, that he was very knowledgeable in Islam. Imam Curtis is an African-American from the city of Philadelphia who reverted to Islam and studied the religion in the Middle East. He is one of the sincerest Muslims I have ever met in my life and I mean to this day and his teachings are true Islam based on facts From the Quran and the Sunnah (saying of Prophet Mohammed peace be upon him). I loved learning from him, he taught me the simplicity of Islam and showed me that Islam is a religion of peace and whole lot of mercy. Any question I had for him he always answered and was very patient with everyone, but he also expected every Sunni Muslim to be on his best behavior. By the time we met he had already been through the con games played on him by so-called Muslim inmates. There was always plenty of con men to go around in every religious group within the prison system just as there was in the free world. There were some religious inmates who were losing touch with reality, for example I had a Nigerian friend who was a Protestant who started to believe that he was a prophet who was able to heal paralyzed people in wheelchairs. When his healing power did not work which was always, he blamed the person in the of not have any faith. This Nigerian was always walking through the prison with his Bible in hand, always condemning anyone who did not follow what he believed. As I said, during my search and in my quest to find the truth as to where my path lay, I studied some of the Jewish and Christian faiths. I am not in any claiming to be a scholar in any religion, but I did learn enough to be able to deal with Jews or Christians in a dialogue. People were always intrigued and interested in trying to find out about Islam but they almost all had great misconceptions about the religion because of all the propaganda that had been spread through the Main Stream Media, Hollywood, politicians and some religious leaders. Whenever I was asked, I did my best to explain true Islam and rather than divide I showed the similarities in all three faiths. I never wanted any part of debating or any misunderstanding but always chose dialogue for better understanding instead, that is if the person I was talking with was willing to have a civil dialogue but if not, then there was nothing for us to talk about. I always pointed out to Christians how Jesus, peace be upon him, greeted his friends with the words of "peace be with you" (Asalamu Alykum) just as Muslims do to this day and how Jesus prayed "and he (Jesus) fell upon his face and prayed" just as Muslims fall upon their faces to pray. To me this was better than trying to point out any contradictions in the Bible, so I dialogued in this manner which seemed to humbled people and bring on better results by showing similarities in our faiths. The things I mentioned were right out of the Bible that did not need interpretations or much explaining because they were clear versus but only needed to be pointed out. At FCI Milan I was going through a transformation because of Imam Curtis' teachings and the kind treatment I was receiving from most of the prison staff. I had decided years ago to become a better human being and being at Milan was a big boost for that which also made me want to be positive role model in the prison because I wanted to show people that Islam is a religion that was unjustly being smeared. Inmates were allowed to shop at the commissary on the weekdays after the 4 o'clock count and on one occasion I had purchased one hundred penny stamps to make up for the increase in the price of mailing stamps. The staff member who took care of me was a new female staff and just started working at the commissary. Instead of giving me the hundred penny stamps she gave me one hundred $1 stamps. I realized her mistake when I got back to my unit so I went back to the commissary and gave her back the dollar stamps and asked her to give me my penny stamps. She had a shocked look on her face, I'm sure she was thinking that inmates were supposed to be dishonest people so how could this be happening. Even though I was changing and becoming a humble individual that did not mean I was now becoming passive so on another occasion at the commissary as I was waiting for my name to be called a staff member working one of the commissary windows named Berdami was one of the few staff who you could say was an asshole at FCI Milan. This asshole was making fun of inmate's names as he was calling us to his window. I was hoping and praying he did not call me to his window because I wasn't going to be able to contain myself if he clowned my name as he was doing to other inmates. I just sat there watching him clowning other inmate's names and not one of those inmates said anything to put him in his place, they just took it with a smile. Unfortunately for him, he did call my name;

Bordami; "Saddadee sadoodee hahahaha"

I walked up to his window and said;

Me; "Boobammi Babami hahahaha I am not one of these coward snitches, I aint scared of you, you are going to give me the same respect I give you whether you like it or not"!

His face turned red and he refused to give me my commissary but that was the only thing he could do which meant nothing to me because I could easily wait until the next day to go back and shop. There was no way in hell he was going to disrespect me like that just because he's a staff and I'm a prisoner and from that day forward he never said anything disrespectful to me. The month of Ramadan is when Muslims fast from sun rise to sun down and that became my favored time of the year. The administration accommodated and respected every faith and allowed all to practice and fulfill their religious duties as much as they could, and they never fell short in their duty. This is what makes the United States of America such a great nation and a person should feel blessed to live in this great nation, sure it's not perfect but nothing in this world is! Do I agree with much of its foreign policies of course not especially the ones pertaining to the middle east, Palestine and Israel in particular! A Muslim is treated better in an American prison when it comes to his religion then he would be as a free man in some of these so-called Muslim countries where tyrants and corrupt officials rule the country. During the month of Ramadan, the administration allowed me to volunteer for work in the kitchen to prepare the meal for the break of the fast every evening for thirty days. One of the Palestinian Muslims I was with at Pekin had just arrived at Milan and when I spoke with him he told me that Frank Calabrese's brother was supposed to board the plane with him but was snatched away by government agents at the airport. I knew Frank Calabrese would want to know about this, so I found him and relayed the news to him. After hearing me out he had a very concerned look on his face but did not say anything other than thank you. It was later revealed that Frank Calabrese's brother and his own son had flipped sides and were now cooperating with the government against him and other alleged Chicago mobsters including Little JM. When Junior from Scarfo's case called Frank Calabrese's brother a Rat he knew what he was talking about, he obviously knew something that no one else knew at the time. My permanent job assignment was at the recreation yard and the rest of my time was spent reading religious and history books as usual, I participated in ceramics hobby craft, worked out and participate in the garden program during the summer months. Another great book to read which contains a great deal of information about the true founder of Christianity after the departure of Jesus, peace be upon him, which I read and would recommend for all to read is "PAUL the Mind of The Apostle" by A.N. Wilson. My telephone Calls were still exclusively for my mother and they went on like clockwork daily, but I now had ration my calls because the new rules of the so-called prison reform only allowed prisoners so many minutes a month, so I called her for a few minutes in the morning and a few minutes in the evening so I could check on her. I became good friends with two stand up European Americans who were from the city of Detroit, one named Casey the other Joe and I considered these two guys to be very good friends and more. Casey was a member of the Detroit Outlaw motorcycle club and Joe was his good friend from the streets. On September 11, 2001, a tragedy happened that would change the world as we knew it especially for Muslims the world over. The morning of Sept 11th I was at work on the weight pile when I heard about a plane crashing into the world trade center and I honestly thought it had to be an accident but a few minutes later I heard about the second plane crashing into the second building and now all thoughts of it being an accident faded from my mind quickly. I prayed to God that whoever the people were that committed this horrible act were not Muslims, not that I was scared for myself but for all Muslim and non-Muslims alike. If it was so-called Muslims who did this than the poor Muslims living in Muslim nations who were already living under oppression by their own corrupt governments were the ones who were going to pay the price. I remember how hectic things were getting everywhere, non-Muslims were blaming the religion of Islam including every Muslim of the world for this horrible act. Not one good Muslim would ever condone such an act nor does the religion sanction such an act. After careful examination by many honest investigators of the circumstances of that day there is a lot to be said about Sept 11th. There are a lot of unanswered questions about the whole thing because a lot of what happened that day makes no sense. Many people to this day are asking for the investigation of Sept 11th to be reopened among those who were asking included family members of the victims and many are calling what happened that day as a "false flag". There was the issue of tower number 7 which collapsed the way-controlled demolitions happen and that tower was not hit by anything, then there were the statements of people who were on the lower floors of the twin towers that said they heard what sounded like bombs going off and some were injured from those explosions. The next morning I was discussing this tragedy with another inmate before going to my job, it wasn't an argument or a debate just a simple discussion. I reported to my job assignment at 8 and about 11 AM the lieutenant's office called my boss asking to find me and send me over to see him. My boss was a very nice and caring African-American woman, she called me into her office and said, "the lieutenant wants to see you, are you okay", I assured her that I had not done anything wrong. It was never a good thing to get called to the lieutenant's office but I knew that I did nothing wrong so there was no need to worry. When I got to the lieutenant's office, he was very polite and respectful, he simply asked me to refrain from discussing what happened on 9 11 because it was too sensitive of an issue. He said it was hard enough to run the institution without having to deal with political or religious conflicts. You must be smart enough to know when it's time to keep silent and not to try and explain yourself so I assured him that I would refrain from discussing it the issue period. But It wasn't always easy not to respond to stupid comments and nonsense, one such example was when a Mexican gang member from California. This guy spoke English with a heavy Mexican accent and was going to be deported and was going to be deported back to Mexico after completing his sentence. He walked up to me at the recreation yard and asked me in his strong Mexican accent "whatt happen"? I was lost and had no idea what he was talking about. This guy lived in my unit so for a second, I assumed he was asking about something that may have happened in the unit like a fight or something. I shot him a confused look and replied, "I don't know, what do you mean what happened". He cracked a smile and spread out his arms to the sides and said, "joo know, New jork"? When I heard him say that my blood started to boil because he was asking me as if I had some sort of connection with those guys because we had the same religion. There was no way I was going to just swallow the shit he said without responding to his stupid question. I let his goofy ass have it by reminding him that Hispanic gang bangers are terrorizing their own communities in this country not to mention the amount of drug flow coming in from the southern of border and poisoning the population in this country, yet I would never dare throw the blame on all Hispanics or the Catholic religion. I told him to look at his file the next time he went to his team meeting, which is conducted every six months, and read the red tag labeling him as a domestic terrorist because of his gang affiliation. After what I said he didn't say another word than turned to walk and as he did, I thought to myself "The nerve of this mother fucking clown". The only way I heard the news was on my headphone radio NPR news and at certain times of the day it was BBC News even though they were biased that was the only two options I had because I was not going to go in the TV rooms. Every time I heard Osama bin laden open his mouth I wanted to reach through the radio and snatch his tongue out of his mouth, so he wouldn't talk anymore because he had no business speaking on behalf of all Muslims. He and people like him were hijacking the religion of Islam with their crazy ideologies. They made threats against strong nations that he could not harm and in return those nations struck back at weak Muslim nations and the only people paying a heavy price were the poor Muslims who were already oppressed. Not all but many of the Arab Muslim inmates were not involved with the Muslim community because they resented the fact that Americans (convert) had the run of the Muslim community. They felt that an American convert had no business leading them in prayer or preaching to those who were born Muslim and whose native tongue was Arabic. Their attitude made me sick because unlike me they knew the religion well before they were sent to prison the only thing these Arab guys were good for was spreading gossip and creating confusion! It was African-American Muslim inmates who taught that I was a Sunni Muslim and what the word Sunni meant, they taught me about great Islamic figures such as Imam Bukhari and Imam Muslim who compiled the Hadith (sayings of prophet Muhammad peace and blessing be upon him). They also taught me about great Islamic scholars who interpreted the Quran such as Ibn Kathir and Ibn Taymiya may God have mercy on their souls. It is truly embarrassing and shameful when I think about how we Arab Muslims had been profiting for decades from operating businesses in African-American community and selling them poison like alcohol pork and cigarettes among other things because we are Muslims and all of that is prohibited in Islam. Not every African American Muslim in prison was true to the religion, of course not there was the con-artists and there was the black nationalist, but most were proud of the fact that they were Muslims and understood that Islam made them better human beings. The ones who always talked black nationalism were usually very sympathetic to Louis Farrakhan's so-called Nation of Islam. When I lived in Jerusalem there were white, brown, and black Palestinians but while there I never ever noticed the differences in people's colors, it wasn't until I came here to the USA that I was introduced to this sickness of noticing the differences in people's colors. This nationalism sickness destroyed the Muslims of the world especially the Muslims of the Middle East and North Africa. There was also African-American Sunni Muslims who pretended to be very nationalist and one easily tell he was a con artist because of his ability to always cause a problem and never ever came up with any positive to help the Muslim community in prison. Any sensible person could see right through him because always displayed hatred for other races in the way he spoke about them. He once asked a visiting Sheikh (religious scholar) a question "isn't it obligatory upon Muslims in the US to fight the government because they are killing Muslims overseas"? The Sheikh who was of African descent was a religious who graduated the top of his class in Hijaz (Saudi Arabia) answered him and his answer made that inmates look stupid for asking the question. The Sheikh's answer was "As for immigrants who enter this country as guests they (immigrant Muslims) are allowed to enter this country after they sign a document stating they will not harm to this nation and that is called Amanna (a trust) in Islam which cannot be broken, and for those born in this country they are free to practice their religion as they please, no one is stopping them from praying and worshiping Allah (God) or forcing you to leave their religion" and explained even further "Even here in prison you are granted more rights to practice your religion then Muslims are in some so-Muslim nations". It is easy to see that every religion and every race have individuals whose only desire is to spread lies, mischief and hatred! After some time at FCI Milan I applied to become a member of a group called JAG (Juvenile Awareness Group) and its purpose was to lecture at risk youth in order to try and steer them away from getting into trouble and ultimately ending up in prison. I met with the staff member who oversaw the group whose name was Mr. Gorman for an evaluation to see if I qualify to be a member of this group. To qualify as a member of this group you had to have a clean prison record, you could not be a child molester, a rapist and an unwritten rule of not being a snitch. Among the members of the group was alleged mafia boss Frank Calabrese, Alan a Jewish college professor who become addict to crack cocaine then turned to robbing banks to feed his drug addiction. There were also about five or six other guys with different backgrounds such as drug dealing and bank robberies. After Mr. Gorman concluded his investigation I was approved and then allowed to participate in lecturing the youth in the prison visiting room every Wednesday evening. Once a year instead of having to deal with at risk youth we were visited by law students from one of the local universities in Michigan. On this visit, each prisoner gave a small presentation about himself then after the prisoners were done the students would get a chance to direct a question to whoever they wanted to ask from among the prisoners. On one such visit, we finished giving our presentations then it was time for the students to ask their questions. The first student who stood up to ask the question was a European American female student who directed it at me, "Being a Palestinian Muslim, how was life for you in prison after 9/11"? When she stood up and pointed at me, I immediately knew what her question was going to be, and I was glad she asked me that question. I first pointed to the fact that some of the inmates on the panel had been with me for many years and knew me very well. They knew that I respected all people and expected the same in return so there was nothing weak about me therefore I was not going to allow anyone to try and intimidate. I also pointed that I was in prison when Timothy McVeigh committed his terrorist act of blowing up the federal building in Oklahoma City where many innocent people including children were killed but no one ever blamed or questioned any of the Irish or Catholic inmates. If the Irish and Catholics were not being held accountable for Timothy McVeigh's actions, then why should I be held accountable for what some so-called Muslims did in New York City. In fact, not even one of the terrorists on those planes was a Palestinian. The whole visiting room broke out in a loud clap after I finished my answer to her question because it was a sensible and logical answer to a good question. What always bothers the shit out of us Muslims is when a Muslim does something wrong all of us including our religion are blamed and held accountable for that idiot's actions. Anytime a non-Arab non-Muslim commits a crime that person is always identified by his name and not his religion, but Muslims are always identified by their religion and not their names in the main stream media. I became the first Amir (head of the inmate Sunni Muslims) and I always tried my best to follow the teachings of Islam to the best of my ability when dealing with the brothers in the community. I had some beautiful American Muslim brothers who were also very supportive in every way. Inmates who convert to Islam tend to become better people and prison officials attest to that fact which can be found in documentaries like "Islam in America". There was the inmate Jewish population which I made sure I treated with humbleness respect, and I could have treated some of them in a rude manner or not even have any dealings with them if I wanted to, but if I did that would have been to satisfy my own selfish desire and played into the false claim that we hate Jews which is far from the truth. I was introduced to a Jewish inmate named Jonathan who was born in Palestine/Israel. When I met Jonathan, I asked him where he was from and his answer was "Israel". I than had to rephrase my question "No I mean your parents, where did they come from"? Jonathan said "O they migrated from Poland". I found out that Jonathan was going to be deported back to Israel after the completion of his short sentence. I made sure to especially treat Jonathan good so when he was deported back to Palestine/Israel he would remember that a Palestinian treated him good and in return he may treat Palestinians living under Israeli occupation justly since he held the upper hand there. I knew if I treated him badly because I had more power than in that prison that he may mistreat other Palestinians back in Palestine where he had more power than them. Then there was the Arabs (Iraqi & Lebanese) from the Shia sect which at the time I did not know anything about their beliefs and thought they were Muslims who had a small dispute with the Sunnis over who should have led the Muslims after the death of Prophet Muhammed (PBUH), but it was much more than that. Another thing I did not know was the Shia inmates were going behind our backs trying to poison the minds of new converts into Islam about Sunni Islam but in our faces, they played like we were all brothers. Their behavior made me want to learn about them, so I could understand why they would want to drive new converts away from Sunni Islam since they claimed to be our beloved brothers. After much studying I found out that the Shia are not Muslims because their religious beliefs were far from the teachings of Prophet Mohammed (PBUH) and they without a doubt hated Sunni Muslims more than anything on this earth. One of the guys who was on the panel of JAG named Tracy who was a Crip from Los Angeles California was released after serving ten years and a few months after his released news reached us that Tracy had been kidnapped, tortured, and murdered. In early 2003 I was called to my unit counselor's office to be informed that I was going to be shipped out to FCI Oakdale in Louisiana where my deportation proceedings would be held. A few days after meeting with the counselor I was told to pack up my property and take it to R&D. I made my rounds to say my goodbyes to my Muslim and non-Muslim brothers throughout the prison. I really hated leaving FCI Milan because I was going to truly miss being around good guys like Casey, Joe, and many of my Muslim brothers plus the staff who were good human beings. Guys like Casey and Joe always made doing time easier because they were always positive and never let things get them down. The next day I reported to R&D and was then transported to a local airport shackled with irons at the waist and ankles. I boarded the airplane at about 10 AM and from there we flew to Indiana than to Chicago, Minnesota and God only knows where else dropping off and picking inmates. Finally, at about 6 PM we arrived at the federal holding facility which is on the airport grounds in Oklahoma City, Oklahoma. I got off the plane and was moved from room to room for the next four or five hours a process that always drained all your energy. The place was packed like cattle with inmates from all over the country because it was a stopping point for inmates heading to prisons in every direction of the country. I spent about a week in Oklahoma before being transferred to FCI Oakdale Louisiana.

FCI Oakdale in Louisiana

I arrived at FCI Oakdale and the drill was the same as any other institution, all arriving inmates are processed through R&D, but this place was different because an announcement was made by the case manager who was processing us, "if any of you guys are affiliated or are members of gangs from southern California such as 18 Street, Suranos, Border Brothers or are member of the Paisa prison gang than say so now, otherwise your life would be putting yourself in grave danger if you are released into the general prison population". A minute or two later a few of the inmates stood and announced that they were members of those California gangs. Those inmates were then escorted to segregation where they would have to sit for a few weeks until they are transferred to another institution where it would be safe for them to be released into the general population. I don't think anyone was ready for what was waiting on the other side of the R&D building. By the time of my arrival at FCI Oakdale I had already served well over 90 percent of my sentence and my security level was low enough that I should have been placed in minimum-security prison but instead I was transferred into this prison. The place was crawling with violent gang members from Texas and the biggest gang there was called Aztecs who were from Al Paso Texas, followed by T S (Texas Syndicate) and lastly M M (Mexican Mafia). As we entered the orientation building the hallway was lined with Texas gang members asking us where we were from hoping they would catch someone belonging to one of the gangs mentioned by the case manager. There was so much violence in this prison that the administration put up fences and metal detectors all over the place. It was like a prison with many prisons inside of it and the tension was so thick in the air that you could slice through it with a knife. There was always an article in the local newspaper about inmates being charged with stabbings, assaults, attempted murder and maybe even murder of other inmates. The Texas gangs were extorting some of the inmates for protection especially some of the Colombians who were passing through there to be deported back to Columbia. There was virtually nothing for inmates to do in this institution because everything had been taken away. Weights, cue balls, and horseshoes at some point had been used as a weapon to assault other inmates hence they were removed by the administration. The world is a small place, I ran into a guy I knew from Chicago who is an older Latin King. I had not seen this guy since early 1990 when we did some business during my drug dealing days but other than him there weren't many people from Chicago there. He was at Oakdale doing time for re-entry which means he was deported to Mexico and came back into the United States illegally. I made friends with two members from the Aztec gang, one called Smokey the other called Flaco who were finishing their sentence and would then be deported back to Mexico. Smokey was about 32 years old and had been living in El Paso Texas since he was a year old, according to him he had no family in Mexico to go back to. The Muslim community at FCI Oakdale was about 25 to 30 members of many different nationalities Turkish, Jamaican, Dominican, Mexican, African, Colombian, Arab and African-Americans. One of the Muslims there was a guy from the country of Sudan who was sick in the head and I say that because he said he was willing to do whatever it took to be able to stay in the United States even if it meant making up lies about other Muslims. Hearing that made me sick to my stomach, so I made sure I stayed the fuck away from this creep. After 9 11 there were Muslims all over the world who were willing to fabricate stories against other Muslims to receive favors from the US and many European nations. I was placed in a dormitory housing unit which was made up of four man or six-man bunk sections. People were always coming and going in this place because of the mass deportations going on, so you had no choice on who was put in your section. One day they placed this fat obnoxious Colombian in our four-man section, he was there for only a few hours before

I got into an argument with him. After talking with the other two guys in my section we decided that he had to go so I informed him of our decision that he had to find another section to sleep in. It turned out that this fat Colombian fuck was paying the Aztecs for protection and if I had not been friends with Smokey and Flaco it could have been a problem for me since they were a super power in that prison. It did not matter how stand up and tough you were because this was real life not Hollywood where anyone could be got. Smokey and Flaco were sent to spoke with me, they asked me what was the problem with the Columbian so I told them that he was hard to live with and asked if they could move him to another section. I said, had I known that he belonged to them I would have brought it to them rather then telling him that he had to go. They heard me out and agreed to move him the next day but asked me not to say anything to him. Sure enough, as promised he was moved out of our section and into another section the very next day. They both knew from past conversations with me that I was also a gang member from Chicago, and we developed mutual respect. They saw that I carried myself like a man/convict rather than an inmate and those were the reasons they did not make an issue out of the fat Colombian situation and trust I could have caused myself some trouble. By the end of 2003 I was moved from the FCI prison to FDC (federal detention center) Oakdale where all the inmates there like myself had finished their sentences and were now waiting to be deported back to their home country. I had already started going back and forth to the immigration court while I was at the FCI and was almost finished with all my court proceedings before being moved to the FDC. My mother hired a Jewish attorney from Chicago who was connected to an immigration attorney near FCI Oakdale. The government was trying to make the claim that maybe I was a Jordanian national and they were pretending that Palestine never existed. As I mentioned before the antiterrorist bill of 1996 killed any chances of any one facing deportation to have a fighting chance in court but in my case, I knew long ago that I could not be deported back to Jerusalem because the Israeli government who occupy my country (Palestine) would never allow me back into Jerusalem, hell they were and are to this day kicking Palestinians out of our land and stealing our properties left and right. The Israeli government with their Zionist ideology claimed that the land belonged exclusively to those people who were of the Jewish faith and no one else had any right to live there! The task at hand for me now was to prove that I had indeed been born in Jerusalem, that I had no connection to the Country of Jordan not that I had a problem with the Jordanian people, but I did have a problem with the game the US government was trying to play. The first thing I did was to get my mother to have my aunt (her youngest sister) who lived in Jerusalem to get me a copy of my birth certificate to prove that I was in fact born in Jerusalem. It took my aunt a few days to obtain a copy of my birth certificate and then mail it back to my mother who in turn gave it to the attorney. It was disgusting to see the US government in court acting like the issue of deporting Palestinians from Jerusalem was a new thing to them. Their attitude reminded me of the days when I lived in Palestine under the occupation of the Israeli military where a Palestinian was not allowed to identify himself as a Palestinian because they wanted to erase the fact that Palestine ever existed. But this time I was getting a taste from those who were supporting the illegal occupation of Palestine which the US government. Back at the prison library at the FDC I quickly went to work on making a file with plenty of information out of the Encyclopedia Britannica among other western sources to prove that Palestine did exist and not only that but had existed for thousands and thousands of years. That Information dated back to the bronze ages and before which clearly proved the existence of Palestine from that time and before. I also included maps from those encyclopedias and Bibles again proving that the area was in fact called Palestine. Of course, that file meant nothing to them, but it meant a whole lot to me and a clear vindication for me as a Palestinian against their injustice of trying to deny me my Palestinian identity. Also, Mr., Gorman who oversaw the Juvenile Awareness Group program at FCI Milan sent a nice letter on my behalf to the immigration court even though it would not help it was a good gesture. I had no choice but to consent and sign the deportation order because I did not want to spend years in prison to fight a losing battle. I had no problem signing it and wished they could send me back to Jerusalem, hell most people of world dreamt of visiting the city of Jerusalem. The deportation order was now official and since I could not be removed from the country I was now going to live under the supervision of ICE for the rest of my life unless the law changed. After that was settled, ICE officials sent a letter to the Israeli Council and one to the Jordanian Council to see if either country would accept me. The ICE agent told me during our meeting at the prison that it is well known the Israelis never respond back to the letters of ICE because if they did, we (Palestinians) would have documentation proving that they were keeping us out of our home land. The Jordanians did answer in a telephone conversation and informed ICE agents that I was a Palestinian and if I was to be deported that I should be deported back to my birthplace not Jordan. I was proud of the guy from the Jordanian Council, that individual could have just said no but instead he acted justly and to be honest I was surprised because the Jordanians or I should say most middle Easterners seemed to dislike us Palestinians and I'm guessing that is because they blamed us for the tensions in the Middle East. I think they feel that if we Palestinians did not exist then there would be no one putting up a fight against the Israelis and they could live in peace with the Israelis. They were forgetting and playing dumb about the fact that Jerusalem holds the third most holy site for all the Muslims of the world which makes it their fight whether they liked it or not. My life had become even more complicated than ever now, not only was I stateless but now I was going to have to live here in the United States with a status of a non-removable deportee until the day Jerusalem is given back to the Palestinians along with a Palestinian country which is unlikely to happen anytime soon. Every week I watched as people from all over the world were deported, there was at least two busloads of Mexican inmates deported back to Mexico each week who were dropped off at the Mexican side of the border crossing. There was also a planeload of Jamaicans, Dominicans, Colombians, and other central and south American inmates being deported weekly. These deportations went on like clockwork every week non-stop. Many of the deportees had been in the states since they were children, and some were as young as one or two years of age. A good number of the people being deported told me they had no place to live once they got back to their home country because the only family they knew was here in the USA and they were worried that they were going to be imprisoned or killed once they arrived there. It was a very depressing situation especially when you're talking about individuals being deported for having convictions for very small amounts of marijuana but there was nothing anyone could do unless the law changed and that was very unlikely to happen. It is now the year 2019 and the law has not changed and from the looks of it there will be no change coming. Things are even worse and getting much harder for immigrants especially after Donald Trump won the election and become the President of the United States of America. My mother was anxiously awaiting my return home, she was more anxious then me for me to be free just as any mother would be for her child. My mother had gotten sick a few times during my incarceration, and she was home alone most of the time tending to her small grocery store. My youngest brother was living with her but during the day he was tending to another grocery store which my mother owned. For some reason I had a panic attack while at Oakdale which had me feeling like crap for a few weeks and I had to deal with it on my own without having to go see the doctor. Finally, in May 2004 after having gave the Friday sermon, the chaplain came looking for me and informed me that I was being released and instructed me to go back to my unit and get my things together then to head to R&D. When the chaplain gave me the news that I was being released it was almost hard to believe and a sense of fear and happiness came over me. I had so many plans after my freedom especially helping at risk youth and that truly was something I looked forward to. I hoped to join an organization that would help steer young people in the right direction and away from the road which led to gangs, crime and ultimately prison. I Had already been told by my immigration attorney at FCI Oakdale that I had to take the Greyhound bus and not take fly home to Chicago. He made that recommendation because he had another Middle Eastern client who got detained at the airport after being released from Oakdale and it took a month to get him released. I took his advice very seriously because I sure as hell did not want to spend another day in jail if I could help it so the Greyhound bus would be my means of transportation back to Chicago. I went back to my unit and gave away most of my belongings to other inmates and only took my legal documents, a pair of sweatpants, a sweatshirt and a pair of shoes then made my way to R&D. From R&D I was transported to the nearest town which was Alexandria Louisiana to a small bus station. At the station I was informed that the bus for Chicago would not be leaving until the next morning so I spent the night in a hotel and the next morning I boarded the Greyhound bus back to Chicago. The ride back to Chicago was long and rough but not as rough as being incarcerated so I was happy and thankful to have my freedom. I arrived at the Greyhound bus station in Chicago at about 5 AM and then took a taxi home. I made it home and knocked on the back door, my mother opened the door and it was so wonderful to see her. My poor mother looked very frail from the times she got sick, but I was thankful that God/Allah kept her alive because I knew other inmates who had lost their mothers while they were incarcerated.

Emad U Deen

Life After Federal Prison

It wasn't hard to see that the neighborhood I grew up in was a different place full of new faces and most if not just about all the people I grew up with were now gone. I loved my neighborhood for many reasons it is the place where I grew up, where I made good and bad memories. It was the place where I became part of a brotherhood (Saints) whom I loved very much and in return received the same back from my brothers. I don't expect anyone who has not lived the life we lived back than to understand what I am saying. I understood that there was no room for me in my hood anymore because I would not be able to relate to people there and had gone through too far on a different path to start a new one to fit in this new thing. It was like a was a foreigner there and the whole scene gave me bad vibes which made want to go far away from there, but I had no choice but to be there. I had a strange feeling that I may one day have to do something horrible to make my bones all over again in a neighborhood filled with new people who had no idea who I was and what I did as a Saint, besides most of these new age gang bangers didn't know or care to respect old Gs! My mother noticed that I was spending a lot of time to myself and indoors and she would say, "Imad go sit in front, get some fresh air maybe you'll see some of your old friends" which I knew was not going to happen because they were gone but I did it anyway just to make her happy. When I sat in front of the house hours passed without me seeing anyone I knew and after a few days of sitting on those steps next door to my mother's store an incident happened in which two young kids started arguing a few feet from where I was sitting so, I asked them to take it down the street. One of the kids, who I would later find out was the nephew of a guy who had become a saint years after I did, told me that it wasn't any of my business. I was pissed off but kept my cool but told him that he should inquire about me from someone who knows who I was. His reply went something like this "oh now you're trying to say that you were a Saint, you ain't no saint" and then rode off on his bicycle. After hearing him say that I smiled and thought to myself "Once upon a time this fucking kid would have idolized" but it did take a lot for me not to snap on that teenage kid. The next day I ran into two good younger Saints who had already heard of me when they met me, I told them about the incident with the young kid and they were able to figure out who I was talking about then told me that they would take care of him. A few days later that young kid walked into my mother's store and apologized to me then whispered to another young kid with him, "that's one of the older boys, he just got out the joint". I heard that this same kid passed away a few months later while at a prison boot camp. I wasn't in prison anymore, but I wasn't free because I still had five years of federal supervised release with many restrictions to complete and had to report to a parole officer regularly. I also had to immediately report to the local ICE office in downtown Chicago which I did and had the pleasure of being interviewed by an ethnically Filipino ICE agent who was trying to interrogate me once again about my birthplace, whether I was born in Jerusalem or the country of Jordan. I wasn't surprised by this minority ICE agent's behavior because I have already come to realize that when a minority is given a position of power in most cases, they seem to want to outdo European Americans by treating other minorities like shit. I didn't want to show him that I was upset but chose to make him look like an idiot fool by simply stating "Do you honestly believe I would have been released by ICE in Louisiana if they had any doubt about my place of birth, there is nothing there for you to find that would change the place of my birth"? A few days later when I reported to my probation officer, I informed him of my plans to help troubled youth, he looked at me for a few seconds than said "I understand and appreciate what you're trying to do but I don't believe that an organization of real value exists". I did find an organization called Cease-Fire but when I got close enough to the organization, I noticed that there was too much politics involved in how it was run which in my opinion was not productive. The guys doing the work on the streets did the best they could with what they had to work with, but it was the people at the top who dictated policy because they had degrees and PhDs that were the problem. Those highly educated people with all their book smarts really have no idea on how to deal the social problems of the people in the disadvantaged areas because most had lived a pampered life. They just don't have a clue nor are they willing to except any ideas and implement them due to their arrogance. I decided that I would try and volunteer my services at the mosque in Bridgeview Illinois to help with their youth who were having trouble. I had been hearing and reading in the news about Arab/Muslim youth from the Bridgeview area who were getting arrested for some major crimes so I thought they could use some help from someone like me, so I decided to make the offer. Unfortunately, one of the people in charge at the mosque declined my help because they felt the parents would not want to expose their youth to the life style I lived. These parents were living in denial and their logic was ridiculous because their youth were already making the local news and you can imagine how much was not. One case which made the news was about Arab Muslim youth who were involved in the robbery and murder of a Polish couple. I was a young Arab/Muslim kid who got involved with street gangs and later drug dealing just like some of their youth are doing now with one big difference, I lived in what is considered a tough ghetto and they live in a suburb with many opportunities for a better future. Most of these Arab Muslims in Chicago are very good at sitting around looking down at other people of other races but they are even harder on people of their own race and religion. Many of these Arab Muslims chose to ignore the fact that one of the best Muslims in the history of Islam and was a very close companion Prophet Mohammed, peace be upon him, is Omar Ibn Al-Khattab, may Allah be pleased with him, who was once upon a time a thug who drank alcohol and even planned to kill Prophet Mohammed, peace be upon him, before accepting Islam. I am in way trying to compare myself to Omar Ibn Al-Khattab, may Allah be pleased with him, but what I am saying is, just because someone was once a thug it does not mean he cannot be a good Muslim. I was truly excited about being released from prison so I could experience how it was to be part of the Muslim community in the free world especially after experiencing the strong brotherhood we had in prison. Unfortunately, that is not how things were in the Muslim community on the outside because there isn't much love or kindness towards each other, if anything there is a bit of hate! From what I could see the community was full of arrogant people who gossiped about each other and could not wait to see something bad happening to another Arab Muslim so they can go out and gossip about it not to mention that a lot did not see anything wrong with cheating each other yet go to the mosque and pray in the front row like they have done nothing wrong! There are some very honest, caring and trust worthy Muslims in the community, but the number is too low there should be a lot more. I would like to point something out that shows how just this government is, a month after my release from prison I received a $35 check from the Federal Bureau of Prisons which was my last month's pay. That shit blew me away that they did want to cheat somebody out of $35 and people wonder why Allah (God) blesses this nation. Back at home I still had to deal with my youngest brother's bipolar attitude and at times dealing with him was like dealing with a total stranger. He had a frown on his face like something was always bothering him when I was around, but he wouldn't act like that when dealing with other people. Hell, I always sacrificed for my family and gave as much as I could and felt it was my duty to do so. But while I was in prison something happened to my brothers and sisters like they drank something that made them cold hearted towards each other and very selfish people! One day While going through the mail at my mother's house I found a letter addressed to me with no return address but once I opened it, I realized it was from a girl I knew from back in the day before going to prison. In the letter, she welcomed me home and wanted to know if we could meet up for a cup of coffee. I called the number in the letter and we agreed to meet her for a cup of coffee and that's when she told me that she was now married to a guy who was once upon a time a connect (cocaine supplier) but she assured me that they were no longer involved in the business. She made a statement about me owing her big time which caught me of guard because she would sometimes get her stuff from me. I asked her how so, since we supplied you and not the other way around and that is when she explained what she meant by saying, "your youngest brother is an ass hole because he burned my people for a kilo gram of cocaine, and they were planning on shooting him for what he did". They discussed shooting my brother and another guy at her kitchen table and when she made a statement to them that went something like this, "Imad is his older brother who work with you and made a lot of money for you guys and never opened his mouth about anyone when he was arrested so that should count for a lot more than a kilogram of cocaine" they agreed with her and let the incident go but the other guy wasn't so lucky he was shot five times in front of his house but survived the shooting. I finally got my driver's license and purchased a used vehicle so I could go back and forth to work at the store with my brother which I hated every minute of it. Working at the store was at times worse than being in prison, I would have chosen prison over having to make a living by having to argue with ignorant teenage kids and there was the issue of selling people liquor and pork. Making a living by dealing in that filth was so far from the plans I had after my release from prison, but I told myself that this was temporary, and we would soon move onto a cleaner business. I was praying five times a day on time and never missed a Friday service but now I was falling so far behind on my prayers, it was difficult to pray and sell people liquor and pork. It's difficult to deal with when you must listen to a 90lb 15year old African-American girl threating to beat your ass and those were her exact word, that shit is hard to swallow for a guy who has been through what I had been through. My patients were being tested by the second with this new me and it was tough to deal with, but I had to be strong to restrain the demon inside of me which wanted to lash out. I understood very well what the repercussions would be if I lashed out which was a long prison sentence and the pain it would have caused my mother. I still had to try and put those disrespectful kids in their place even though I knew it would not do any good and sometimes it made things worse. There are some people from your past that you do not want to see and one afternoon a familiar face popped up in the store and it was my old drug supplier Ricky which caught me off guard not to mention the surprise of seeing him after all the years that have past. Ricky came into the store and stood next to the newspaper rack then started shuffling through the pages of the Chicago Sun Times newspaper, so I came around the counter to greeted him and see what was on his mind.

Me; "Hey Ricky how are you doing and how's it going"?

Ricky; "Good, how are you man"?

Me; "Good, is everything all right"?

Ricky; "Yes I need your help"

Me; "My help, how can I help you"?

Ricky; "I have a lot of shit but I can't sell it. I give one guy a kilo and a month later he give it back to me, he say he cannot sell it because he scared"?

Me; "Man I'm sorry but I can't help you with that I want nothing to do with that business, nothing whatsoever not even in a conversation".

Ricky; "Maybe you know someone, a good guy you can connect me with, and I also have a lot of Motta (marijuana)".

Me; "Na bro I'm sorry, like I said I can't help you, I don't know anyone and if I did, I wouldn't hook you up because I would get the same punishment if you guys get caught and someone mentions my name". Ricky stood there for a moment than shook my hand and left the store. A month or so later Ricky was back again, and we had almost the same conversation all over again, but I made sure I cut it real short with him. I was very clear in our first conversation that I was out and wanted nothing to do with that business so now I was spooked because he should have stayed away and not come back after our first conversation. It seemed that I had to get Ricky to understand that I was serious about my position, that I was done with the drug trade! After Ricky left, I went to visit the Old Mexican at the Tavern where I first met Ricky for the first time and asked the him to tell Ricky that I was out of the business for good so he must to stay away from me! The old man assured me that he would speak to him and that I do not have to worry about seeing him again and to this day I have not seen or heard from Ricky again. My relationship with my brother wasn't getting any better, on the surface it looked ok but beneath the surface it was anything but ok. He was hiding something inside, but I had no clue what it was or what it could have been. One thing for sure is that he was always frowning when I came around, so it was a matter of time before we started to bump heads and argue until we got into a physical altercation. Than there was the issue of us trying to get our mother to agree on selling the store and get away from selling liquor and pork. I tried explaining to my mother that working at the store with all its bullshit and having to deal with my brother's attitude was making my life a miserable hell.

Unfortunately, with the passing of time I also fell in line with what my family was doing and forgot about the unlawful sale of lottery, liquor and pork. I even convinced my mother to put a meat counter and brought in T-shirts, socks, hats to boost the daily sales at a much higher profit. I even connected with guy who was fronting me boxes of gym shoes for $25 a pair which I sold tons of them boxes at $75 a pair. The liquor counter looked like crap, so I brought in a friend who built a beautiful glass liquor counter which changed the look of the store and gave it a very respectable look. The business was doing between 13 to $1700 a day and up to $3000 on the first of the month but after my ideas the sales were as high as $4000 on regular days and as much as $8000 on the first day of the month which was a big jump. I also had African-American friends who were holding private club parties who would purchase six and $700 worth of liquor at a time. In a conversation with my middle brother he put the change at the store in these words, "if it wasn't for you Imad this store would still be considered as a chips and pop store". My baby brother had been at the for years and never made much changes there he was happy with selling a lot of candy, pop, and hot chips with cheese. I was living at home, so I didn't see the need to take more than a $100 a week because we were a family and all the money was put into one pot so at the end of the day everything belonged to us (our mother, me, and my youngest brother) which was an unwritten agreement we had. My middle sister was working as a cashier at the store, she was a naïve kindhearted person who did things at the store that jeopardized all the hard work we were doing there. For example, I caught her selling someone liquor on their link card one day then I pulled my brother and mother to the side about what I caught her doing. After that the three of us decided that she should stop working at the store and to be honest I hated to see her therein the first place because it was a rough place for a guy let alone girl. My brother had been complaining to me about how he had to play blind with her while I was in prison because he needed her help at the store. There was also a young African-American kid called Ron who was a good friend of my brother working the register for a few hours in the evening. This kid did not have another job but was able to pay his rent, phone, eat good, and dress-up his Chevy Z28 with what my brother was paying him for those few hours, so a red light kept popping in my head that something was not right with this picture. I thought maybe him and my brother had something going on the side but one night as we drove home I asked my brother a question about Ron "how much are we paying Ron a week to work those few hours at the store" he said it wasn't much because he owes us for a hotdog cart and that is the way Ron was how he made his living. Once I heard that I said to this, "well he hasn't worked the hotdog stand in a while and does not have any other job so how is he able to pay rent, his phone bill, food and spends money on other things without any income, doesn't this strike you as being odd"? I could see my brother was thinking deep and hard about what I just said because knew exactly what I was getting at and he knew I was making a lot of sense. The next day we started watching Ron and sure enough we caught him stealing from the lottery money and God only knows how many years he had been doing this. I could not figure out how my brother how my brother did the deposit for the lottery every week and never ever said anything about being short. As I became friends with customers who lived around the store, some of them them felt comfortable enough to tell me they felt that my younger brother was envious of me and sounded ridiculous. I felt like they were fishing to see if there were problems between him and me or they were just looking to stir up trouble between us. There something wrong with him which was clear by his actions but him being envious of me never crossed my mind at all. He seemed threatened by my being at the store like he felt his powers were dimensioning or something and I felt that because he always wanted it to be known that he was in charge and in control of the business. He always behaved like an arrogant asshole to some of the salesmen which was very embarrassing for me to stand there and watch him act like that. Even though my brother went to good Catholic schools he really didn't know anything about politics, history, or religion! Whenever I tried to have a conversation with him about one of these three subjects, it was like I was talking in Chinese to him. I would have intelligent conversations with educated customers or salesmen and my brother would stand there looking lost because he was unable to participate in those conversations. At the time I thought he would be proud that his brother was able to hold his ground in these conversations given that I had not even finished high school but instead it was eating him up inside and help brew the envy in him. He constantly complained to me about how he had been a prisoner in the store and how he was missing out on life for not being able to spend time with his daughter. He said he had help mom out with the store for years and now I should take over the business which is not what I wanted to hear, hell I was trying to get out of there not get stuck there. Greed had already cost me almost 13 years of my life which was much more important than all the money of the world and being in that store was not worth any money. My brother always wanted me to speak to our mother to try and convince her to sell the store, which I did because I felt this was the best course of action for all of us, but it always turned into an argument between me and her. When he played on my sympathies and asked me to talk to our mother His intentions were to turn me into the bad son who came home to give away everything we owned because I was too lazy to work in the store while he on the other hand was the good son who ran the store for years and never asked her to sell the store so he didn't want to work there. This created a problem between me and my mother, but he was the good kid who never talked to her about selling the business and played it off as if he had nothing to do with it. He tried to run the same thing on me again about approaching my mother but this time I declined to do so and told him that he would have to bring it up to her himself this time because I was done discussing it with her. After I said that to him, he gave me the impression that he was going to talk to her, but he was lying because he never did. We got into an argument on the telephone not long after this conversation and it was at this time that he said the most disgusting thing one can say to his blood brother over money which is when he threatened to send me back to prison and his exact words were "I am going to send you back where you came from" and that is how manly he is. This is My blood brother saying this shit, I had never done anything to him, to utter such words out of his mouth is beyond comprehension. On the other hand I was keeping him out of jail, he beat up to Palestinian brothers with a baseball bat in the store. They called the police then me to tell me what my brother did to them, I hauled ass down to the store from home and arrived there in time to convinced them to tell the police that they did not want to press charges against my brother. I walked into the store and found my brother standing with a police officer over the computer because the officer wanted him to replay the recording from the camera to see if my brother did hit the guys with a bat like they were claiming. I could see my brother scared and was stalling so I told him to forget trying to find it because the brothers were not going to press charges and when my brother heard me say that he looked like he wanted to fall on his knees and give out a long sigh of relief. If I didn't show up at the store and talk the two brothers out of pressing charges my brother would have been arrested and charged with two assaults with a deadly weapon or aggravated battery with deadly weapon which meant prison time because he was a convicted felon already not to mention a possible law suit. He thought he was the only one to ever work and provide but he forgot that I had worked and provided for the family long before he ever did. He was stressing me out so much that I started to suffer from anxiety which eventually evolved into panic attacks. Anxiety and panic attacks are two fucked up things for anyone to go through and I would not wish them on anyone. The attacks got so bad that I had to be transported in an ambulance to the hospital because it felt like I was going to die from a heart attack. One afternoon as I was running the store, I received a visit from an older GD friend of mine who I had met at FCI Pekin who informed me that the police found the G D board member who wanted the meeting in Pekin prison in the truck of a car on the southside. He was kidnapped, tortured and murdered than they wrapped him in plastic and left in the truck of a stolen car. Another victim of this fantasy about trying to lead his own gang, gangs that no longer honored older leaders who were imprisoned, and they were willing to murder them if they came around trying claim their positions of power after being released from prison. This was just another example of how fucked up things were on the streets and a warning for me to stay the fuck away from people and that is exactly what I did. This is how ignorant my brother was I purchased a vehicle that was worth $40.000 on payments and this idiot said in front of the salesman that this truck was for me doing 13 years in prison. What really made his statement so ridiculous was the fact that the truck was purchased through a loan which meant I had a monthly payment, so I paid for as I was working at the store. Dealing with my brother was a very hard task to do especially having to overlook a lot of the ignorant statements that came out of his mouth. I was always honest with my mother and I did tell her on a few occasions that if something happened to her my brother would do anything and everything to keep everything, but she would always say "no Imad your brother is not like that, he would never do that". I was trying to get her to understand that Islamically she had to get a Will done or it was going to cause a problem amongst her children if something happened to her. I did not want to push the issue because I knew my mother hated talking about death and like a lot of people hated the subject. But deep inside she had some doubt about him because she started giving me a few thousand here and there to put away which turned into a good amount of money. I gave the money to a few friends to hold for me and never spent it and to this day I still have that gift from her but now it belongs to my little girl who was born in January of 2014. I collected the money not to long ago from my friends and put it into an account for my daughter's education. I truly did not want to push the issue with my mother about not having a Will for another reason and that is because her health was deteriorating rapidly, she was having breathing problems and I think she was also having a lot of panic attacks. How would it look me talking about a Will while she was that sick, sick enough that at times I feared losing her at any moment? But Somehow, I felt that my mother was strong enough to pulled through as she had done so many times in her life. Unfortunately, while we were dealing with my mother's rapidly failing health my baby brother was plotting and planning how to get rid of me out of the store and whatever else we owned, so he could keep everything for himself. I am sure brothers and sisters have been doing thing like this since the beginning of time, but it is happening on a very large scale these days. I don't think I have to try hard to convince anyone that the thing called family has changed tremendously is not what it once used to be. I was tending the store one morning on the weekend in 2007 when I received a call from my brother-in-law, my middle sister's husband, the same sister who once worked at the store with us. He called with some very dreadful news and it was to say that my sister had passed away in her sleep. I could not believe my ears when he told, my mind was racing in every direction trying to figure out to convince him that maybe he was making a mistake and if he was sure. A minute or two later I had to accept the reality of the situation which is my sister was indeed dead and had been for hours before anyone had any idea. Now it was up to me to call my mother to give her the heart crushing new that her daughter who was her best friend was now dead. I took a few minutes to gather myself getting the nerve up to call her, I kept thinking how do I break it to her and how was I going to help her deal with the pain brought on by this tragedy. When she answered the telephone, I greeted her and told her that I had something to tell her, but I needed her to be strong. I heard the fear in her voice when she said, "please tell me I will be strong Insha Allah (God willing)". It was not easy, but I finally brought myself to tell her that her daughter/good friend was dead in Arabic. I will never forget her reaction and what she said, she handed the telephone to my niece and in a panicky voice said "Ceci Fatimah is dead, is dead" in very broken English and those words play in my head over and over to this day, I ever forget the pain and panic I heard in her voice. As I said they were best friends because they were both caring, kind and had loving hearts. The circumstances surrounding my sister's death are complicated, I was not going to discuss it in this book but after some serious thinking I decided that I would because I am hoping the story may help someone else not make the same mistake my sister made. After the call to my mother I called the mosque in Bridgeview Illinois and got the number to the funeral home which accommodates Muslims in Islamic wakes and burials. I called the funeral home and informed them about the death of my sister and where her body was being held which was at the morgue in the Township of Deerfield. We buried her the next day according to Islamic traditions where the body is washed as if she was being readied for prayer than she was wrapped up in a white cloth and placed in the coffin. There is no clothing or jewelry permitted on the body and immediately after the noon prayer then funeral prayer is conducted at the mosque then on to the cemetery for burial.

There is no doubt the death of my sister took a devastating toll on all of us, but it really crushed my mother and I believe from the stress caused her health to deteriorate even further. My younger brother was so distraught that he was unable to work for at least a month or maybe even more, he attempted to come to the store but was unable to keep himself together, so I send him home to rest up. Tragedies and Death tend to bring families closer together and promises are made to keep strong ties from that day forward. Unfortunately, those promises last for a very short time before people forget and go back to behaving as they did before such as not speaking to each other and holding grudges over the silliest issues. Before the death of my sister me and my youngest brother decided to start a mobile truck washing business, we purchased two international box trucks and equipped them with water tanks and pressure washing machines and that was the easy part of starting the business, but the hard part was to go out and elicit clientele for the business. It was a very slow process because there was a lot of competition out there and on top of that it was a seasonal business because it gets too cold in Chicago to wash trucks outside in the winter. I would wash whatever customers wo had during the weekdays and if we had any weekend customers than my younger brother would wash them but most of the time the trucks were just sitting around collecting dust. I had been thinking during those days about the insurance policy covering the store, specifically the amount of coverage we had. I had some concerns because of bad things I had been hearing about the Palestinian insurance agent who had the policy for the store. I was advised by some Arab salesmen that we should be very careful with that insurance agent and to take a very close look at our policy. I approached my brother and questioned him about the insurance policy and to my surprise I found out that he did not have a clue. The next day I called the insurance agent and was informed that the policy was only for $175,000 in total, hell the property by itself was worth more than that. I requested for the agent that immediately come to the store to be able to see for himself that the policy was way off so he could correct his mistake. There was the building which was paid for, about $250.000 in liquor stock, the groceries and cigarettes inventory, brand-new refrigerators, and freezers. The policy should have been close to a $1 million so I asked him how he could justify a policy of $175,000 yet he was collecting over $8.000 a year. Paying that amount of money for coverage should have been for a million-dollar policy but he just stood there looking stupid because he was caught, he had been stealing from my mother for years and my brother never had a clue. After that meeting the policy was boosted up to, I believe to almost $1 million in total and we wanted him to include theft in case of a burglary. Not long after the old policy was corrected our store was burglarized through the storage area, but the alarm never went off and the burglars stole $80 to $90.000 worth of high-end stuff such as Remi Martin, Hennessey, and Grey Goose. It turned out that the moron from the alarm company had forgotten to connect the motion sensor in the storage area. When we called the insurance agent and informed him of the theft, he began to act in a manner which gave us cause for concern. My worst fears came true because he informed me that he forgot to include the theft by burglary into the insurance policy even after I made sure to repeat myself over and over than made him say that he understood what we wanted. This is precisely what those Arab sales people warned me about when dealing with this guy, he charged people for the best coverage but gave you shit coverage then he would pocket the extra money. I had the insurance agent come into the store and recorded a conversation, with his knowledge of course, between him and us in which he admitted that it was his mistake and he promised to rectify the situation even if he had to pay us for our loss out-of-pocket. While in prison you always become friend with some good guys who you would not mind having for friends once you are free, so you exchange information at some point then you try to hook up with each other on the streets. While at FCI Pekin I met an African American guy from the southside not far from my neighborhood who was a member of the Gangster Disciple (Folks) and was a standup guy. Me and this guy got along well so when I got out, he came and found me at the store and he also met my brother and sister. One day when he came to visit me at the store and asked me to do him a favor, and the favor was to use the store as a reference which was a reasonable request. He filled out an application somewhere and the place was supposed to give us a call for a reference, so he left a paper with his full name and telephone number on a small paper than taped it next to the register. A couple of months after my sister's death my brother approached me and said one of my sister's friends told him a story that he thought I should hear. My brother knew some of my sister's friends, but I did not nor do I have the desire to know any off them because they weren't the kind of people I would deal with. That evening I heard the story over the telephone from my sister's friend who was a homosexual heroin addict, he said that he asked my sister to get him a small packet of heroin from a black guy who drives a blue sedan Infinity and the person he was describing was the GD who was my friend from Pekin prison. The GD friend was one first people I called the day I found out my sister passed away because we were that close, and he immediately came to visit me at the store and just about cried his eye balls out. My sister's friend who told me the story about the black guy was a white kid from the suburbs of Chicago and was a long-time heroin user, he told me that he warned my sister not to play with the heroin because he knew that she never used it before so he thinks that she did not listen and played with the stuff and that is how she lost her life. It was hard for me to believe this junky that my friend would ever give my sister plus I would not have had any dealings with him if I knew he was dealing in junk. I called him to the store and confronted him about what my sister's junkie friend said about him and he swore up and down that he did not nor, would he ever do shit like that. I will say this, me and my brother did discuss the possibility of killing my G D friend after hearing what my sister's junkie friend had to say. Killing him would have been very easy because I could have lured him to come to the store one evening and took him to the storage area where we sometimes worked out at and shot him in the head with a small caliber pistol and no one would have heard a thing but what if it the junky was making the story up. My friend did say that my sister got his number from the paper he left by the register and they hung out with her friends a few times in down town but that was it than he accused my sister's gay friend of trying to throw the blame on him. Looking back on everything now and especially how things turned out with my brother I am glad I was not positive about my GD friend because I would have killed him back then and I am almost positive about one thing he would have turned me by now. It is easy to feel that way about my brother because of his statement about sending back to prison and threatening to call the police on me when we had an argument. I honestly believe now that had he been able to point to a crime than he would have had me arrested so if I would have done something to my friend than he would have surely turned me in by now. This is the first time I discuss the true nature of my sister's death, we of course wanted to hide it from people and especially from our wonderful and caring Arab/Muslim community who seem to thrive off other Arab's/Muslims misery. The only expectation out of most of our so-called Arab/Muslim community is that they will gossip and spread your misfortune all over the streets. The sad thing is that most have no room to talk about anyone, so here you go my so-called Arab brothers and sisters have fun with this information I just revealed to you. Take a good look at yourself and you families my Arab brothers and sisters before you talk about others, is it a wonder why we are in such bad shape as a community? When European society was once upon a time living in darkness it was Muslim knowledge that brought them out of darkness and into the light. These days Muslim societies are the ones living in darkness because we have really abandoned true Islam and our hearts have become hard for one another, and that is a clear indication that Allah (God) will give Islam to better group pf people who deserves it! I am sure Chicago Arab Muslims will probably label me as a "Self-hating Arab" just like some Jews do to other Jews simply because they say they are wrong for their treatment of the Palestinians people. They can call me whatever they want I been called worse by better people, behave justly in your dealings with Muslims and non-Muslims and Allah (God) will change our condition. One morning I headed out in the wash truck to handle some work at O hare airport, while waiting at the back gate for an escort I received a phone call from my brother. When I answered the phone, I couldn't not understand what he was saying because he was rambling hysterically. For a moment I honestly thought something bad had happened to my mother, but I was eventually able to get him to calm down, so I could understand what he was trying to tell me. He told me that he caught his daughter sneaking out of the house at night, that she was hanging out with the boys (Saints) in the neighborhood and when he confronted her, and she ran away when he turned his back on her. He started blaming our poor mother because we lived in the neighborhood and he was in the store so much that he neglected his daughter, as if my mother was twisting his arm to do either thing. I calmed him down and promised him that I would go looking for her in the neighborhood and bring her home as soon as I was done with my work. I finished my work and was back at the neighborhood looking for my niece and was able to locate her a with one of her girlfriends. I grabbed her then called my brother to informed him that I had his daughter in the car with me, so we could meet somewhere to talk. We decided to meet in the parking lot of a nearby Starbuck, when I arrived my brother and her mother were there already so, we talked for a few minutes and then she took off when them and I went my own way. I did some investigating and found out who she was hanging around with from the Saints than I approached the guys and asked them to stay away from her. Out of respect for me they agreed and promised not to have any more dealings with her. My brother was so upset with his daughter that he stopped speaking to her so me and my wife took her in to live with us until things cooled down between her and her father. My wife took up the task of taking her to school and then taking a break from her job to go across town and pick her up after school and this went on for a few months until things cooled down and my niece was able to go back and live with her father. During those months my brother was constantly calling my wife to thank her repeatedly for being there for him and his daughter in their time of need. Unfortunately, it did not take long for my brother to forget what my wife did for him and his daughter. For some strange reason he stopped speaking to my wife and even started to badmouth her to his daughter. My niece was still speaking to my wife and she is telling my wife all the bad things my brother was saying about her. In late 2009 my mother's health took a turn for the worse, she was admitted into Christ Hospital. I visited my mother at the hospital after work and tried inquiring about her diagnoses only to find that my youngest sister had placed a password at the hospital so there was no way to get any information about my mother's condition without the password. My sister convinced my poor mother to agree to this bullshit arrangement which made no sense what so ever to me, I mean what the fuck is the purpose of doing that. I tried explaining to my mother about this stupid password idea but in her condition, it was no use pushing the issue, so I had to just leave it alone in order not upset my sick mother. Since my release from prison I noticed that my youngest brother and sister bullied my mother into agreeing whatever they wished and when I mentioned it to my mother, she would say that if she did not go along with my youngest sister than she would stop speaking to her. The hardest thing to digest was how my youngest sister who hardly came around was now in charge of my mother's medical issues. This was the same sister who cried and complain about my mother because she always said everything belonged to me and my youngest brother. My mother had good reason for saying that because it was me then my youngest brother who provided and never took like my other brother and sisters did. My mother was released from the hospital, but her legs still had fluid in them. I asked her what the doctors said was the cause of it and why did they release her because her condition had not changed. She would say that my sister was talking care of it so be patient and give my sister a chance. I tried to convince my mother that we needed to get a second opinion, but she was so brainwashed by my two siblings that I could not get through to her. She would say my sister is taking care of it so be patient and give her (sister) a chance. Even after her release from the hospital my poor mother would call my youngest sister for days at a time without an answer and she only visited my mother a time or two in that year. My youngest brother knew it was necessary to stay on my youngest sister's good side because the liquor license at the business was in her name and there was no way his name could be on the liquor license because he was a convicted felon. While working at the store, there were people that I would borrow money to and or give food on credit until they received their money than they would pay me back. Many of these were poor ladies with kids and on a Sunday morning two of these ladies came in to get credit. One was older women who wanted to barrow $5 and the younger one wanted to borrow food. For some reason they got into an argument in the store than they left and took the argument down the street to the next block. There is no doubt that younger women was the aggressor of the two but the older women sliced the face and neck of the younger one while defending herself on the next block. The Older women was arrested and charged with assault with deadly weapon or attempted murder I'm not sure which, but I found out that the State was trying to give her a twenty-seven-year sentence for the case. Months later a public defender called me and asked if I would testify for the defense on behalf of the older women. I told her that I would, and the day came so I went in to testify and found the State was telling a lie and I told the truth exposing all the lies being told. After my testimony for the defense I let the courtroom and headed back to store than as I was pulling up in front of the store my cell phone rang, and it was the old lady's attorney who called to thank me and tell me that the judge believed my testimony and found the old lady not guilty. After having spent over a year in Cook County Jail the old lady was released than she came to the store and gave me hug. The State was mad at according to what the younger lady told me, she said they wanted to know if I was breaking any laws at the store. In March 2010, my brother approached me while we were standing in the store and asked me if I wanted to just concentrate on the truck wash business and he would stay in the store and handle things himself which was odd coming from a guy who regularly complained about being in the store but I just took him at his word and was actually feeling bad for him. I was happy at the thought of being away from the store, but I hated leaving my brother in that store seven days a week. He assured me that it was okay because it kept him busy, so he did not have to think about his daughter who was still giving him problems. That night when I got home at home, I mentioned to my wife the conversation I had with my brother. Once I finished telling her she immediately said without any hesitation, "your brother is trying to cut you out of what you have coming, he figures your mother is really sick so he figures she will not be around much longer". I got into a argument with my wife for saying that about my brother. Whatever arguments and disagreements I had with my brother I did not think he would stoop low enough to be thinking about cheating his brother at a time like this. But I would soon find the truth about my brother's true intentions and learn how much of rotten person my brother turned out to be. A day or two later I called my brother at the store to see how he was doing but he started acting very rude with me, so I went straight to the store to talk face to face. When I walked in, he was on the phone and I am sure it was with my youngest sister because he said "O he just walked in" referring to me. Immediately he started to use profanities and threatening to call the police on me and have me arrested. I thought about what my wife said and how right she was about my dirt bag brother. He was going to call the cops and say what, he was being a moron because my mother was alive, so I had the same right to be there in the store as he did. I tried speaking to him in a very humble way, but he just kept on because he was thinking about money and materialistic things which were much more important to him than his own brother. He continued his aggressive behavior, so I turned around, which I did not have to do, and started to walk out when he suddenly yelled out to me while laughing "we are plotting on you, ha ha ha ha ha". I'll never forget the look on his face while he was saying that, it was as if I was looking at someone, I never knew who was blinded by greed. I left the store that day and never looked back, I kept on moving forward with my life and the best I could with the truck wash. No long after the encounter with my brother I went to visit my mother and during she asked me to move back into the apartment upstairs from her so I could be closer to her. At first, I was reluctant to do so because my brother was living in the same building which meant I had to deal with his ignorant behavior, but I finally agreed with my mother. My brother found out that I was moving in back upstairs and he immediately rushed home pouting to my mother like a baby like the house belonged to him than he tried giving my mother an ultimatum by saying, "If he moves in than I am moving out". My mother flatly told him this "do whatever is pleasing to you" which broke his little silly pride and sent him on his way back to the store. Of course, he never moved out and just as I expected he started acting like a jerk every chance he got towards my wife without ever saying anything disrespectful to her. He behaved like a jealous child he was also being a jerk to her kid throwing away his toys in the garbage which he did while no one was looking. He was lucky that I had more sense than he had but most of all he was my blood brother so he there was no way I was going to have that on my conscience otherwise he would have had a very nice surprise waiting for him when he went home on one dark night. What can I say for a guy who turns on a woman who was there for him and his daughter in their time of need other than he is spineless and a low-class individual. It was decided that my mother would go live with my sister, the oldest of three girls, who lived in Lockport Illinois so she can take care of her. Not long after my mother went to live with my sister me and my wife decided to move out because my mother was no longer there. There was no reason for us to stay in the same building as my brother because we did not want to deal with his rudeness, ignorance, and childish bullshit so we moved out and rented an apartment on 34th street. I did not want to let things get so out of control between me and my brother that one of us, so decided to take the higher ground and leave. In September of 2010 my mother's youngest sister came from Jerusalem to visit us and during her visit my mother sat us down and explained to my brother in front of my aunt that if something was to happen to her, she wanted everything to be split in half between me and him. She also instructed us to help our brother and sisters if they needed help. When my mother was done talking my brother responded with this, "Mom I already know that, you don't have to say that to me". My mother consistently tried getting me to go back to the store, but I refused every time she mentioned it. I am guessing she figured if I went back than I would secure my position if something happened to her, but all my mother had to do was get her will done! My mother was going back and forth to the doctors more often but not getting any better and now she was permanently attached to an oxygen tank to help her breath. My poor mother suffered most of her life at the hands of my father was now suffering from her deteriorating heath and I could see the fear in her eyes every time I looked at her face from uncertainty. We were all scared at the thought of losing our mother and we hoped that she was somehow going to eventually pull through and that was especially true for me because I had no way of knowing what she was suffering from and how very serious it was. It was the pass word that my sister and brother put in place that kept us from knowing anything and like I said they convinced our mother that this was the best course of action to take. I did not want to argue with my mother about the pass word, as for my two-siblings who placed the pass word with the doctor I must ask what the purpose was of doing that other than it being a part of the plot that my brother mentioned to me during our argument. I was driving down Interstate 55 one day and happened to pass my mother and brother as they were heading to a doctor's appointment. I looked over and saw my mother looking at me which put a great big smile on my face, she was smiling at me and throwing kisses at me with her hand, every time I pass that section of the I 55 I visualize that moment in my head wishing I could have my mother back. I was working one cold November morning when I received a call from my youngest brother who gave me the dreadful news that my mother was taken to Rush hospital and was unresponsive. The doctor requested the family to be at her bedside which was without a doubt a very bad sign. I couldn't think straight; fear and hysteria took over me after hearing about the doctor's request which basically told me that the end was near for my poor beloved mother. It was not hard to read the writing on the wall and the reality of my mother's grave condition was hitting me hard, it is a day that in will never forget. I could not drive myself to the hospital because I did not have a vehicle on the job site, so I called my boy Y B to pick me up and to take me to the hospital. YB is one of my younger boys (Saints) but he is not a product of today's men, he is a man's man and he is one of the most honorable individuals I have come across since my release from federal prison. By the time YB's arrival I was distraught crying and mumbling to myself, this was the hardest thing I ever had to endure in my life. I jumped into YB's car and we headed to Rush hospital and the closer we got to the hospital the more helpless I felt. I had been down many rough roads in my life but never one that is as rough as this one, what can be harder than the thought of losing your mother. I got out of the car and walked into one of the buildings and approached what looked like an information counter. At the counter were two people a female and a male security guard, the guard asked what he can do for me, but I was chocking up so badly that I was unable to get the words out and eventually was able to ask him where I could find my mother. The guard directed me to the intensive care unit, and I believe I was the first one to that morning. I wanted to see my mother immediately, but someone said that we had to wait for the doctor to come give us an update on our mother's condition first than he would give us the green light to see her. By this time my wife had arrived and was trying to calm and comfort because I was in a panic mode. I was still crying, talking to myself and tapping the top of my head with my knuckles and not listening to anything or anyone. Eventually the doctor came out to the waiting area and informed us that our condition was Critical, but they were going to do everything they can to help her. I was starting to feel a bit better but more anxious about seeing my mother no matter what her condition was. I asked the doctor if we could go in to see our mother and he gave us the okay to do so. When I entered my mother's room, I seen tubes running everywhere in my mother some in her chest others her arm and the rest of them shoved down her throat. Reality was starting to set in, I knew it was going to take a miracle from God for my mother to pull through but there was always that little bit of hope to cling onto. I started to call out to her "yumma, yumma" finally she opened her eyes and that brought me to tears again. My mother's condition brought me and my brother back to speaking terms, so it seemed we were pulling together for the first time in a while. I had been through too much shit in my life to hold a grudge against my own brother for mere words especially at a time like this. I decided to stay with my mother 24 hours a day, but my poor mother was out of it most of the time. I took up the task with pleasure of helping the nurses keeping my mother clean since she could not get out of the bed to use the restroom. It was so hard to see my mother being so helpless when she was strong enough to moved mountains in her younger days. The doctors tried removing the tubes from her mouth to see if she would breath on her own but that only lasted for a few hours at best than they would have to reinserted them back in so she could breath properly. I slept in a chair next to her bed during the two weeks and she was getting delusional saying things that were not making any sense, she thought we were at home so she would tell me and my brother that we should go to our rooms and go to bed because it was late. It's heart breaking to recount what happened in those days, but it must be included in this book. By Allah (God) who holds my soul in his hands knowns that I would have given her whatever life I had left and would have been more than glad to take her place if I could have. It was a horrible feeling to be there next to my mother and not be able to do anything to help her, yet she was always there for me in my time of need. It was during those dreadful days that I found out my mother was misdiagnosed when she was admitted into Christ Hospital. Thanks to my two ignorant siblings who had a hidden agenda for taking advantage of our poor sick mother and making her agree to implementing a pass word so I could not enquire about her diagnoses and treatments. Because of their greed my poor mother suffered for well over a year without any treatment for congestive heart failure. On December 5th 2010, I woke up in the chair next to my mother's bed and found her surrounded by nurses. I jumped out of the chair and frantically asked them what was going on, but they were too busy working on my mother, so I stepped out of the room and into the hall. A minute later a nurse approached and asked me to get on the phone to speak to my mother's doctor who was a very nice Indian guy. As I was walking away from my mother's room I looked back and seen my mother reach her hand up for the nurse's closest to her looking for comfort as she was dying, and the young nurse grabbed it and started to comfort her. I got on the phone with the doctor and he informed me there was nothing else anyone could do for her than apologized to me, but I kept trying to convince him that there must be something that could be done but he kept apologizing. I was on the phone with him for a minute or two and by the time I got off the phone my poor beloved mother was gone to where she can rest in peace Allah willing. The doctor told me that she had gone too long without any treatment for her heart troubles and that brought me back to thinking about my brother and sister with their bullshit pass word. I so mad thinking about what they did to my mother with their greed but what can I do they are my brother and sister and my mother loved them as she loved me. I am sure they have conditioned themselves to believe they have done nothing wrong for worldly gains, but they won't be able to that forever and it will eat them up from inside out. I the funeral home that handles Islamic wakes and burials and arranged for them to pick up my mother's body from Rush Hospital and they did an hour or two later. I called my aunt back in Jerusalem to give her the bad news about my mother's death and she just about cried her eyes out. As I made my way to the funeral home with my wife I felt a panic attack coming on, but it didn't really hit me until I was in the lobby of the funeral home. I became dizzy and was unable to hold myself up, so an ambulance was called, and I was transported to a nearby hospital. Even though I was pretty much out of it I was still aware of what was going on around me and I noticed my youngest brother just standing there, he never made any attempt to see if I was okay. At the hospital, they placed an IV in my arm and diagnosed me with anxiety, fatigue and dehydration. My wife stayed with me for a few hours until I was released from the hospital. The next day we had the wake for a few hours and by noon prayer we were at the mosque where the Imam led the funeral prayer over her body and from there it was to the cemetery where she was buried at Evergreen Cemetery. My youngest brother stopped speaking to me immediately after my mother's death and the reason was clear, he had property and money on his mind, and he had no intentions on giving anything from my share. I called Jerusalem and spoke to my aunt and as we were talking, she asked me how my brother was doing so, I told her that he had speaking to me after as soon as my mother passed away. My aunt told me that my mother never did the will even though she intended on doing one after her visit in September. She advised me to put my trust in Allah (God) and ask God/Allah to guide him to do the right, she also asked me to call her back in a week because she was going to call my brother to see what his problem was. A few weeks later I called my aunt back, according to her my brother had the audacity to tell her that my mom wanted him to have everything, but she reminded him of the meeting we had in September. After my aunt reminded him of what my mother instructed us to do, the only thing he could say was "yeah ok you are right and it's up to me if I do or don't do what my mother wanted, anyway my mother is not here anymore". After hearing what he said my aunt told him that she won't be speaking to him anymore until he does the right thing. I eventually called my religious teacher and friend Imam Curtis to tell him of my mother's passing away. I was definitely in need of his religious guidance at a time such as this. Imam Curtis knew how close my mother and I were by our many conversations, so he gave me religious consultations and advised me on how best to deal with this terrible situation. One of the things the Imam advised me to do was to ask Allah (God) while in prostration to let me see my mother in my dreams. I did just that every time I prayed, and I begged Allah (God) to let me see my mother in my dreams just as the Imam had instructed me to do. A month and a half after her death I had my first one and, in that dream, I walked into what looked like a mansion which had two sets of stairs leading to an upper floor and on the upper floor was a big door which was dark in color. While I was looking up at the door it opened, then my mother came out carrying a baby wrapped in a white cloth. I addressed my mother, "hi mom" she looked down at me and answered with a simple "hi" but she kept walking without saying anything else and that was it for that dream. I had a second dream about three months after she passed away and, in that dream my phone rang, but the weird thing was that the ringtone was the same exact ringtone that I had on my telephone at the time. Anytime my mother called me, she had a habit of dragging my name out instead of saying "Emad" she would drag my name out with joy like this "EEEMMMMAAAD". I answered the telephone;

Me; "hello"

My mother; "EEEMMMMMAAAAD"

It felt so real and why wouldn't it I had no idea I was dreaming! To this day I remember the great joy and excitement I felt from hearing my mother's voice.

Me; "Mom Keef halik" (how are you)?

My mother; "Alhamdullah" (praise be to God) "keefak inta" (how are you)?
Me; "Wayneck yamma, wayneck" (where are you mom)?
My mother; "Maa lek yakhi roo' yakhi" (what's the matter honey, calm down honey).
Me; "Waynik yakhtee" (where are you honey)"?
My mother; "Itkhfsh ana foo'" (Don't be scared I am upstairs).

I started to say something else but she was gone and the dream was over just like that. I did not wake up I continued sleeping but that morning I woke up feeling unbelievably good not knowing why because I had forgotten about the dream and it had not come to me yet. I walked to the kitchen and started to make a pot of coffee while my mind was racing trying to figure out why I was feeling so good given the fact that in those days I would wake up daily in a daze from the thought of having just lost my mother. Then it hit me, I remembered the dream and that caused me to pause and go into a deep trance for a few minutes and the dream was playing over and over in my head. I had to call Imam Curtis and tell him about the dream and when I did reach and tell him, he was elated and congratulated me saying "Allah (God) answered your prayers and allowed your mother to assure you that she had made it to heaven". Many people would probably just dismiss this as my mind playing tricks on me or that I cause myself to have that dream by over thinking and I respect their opinion even though I believe they are wrong. That was the last dream I had of my beloved mother and that was 8 years ago. A few months passed after my mother passed without hearing a peep from my brother, but I left him alone because I want to push and beef with him right after the death of our mother. I text my youngest sister to see how she was doing and mentioned to her that me and my brother were no longer talking. I told her that I knew why he stopped speaking to me because it was self-explanatory, and she affirmed my suspicions with her ignorant answer. What else should I expect from a daughter who was asked after the passing of our mother why she stopped answering our mother's telephone calls and her answer was that she did not want to get too attached to her own mother because she knew our mother was not going to survive. Our mother carried this creature in her belly for nine months than sacrificed and cared for her until she was old enough to care for herself and this is her excuse for not answering the calls from her sick mother. A few days later I contact an attorney and explained my situation to him, and that attorney sent my brother a legal letter. I waited to see what type of fraud my brother and sister had been working on "The plot". In the meantime, my baby brother was bad mouthing me to people telling them that my mother hated me and how I was a bad son to her. My brother looked like a fool saying these things because he was saying this to people who knew that me and my mother had a great relationship. After a month or more I received a telephone call from the attorney telling me to come into his office that he received what was supposed to be my mother's will. I didn't have to look at it to know the will was without a doubt a complete sham, so I went to the attorney's office and found that everything we owned was left to my youngest brother and youngest sister (the plotters) and I was cut out of everything. The notary on the will was none other than the scumbag Palestinian insurance agent who owed us almost $100,000 for the theft of the liquor which he was supposed to cover from his pocket because he did not add it to the policy. I called the agent and asked him "you notarized my mother's will"? His reply was that he couldn't remember doing it because he does so many of them. Two days later I walked into his office to discuss my mother's will but this time his memory was sharp as a Ginsu knife. He told me that he remembered the day my mother came in, then pointed to the seat I was sitting in and said, "Your mother sat in the chair you are sitting in". He was so nervous while talking to that he started to tell me a story about someone doing some notary forgery in his name and he was getting blamed for it, a story brought on by guilt of a crook. There was only one way to prove that the signature on the will was not my mother's. Me and my wife did not have much money at the time, so I decided to sell the Nissan SUV and cut down on expenses which weren't much anyway. There was the money my mother had been giving which was with friends but there was no way I was going to touch that because I wanted to use it down the line for a business or something like that so, I pretended it did not exist. I was still working the truck wash but that was only seasonal work and the money from that business came in very slow. As I said before that I was not taking any money while I was at the store other than the $100 a week which was mainly used for gas in my car. On the other hand, my brother and sister had all type of money at their disposal they had a safety deposit box with hundreds of thousands of dollars, two bank accounts with tens of thousands of dollars in each, $60,000 which was at my sister's, the store was making thousands weekly, the apartment building on wood street where we grew up and all my mother's gold which was worth well over $150,000. After discussing my situation with a friend he encouraged me further to prove that the will was fake. I had just lost the best thing in my life (my mother) and my two siblings stole everything we worked for but that was not enough for them now they were spreading lies about my relationship with my mother to try and cover up their plot. Finally, I decided to take them to court to prove that this so-called will was a sham and the signature on it was not my mother's. For a minute I contemplated on using some of the money my mother had given me but fortunately my friend who is the head of the IMAN organization in Chicago connected me with a Pakistani attorney who would only charge me a few thousand dollars and would even allow me to pay him a little at a time. Other attorneys I spoke with wanted $30.000 or more to take the on case and represent me in court. My attorney filed the proper documents in court contesting the will and asked that my brother produce my mother's Social Security card and driver license for examination against the signature on the will. My attorney hired an ex-Department of Justice handwriting expert to examine the signature on the will and the two other documents with my mother's signature. Not long after the hiring of the handwriting expert I received a text message on my telephone while I was sitting at home from an unfamiliar number and the text message read, "can we talk"? I asked who was texting me and it turned out to be my youngest brother. As we were talking, he offered to pay me $50,000 to drop the case, according to him the attorneys fees were killing him so, he would rather give me the money. I refused his insulting offer because it was his fear of the hand writing expert that made him text me with that offer. I wanted to prove that the signature on the will was a forgery and that was my goal not his pay off money but after that I wouldn't care how the case ended. After thorough examination of the signatures on the Will and the two ID cards 5 handwriting experts concluded that the signatures on the ID cards were from the same person but the Will was not signed by my mother hence it was forgery. After that my brother and sister felt the heat so they spent more money on another attorney but as far as I was concerned, I proved that they forged the will and that was my vindication from the lies they were spreading about my relationship with my mother. When the time came for the judge to rule, he ruled that I needed more evidence than just the handwriting expert who were saying that the signature was forgery. It wasn't hard to figure out why the judge ruled against me with that bogus ruling and that is my brother and sister had access to big money to hire older top dog estate attorneys who knew their way around the system, but I had one new young very nice and timid Pakistani attorney. The only other evidence for me to get would have had to come from God and that was not going to happen. My attorney informed me that I could appealed the ruling, but I didn't because I had achieved what I was after and that was enough for me. I had planned on going after the insurance agent for betraying his public trust by using his notary powers to forge my mother's Will but found that his only punishment would only be a $5000 fine. That punishment was hard to digest, a $5000 fine for doing something that evil which tear families apart yet a person can get a year or more in prison for forging a check worth a few hundred dollars. My youngest brother and sister took everything with that fabricated/forged will and that is something they will have to think about for the rest of their lives, but they will somehow have to answer for their actions in this life or in the next. Most people including my two siblings do not believe in the next life even if they say they do. The disturbing thing is that they are clueless about the seriousness of their actions which was a crime against their own souls because they betrayed their mother after she passed away. It may sound like I hate my baby brother and sister because of the bad things I say about them but the is far from the truth. I love them both and the things I say about them are the truth so, I hope and pray their hearts become soft and loving and they think more in terms of being a family rather than loving this world and its material gains only. Me and my wife struggled for a few years busting our backs to make a life and in 2012 we were able to purchase a small family home on the south side of Chicago in an area where Chicago police, Chicago firemen and other city workers reside which makes it a great place to live and raise your kids. My wife works for a hospital as a coordinator for an Avon program that helps patients with breast cancer. We live a simple life and we have our ups and downs like most people, we are not perfect like everything else is not perfect. In the last few years I reached out to my father but every time I see him, I realize more and more that I cannot forget what he did to our family especially my mother. I just cannot get it out of my mind when I look at him or listen to him when he speaks. I am a person who forgets and forgives easily without holding a grudge but what my father did to my mother is something I can't forget so my attempts at kindling a relationship with my father is always cut short by those feelings. Unfortunately for him he is financially broke and finds himself alone with his children wanting anything to do with him at all. In 2013, I called my wife morning while she was at work and she told me that she was not feeling well. When I heard that I my response to her was, "maybe you ate something that is not agreeing with you" but her answer was "maybe I am pregnant". I honestly thought she was playing around so I told her to stop playing that she was not pregnant but to my surprise she said, "Well I am pregnant". The news of her pregnancy scared the living daylights out of me, because I was 47 years old and the world, we live in is not a place to bring a child into as far as I was concerned! My wife is a few years younger than close to mine which made her pregnancy a very difficult one and from it she developed diabetes. Also it seemed like every few weeks she was admitted into the hospital which I found out after she gave birth that the doctors feared the baby may have been dead because the baby had not made a moved for a day or two only to find out that the baby was fine. The doctors also told my wife that the baby was more than likely going to need open-heart surgery after she was born which is something my wife hid from me in order not cause me any distress. On January 8, 2014 she gave birth to a healthy beautiful baby girl at the University of Chicago Hospital, but the doctors chose to place the baby in the intensive care unit for close observations to keep an eye on her sugar level. I went to see my little girl and performed the Islamic tradition of calling the Ethan (Muslim call of prayer) in her ears. When I saw the baby's face it brought me to tears because she looked identical to my mother and there is no exaggeration when I say that. My wife and I knew the baby she was carrying was a female so we had decided to name her Fouza after my beloved mother. A few months after the birth of my baby girl as I was sitting in the living room watching TV, the dream I had of my mother carrying a baby popped in my head and thought "WOW" could it be a sign That I would be having a child in the future, Allah (God) knows best. My little girl is a mini version of my mom she acts just like my mom in every way which makes me love her that much more. The name Fouza means "Success" in English and she is now 4 years old and I wish so much for my mother to be here so she can meet her because there is no doubt in my mind that they would fall in love with each other. I hope and pray that one day me along with my brothers, sisters can be a loving family to each other Allah (God) knows I have tried reaching out to them without any success but will continue to try because that is what our beloved mother would want. I know why it is hard for my youngest brother to face me, but I told him through messages on any occasions that he is my brother and I do not care about the money and properties. We all know from history that the world has always been a scary place but now in 2018 the world is scarier and more dangerous than it has ever been. What makes it scarier is that most of the world leaders are the worse kind of people and It takes people to put them there so what does that say about people in general. There isn't much trust or loyalty left among the people and there is so much false pride that it is causing all kinds of hate between the races. I am now 51 years old and one of my worst fears is the thought of not being around to see my Fouza get an education and is old enough to take care of herself. I constantly worry about her and always pray that Allah (God) surrounds her with the best of people, and for Allah (God) to bless her with good husband who will take good care of her and never abuse or harm her in anyway Ameen. None of us are perfect and we never will be, I have made many mistakes and will continue to make them but at least not the ones to send me to prison. The part of my life which involved the use of crime and violence to hurt people has long been put to rest. I will admit, people these days make me want to go back to the old me especially those who are supposed to be your friends who turn out to be treacherous back stabbing chumps, but I can't so I exercise much patience and sweep the shit under the rug. I am scared that if I do something to one of these so-called men than there won't be any turning back because I will want to keep doing it. When my mother looks down on me, I pray that I am making her proud of me especially of the way I have been handling situations with my brother and sister. It has been years now since I spoke to at risk youth but every now and then I reach out when I think I found a good organization, but it always turns out to be plagued with politics. People need to know and understand that prisons are now big business especially with the that privatization of prisons by the government. I recently read an article about a juvenile judge who was convicted and received a 40-year prison sentence for taking money from private prison officials to convict all juveniles who appeared in front of him then giving these kids heavy sentences, so the money keeps rolling in. It's a no brainer just like cattle farms need cattle to be in business, well prisons need human bodies to stay in business and these bodies come from among the poor people! As for abusive husbands and fathers, they need to understand that in the end their evil actions will catch up to them and they will find themselves by themselves living a lonely miserable life in their old age as many do including my father. My advice to the abused you are strong enough to take their abuse so that means you are strong enough not to except it and do something about it, like calling the police and you will find that they are cowards who take advantage of those they deem week. That is what we should have done about my father long ago, maybe my idea which was to shoot and kill him was not the correct way but reaching out to the system would have helped and maybe could have stopped the pain and suffering he was inflicting upon us especially against our poor beloved mother. Now he is old with no one to beat on playing the loving father roll because he has no one to turn to and is financially broke. He has forgotten all the physical and mental abuse he bestowed upon our family and especially towards our mother than abandoning her and leaving her to be by herself after my arrest. He left her to chase another woman and wasted all the money we had on her and other people. He gave away our business for a $130 thousand in payments to my shyster brother in law which he had no right to give away. He abandoned me like he did the rest of the family other than sending me a sending me a $135 one time than harassing my mother to give it back to him which she did. Let me be fair to him and again mention that he visited me one time during my 13-year incarceration. I tried to forget and be there for my father after my release from prison, but I just cannot overcome all the shit he did to my mother, hell it is hard to just look at him! Recently I reconnected with my old friend Green Eyes who is still incarcerated in the Illinois Dept of Corrections serving out his 103-year sentence. He has served about 29 years but after speaking to him via telephone I found that his 103-year sentenced was reduced to 60 years by the governor because he had the highest sentence for a drug case in the history of the state of Illinois. I was glad to hear that good news, but I believe he should have been released because has way too much time for the crime he was charged with which was a nonviolent drug case. I thought it was real petty on the part of the State government to make him do another 2 or 3 years after giving them so much time for a nonviolent drug case, but they hold all the power in their hands so it does not really matter what any of us think or how senseless their decisions are because they do as they please. In one of the many telephone conversations with Green Eyes he reminded me of the incident which I mentioned earlier in which we almost got shot up by someone who was in a car next to us and I thought they were from the La Raza gang, as it turns out I was wrong. Green Eyes told me about a conversation he had with a Latin King from 51st and Ada a few years back in another prison in which the guy mentioned the incident at stop sign on 47th and Hermitage saying he almost took my head off had I looked back seen him then ducted my head. There are somethings you are told by people in your life that are hard to forget such as good advice, I will always remember being told by older guys as a teenager that I should stay in high school and to enjoy the experience because later in life I will regret it if I don't. These guys were speaking from experience and I did not take heed I just wanted to be a grown up by being stupid and the only thing I could say is I should have listened! I wish I could bring time back because I would not miss one day of school and live one day at a time by behaving my age, unfortunately we all know that I can wish all I want but time does not go back. Thinking back, as a teenager I thought going from 15 to 30 years old is a hundred years apart but as all of us grownups know now, it happens like the blink of an eye. It is so hard to believe and understand how fast time has passed us all by, how fast I went from 15 years old to 52 years old because it seems like yesterday. I had chosen a path in life where if you did something to me, even a mere word that offended me than I would make sure you paid the price so training your mind to change paths after so many years of being on the same path is a difficult task but it's something that has to be done if I want to enjoy the rest of my life as a free man. I have been dealing with anxiety and panic attacks since 2004 a few months before my release and up to this day and believe me when I say these things are brutal. Simple daily tasks a very difficult thing to do from this anxiety stuff and believe me when I say that it is one of the hardest things, I have had face in life. People around you whether family or friends do not understand what you are going through because it is hard to explain and harder to understand. You go to the doctor and he does all this testing, and everything comes back normal, but you don't feel normal because one minute you are dizzy than your stomach is in knots, racing heartbeat, shortness of breath, shaking from chills and so on. To me it seems like most doctors are not interested in truly treating people with my condition because they do not understand it either. They pretend to listen when you're trying to explain it to them, but they only want to prescribe you medication because they are encouraged to do by big pharma and in many cases that seems to cause more damage than help. I had to start doing my own research for my condition while dealing with doctors so they can see that I have been researching and they cannot just tell me anything. Millions suffer from anxiety in this country and from the looks of it many more will have it due to economic stress. I been through a lot and was able to handle every bit of it but anxiety and this panic attack stuff I would not wish on my worst enemy. With this anxiety condition hanging over my head it has not been easy writing this book because I had to recount things I would rather forget about. I never would have ever thought about putting my life story down on paper, but many people who heard some of my life experiences encouraged me to write a book. How does someone like me even begin to write a book without having much education is not an easy task at all but never the less I am trying my best because I do believe that I have a story worth telling. The first person to encouragement was a Syrian medical doctor that I met at a fund raiser for my friend's IMAN organization in Ann Arbor Michigan. My friend told the doctor who was sitting next to me at the table to listen to my life story, that the doctor would find it interesting. So, the doctor looked over at me and said, "Please tell me a little bit about your life". I gave him about a 10-minute summary of my life, after hearing what I had to say the doctor grabbed my arm and took me to my friend then said to him, "This guy needs to write a book about his life".

When I heard the doctor say that I thought to myself "What the hell is this guy talking about". That was the first person to give me encouragement, and there were other people I met who came from all types of backgrounds that said the same. One big cause of my anxiety is that I am still learning how to accept and overlook the dirty stuff people do which is something I would have never let slide once upon a time in my life. It has become harder than ever to deal with men these days because most men have lost their dignity and honor, and most cannot be trusted but you still must deal with people in this life and that is a great source of stress for me. I recently found out something truly crazy which is the US Government considers Middle Easterners White People and that got me to thinking. I am not saying that it is a dirty thing to be called a White person or a person of any other color, but I am saying your entertainment industry has been labeling us terrorists, dark dirty desert people who sit around in tents and plot treachery. They taught the people of this great nation to call us terrorists, sand niggers, towel heads and camel jockeys but did you ever tell them you consider us White people just like you are? No of course not but It finally came to me, Jesus peace be upon him has been turned into a blond hair blue eye white man with Michael Angelo 's painting and then there are the Jewish people of Eastern and Western Europe that are ethnically White who you have been helped by European Nations to take my country, claiming that it belonged to their forefathers which is lie because their forefather were Europeans just like they are! They did not include us into the white race to legitimize us but rather to legitimize their lies. Going back to when I was in Federal prison one of my European American friends who was a Seventh Day Adventist called me a sand nigger jokingly. I look at him and said, "I guess if Jesus peace be upon him was here with us now you would call him a sand nigger also". After having said that to him he had a puzzled look on his face, so I said, "Jesus peace be upon him was born a few miles from where I was born so if I am a sand nigger than he has to be one also". We live in a world full of people who have been brainwashed for many years with so much misinformation that 90% of the information of what people know about world events is based on pure lies. It is simple, one side of the story has been told and it is a lie and a lie told enough times becomes the truth! The same thing goes for religions people are too lazy to open their religious books and study "truly study" they listen to their spiritual leaders and never bother to investigate if what they are being told in these sermons is in fact true. So they would know if what is being said in those sermons exists in their religious books or whether it is just the spiritual leader's own opinion. I stopped trying to keep up with world news because it is so depressing Ukraine, Syria, Iraq, Palestine, Libya, Yemen, West Africa, Ukraine and so on. Spilling of human blood and taking human life means nothing at all and there seems to be a contest for who can spill more blood. Killing each other has been around since Able and Cain that we all know, so I am in no way pretending that it is a new thing, but I am saying that it is way out of control and people think it is ok if nations/governments are doing it. We all know the horrors recorded in history books and others on film that seem to do not do us any good because every decade or two we seem to repeat history. We hear of one group of people butchering another group out of greed, false pride and most of all stupidity. Whether it is about the color of one's skin or their religious beliefs people must butcher each other and at the same time pretend to be civilized. Same game different players Stalin, Lenin, Hitler, Mussolini, and now Bush, Netanyahu, Saddam, Putin, Assad, Maliki, Sisi and Mohammad ibn Salman of Saudi Arabia and others. Assad the tyrant of Syria along with his Iranian and Russian masters are and have been butchering Syrian Sunni Muslims and using chemical weapons and the so-called civilized world stands idly by play deaf, dumb and blind. Let me make something very clear, something that most people should already know but don't and that is the so-called United Nations is a worthless organization plagued with hypocrisy. We ordinary people are not free from blame we too have stained our hands with the blood of innocent people because most of us allow our governments to support tyrants who butcher their own people or their neighboring countries because of selfish interests. As for the Muslim world, we are our own worse enemy because most of us have a disease in our hearts that makes us hate one another and seem to wish ill will on each other. Our hearts are full of malice and arrogance, many of the men gossip more than bad women do and we give Islam a bad image while pretending to worship Allah! Allah has turned his face away from us Muslims because most of us are hypocrites who hate to see anything good happen to another Muslim! Muslims who read what I am saying here may not like what I am saying and to that I say, "I don't care because what I am saying is the truth"! Allah (God) gave us the best religion with the best example (Prophet Muhammad peace and blessing be upon him) but we just spit on it and for that we are suffering the world over, but he will replace us with a better people who will love and follow the religion of Islam with good and true intentions. I am begging non-Muslim to please not Judge Islam by the way some of us so-called Muslims behave but rather go out and investigate the religion of Islam for yourself study the Quran and the Sunnah (teaching of Prophet Muhammad peace be upon him) and Judge for yourself and you will find that Islam is innocent of what it is being blamed for.

UPS Deal Tunes
into an Ordeal

One of my best friends from my childhood days came looking for me a few years after my release from prison maybe sometime in 2008 or 2009. He got my telephone number from another childhood friend than gave me a call while I was still at the liquor store. In that conversation he informed me that he was interested in opening a business with me suggesting we open a liquor/grocery store like the one my family owned. When I heard him mention the Liquor store idea, I discourage him from even thinking about getting involved in that kind of business because I did not want anything to do with a liquor business. He went silent for a second than said that he held a high position at UPS and if I knew any trucking companies willing to take on work from UPS as contractors for a fee. He informed me that he needed to do something because he was having trouble trying to keep up with amount of debt he owed. The tenants in a building he owned were unable to pay the rent and he had to pay the mortgage out of pocket and this all due to the recession which hit in 2009. He also told me about his student loans which he also owed on, and his sister had him in bind because she took a house in his name and was going into foreclosure. He basically begged me to come up with something that would make us both money which was easy to me and it had to do with his suggestion about getting work from UPS for a trucking company. Unfortunately, there was one problem with that idea because he was petrified of anyone finding his identity if I hooked him with a trucking company because he knew that would cost him his job. He wanted me to handle all the details while keeping his identity a secret and I promised him that I would. I told him that I would go out and scout around with some of the trucking companies I was familiar with. I started inquiring with a few trucking companies to see if they would be interested and they were of course very interested. The hard part was having to except and take a chance on the deal I had worked out with the owner of the company because it was based the honor system. We didn't have a signed contract or anything like that so I had to take him at his word, that he will pay my friend at UPS when the time came for him to pay up. Honestly, I was not going to be making any money from these deals at that time, I did it so he could make a few dollars to catch up on his bills. I was looking at the bigger picture which was supposed to come down the line and all we needed was patience. The first UPS venture was with a Palestinian guy who owned a small trucking company in Summit III and with the help of my friend at UPS he was able to get work during the months of November and December in which his trucking company $85,000 from 5 or 6 weeks' worth of UPS. He made me a promise of paying my friend 10% of whatever he made but unfortunately the guy went back on his word when it came time to pay. I had to chase the dirtbag for a few months and was only able to collect $3000 for my friend and I only chased him because the money was not mine plus, I told my friend that this guy could be trusted because I prayed with him many times, so he was a God-fearing person which taught me a hard lesson about so-called religious people. When my friend from UPS heard about the $3000, he was disappointed and upset so he told me to tell the Palestinian owner to stick the $3000 in his ass. I still took the money from the Palestinian guy and held it for my friend from UPS because I knew that when things cooled down he would want it. About 8 months after that incident I had a telephone conversation with my friend from UPS and in that conversation, I told him that I had collected the $3000 for him from the owner of the trucking company and if he wanted, he could come to my house and get it. The next day he came to my house to get his money and noticed that I had a custom-made Harley Davidson painted in an American flag style paint job. I had just picked up that bike in a great deal because the owner had well over 30k invested but he sold it to me for

$7500. The guy was losing his house during that time when foreclosures was at all-time high. Originally the guy was asking $18 K for the bike, but the country was in trouble and people didn't have that kind of money, so he kept dropping the price until I bought it for $7500. He wanted to purchase the bike from me, but he didn't have the $7500 so I told him that I wasn't planning on selling the bike but since he is my childhood friend than I would keep the $3000 we could work on the $4500 down the line. He was shocked that I did that for him, but he was my childhood friend who was worth much more to me than materialistic things plus I was not going to lose because I knew he would pay me the remaining. Within days after taking the bike he called me and wanted me to try again with another trucking company, so I did the second venture was with a Bulgarian guy who owned a trucking company in Elk Grove Village. The guy did the same work as the Palestinian guy did but was honest and could not pay 10% but he paid what he promised to pay, and this is how my friend paid me for the bike. He basically got my motorcycle for free but unfortunately, my friend at UPS was unable to keep giving the Bulgarian guy any more work from UPS after the peak season because he was still scared to stick his neck out any further and expose himself but at least the motorcycle was now paid for. The problem with my friend was that he was making a lot of promises to me which in turn I made to the owners but at the end of the day he would renege on those promises because he was afraid of getting caught and losing his job. Finally, he got his nerve up that he wanted to invest some money in a trucking business with my wife in which he would obviously going to receive half the profits. Our friend guarantied her that he would push harder to keep UPS work coming and much of it would pay by the hour. There were two reasons my wife offered him half of what she was going to make, the first was that she grew up across the street from him and the second because she knew about his financial troubles. The third venture was with an Italian guy who owned a small company in the city next to the neighborhood I grew up in. I explained the deal to him as I did to the other two guys before him but this time, I added that my friend from UPS was offering hourly pay during the peak season. When the owner of the trucking company heard what I had to say he did not hesitate and jumped at the chance. He agreed to take less of a percentage from my wife and friend than other companies take from owner operators. The work started in October for the peak season and they mainly did regional work (Indiana, Ohio, Missouri, Minnesota and Iowa) which paid by the load but when January or early February came around, they started doing local work (city work) for UPS so our friend at UPS finally stuck his neck out and made things happen. That local work paid by the hour just as he promised but they weren't the only companies doing this kind of work for UPS there were other companies who have been doing this work for decades. Everyone was happy because everyone was making money especially my friend, he had it made because he had his long-time job at UPS where he got a check with full benefits and at the same time every week, he received a check from my wife for majority of the profit so she could be happy. A month or two later he started to get really greedy, he saw money coming in so he started acting like he should be getting more money even though he was getting most of it he was pretending not to understand that my wife had overhead such as truck repairs, high way tolls, insurance and so on. She did all her expenses then gave him half of what was left but he always craying and complaining that he should get more. She got tired of his crying and invited him over to the house, so he could do the paper work himself. He came by the house and when he was finished, she looked over what he did, and she found that he had cheated himself which she showed him while he stood there looking like an idiot. He had the audacity to tell her that he wanted his weekly money in cash which she was not going to agree to, so he asked her to the first few checks in one of his tenant's name until he opened a corporation which he eventually did under someone else's name. That year he received a nice piece of change from my wife which was mostly paid to the company he owned under another person's name, but she had the 1099 mailed to his house and when he received it, he called her number by accident thinking he was calling her book keeper. He said that he only received half the amount of money claimed on the 1099. When he realized his mistake, that he was talking to my wife he quickly tried cleaning it up, but he already said it and she heard him loud and clear. I helped this crud purchase his first even if we knew his greed was driving to do something for himself alone because it did not matter to us what he was trying to do on his own if my wife was still making some money. I even helped him find drivers for his trucks which is not an easy thing to do. To make a long story short he opened another company and still has a few trucks with my Italian friend who I eventually introduced him to because he got comfortable and was not scared anymore. I verbally checked his ass on occasions, and he is fortunate we are living in different times or I would have fucked his ass up for the greedy coward shit he pulled. We are no longer on speaking terms and I hear he is all over the place now, taking money from whom ever pays he no longer has any fear of losing his job I guess his greed is blinding him. He has even tried turning my Italian friend owner of the trucking company against my wife by cutting her trucks out of UPS work. A short time back he had one of his drivers call one of my wife's drivers with a job offer which furthers proves that greed is blinding the hell out of him but of course the coward denied trying to do this when he was confronted about it. He a lucky scumbag because if I was like him, he would have been exposed to UPS and lost his job for the underhanded stuff he did. Nothing is in his name which is easy to do, so he feels safe but somehow some way his greed will get the best of him. Even my Italian friends at the trucking company developed that lying sickness brought on by greed and because they know that my wife and I are no longer are dealing with my old friend at UPS so they sometimes try pulling underhanded whenever they think they can. They try lying to my wife about that rates and claim the

UPS work they are now getting comes to them through someone else other than my old friend at UPS, but we always catch them when they are lying. Never the less they are still better people to deal than most other companies who would have broken their word within a few months. It is a fucking shame when you think about the fact that it was me who hooked these people up together and from that they both (my Old friend at UPS and my friend at the small trucking company) have made more money than they ever dreamt of making in these few years but they easily forgot who helped them get there. People these days are fearless, they break their word, steal from you and go around doing as please to people because they know damn well that there are no repercussions. Things changed and change is not always good, kids have no respect or fear what so ever and adults are just as bad, and God forbid if you stand up for yourself or for what is right then they will threaten to call the police on you. It has been 14 years since my release from prison and the world seems to only get worse by the day and every time you think shit cannot get worse something else happens that shows you how wrong you are for assuming that. Much of the world is on fire by tyrants waging war against their own people who are seeking to live a life of freedom. It is clearer than it has ever been that the worse people are the leader of the people which is the case in almost every nation. The regular Joe Ordinary is fucking disunited and behaves like crabs in a bucket every time one is ready to escape another reaches up and pulls it back down into the bucket. Most of us do not get involved, using weak excuses like "We have no power to do anything, what can we possibly do" and that is by far the sorriest cop-out ever. We all know politicians running for office are no good, yet people elect them anyway because we the people have become like sheep. How does a candidate spend millions Jof dollars on a job that only pays 80 or 100k what is it that we common folks are missing here, are we that stupid that we cannot comprehend or is it that we just gave up because we are that weak? I met and have dealt with a few new people since my release from prison and a few turned out to be great but others who I thought were good turned out to be spineless pieces of shit. I am talking about the ones that I helped since getting out which was my mistake because I should have never let them get close to me let alone help them. Helping disadvantaged communities with big educational and anti-violence programs should be of top priority. Enough of the same shit talk from politicians about we need to be tough on crime because we have been hearing it for decades and it has not done the nation any good. Those people out there sincerely trying to bring a positive change in our disadvantaged/gang infested neighborhoods are getting enough funding to be able to make a dent because the system would rather build prisons and wasting billions of tax dollars. The government is allowing manufacturing jobs to leave the country and replacing them with corrections/prison jobs especially for those leaving the armed forces. To make things worse many kids are out here having to raise themselves who left alone to have sex at a very young age only to become pregnant than give birth to children. Now they are no longer going to school, so they are uneducated children who are having children and have no clue how to be a parent! I met some good young brothers (Saints) since my release unfortunately they are no longer with us which is sad and let me name a few Smiley, Macho, Baby Pit, Sandro and there are others so please brothers forgive me and may you all rest in peace. I am never ashamed to talk about my past because I believe it will help young people make better decisions when they are faced with the same situations I was faced with. My affiliation with the Saint of 45th street was a bitter sweat chapter in my life that I cannot change which I understand but am not ashamed of it either. I am glad and thankful to the people who encouraged me to write and publish a book about my life story. There is a misconception among today's young especially many gang bangers and that it is a gangster is disrespectful to civilians and pushes his weight around because he is part of a gang. Back in the day things were not that way because the majority were tough before becoming gang members and tough does not mean if you are able to shoot people because that is a small part of it believe it or not. I am not saying that every young person involved in gangs disrespectful, but a lot have the wrong conception about the image of a gang member. Snitches are roaming neighborhoods as if they've done nothing wrong and are still allowed to be involved within the gang when all they are is RATS. It is self-explanatory when a guy who just got out of prison and is on parole or probation with a few convictions gets arrested with guns or drugs but is released or is given a very short sentence when we all know how merciless the courts are these days when it comes to sentencing repeat offenders. It's easy, they are nothing but informers who cooperate with the authorities on their brothers, then after serving that short sentence they're back on the streets playing gangster again and more than likely they are the ones pushing others into breaking the law. The government took all the real gang leaders down in Chicago when most were already in prison to crush gang activities but instead, they caused more harm than good. By doing this they gave a lot of the fake gangsters what they wanted which is for gang banger to do as they please without any repercussions! You were held accountable for your actions back in the days but that is no longer the case and therefore gangs banging is out of control now. I hate to use this analogy but what would be the state of the US Armed Forces if there were no sergeants, lieutenants, captains, colonels, generals, or the president? Gang leaders and their rules kept most of their members in line whether you like it or not. I am in no way condoning gang banging but gangs have always been a part of society and leaders with established rules kept them in line where they kept death and destruction directed at each other and away from civilians for the most part. I have heard this but don't know where this came from that gangster rap is part of the cause which creates violence which I believe is bullshit. We should give rappers like Snoop Dogg, Ice Cube, Jay-Z and other credit for where they came from and where they are today. They worked hard and made plenty of money from their art and that is exactly what they are is artists so, credit should be given to them for their success. I myself don't know much about rap music unless you are talking about old school rap like Grand Master Flash, Kurtis Blow, The Fat Boys, Run DMC and so on. Sure, the message was different but then again, the music of the 60s is different than the music of the 70s, 80s or 90s! If we are going to blame these new rappers for our social problems, then we should start with Hollywood first especially for creating movies such as "Scar Face" which was played by Al Pacino and many people idolize the character even now. Blame can be directed in many directions, but I believe most of the blame should fall on the backs of those governing this great nation from the smallest position all the way to the top. I have had the pleasure of being acquainted with an individual who is trying to make a difference in the inner city who happens to be the owner of the Back of The Yards Café who is very active in the Back of The Yards area. Another Brother is Rafi who has been involved with Cease Fire for many years and is very serious about trying to make a difference. Also, I became acquainted with a good brother X M who is a very active member of an organization called ICAN (incarcerated children's advocacy network) which is fighting for fair sentencing and to putting an end of imposing life sentences for juveniles. As for me, I do one on one here and there but I don't see any hope in finding an organization that I can be a part so I could share my life experiences and opinions for the purpose of helping at risk youth. Believe it or not most of these organization to help curb gang violence are so underfunded that those already there do not want to bring in anymore help even if that person would be a great asset to the organization. To fully invest in such organizations is not a waste of tax money after all we all should want the best for this place we call home. What good is sending people to prison for decades for non-violent crimes and warehousing them with no education programs what so ever.

And this is exactly what is and has happened to many people including my friend Green Eyes who suffered much in his life time. This is a guy who has served 29 years of his life in prison for a non-violent crime but not only that, his mother was shot and killed while she was sleeping with her child Green Eyes who was asleep in her arms than a year or so after he was sent to prison his brother was run over and killed by white suburbanite kids who tried robbing him for an eight ball of cocaine and lastly his only other brother shot and killed a guy after getting into a physical altercation and was sentenced to 38 years in prison. Green Eyes was not the only old friend that I was able to reconnect with, I finally was able to hook up with my friend/brother Tommy from New York. Me and Tommy speak regularly, he has been out of prison for 10 years and since than he started a program giving senior citizens the opportunity to have a workout program. About six months ago I found out some bad news through a friend that alleged mob hitman Harry Aleman has passed away in state prison from lung cancer. Little JM, Frank Calabrese and other alleged mob figures were found guilty in the criminal case "Family Secrets" and I believe most received a life sentence in prison which is basically a death sentence for these old guys. Frank Calabrese has already passed away a few years ago in whatever federal prison he was being held in. At the end of the day if you are living your life on the wrong side of the law, there are only two options if you don't get right and those two things are prison, death or both. A word of advice to the young bloods, life is great if you stay in school to get an education and stay out of shit than find a good job so you can make a good living and enjoy life as it should be enjoyed within the law.

Why such easy access to Europe and USA for Palestinians?

Not many Palestinians including me ever thought as to why it is so easy for us to get accepted for migration to Europe or the USA, but it is now clear to me why it is so easy. They do so in order to help in the ethnic cleansing of us Palestinians from our forefather's land (historical Palestine) so they can make room for Zionist Jews arriving from European and the USA. When they grant us visas to leave our homeland, they of course want us to feel like they are doing us a favor allowing us to migrate to their lands! The favor is purely meant for the Zionists Jews who have been illegally occupying our land for over seventy years now and they continue to migrate to our land mainly from Eastern Europe and the USA! Personally, If I could bring time back I would have never left Jerusalem and would have rather been shot and killed by a Zionist. We were in Palestine living a very poor life, but we were a good family who loved each other and lived in the Holiest place on earth with a great culture but look what happened to our family we lost our culture, identity and for most of the family our religion. Even though we did not know anything about it there was a great chance that we would have learned it at a young age even here in the USA if our father was a better person. When I say these things, I am in no way saying I hate this great nation, but I am saying preservation of my heritage and religion (Islam) is much more important than all materialistic things the world has to offer. I am positive that my family would have never left Palestine if the Zionists would have left my father alone to live his life as a free man to be able to work and support his family. I always wondered to myself even as a child "why are we dealt such a terrible hand of being prisoners and to humiliated in our own homeland by these people (Zionist)". Growing up in Jerusalem under occupation I looked at these Zionists occupier as evil people because they behaved as such and I blamed them for all our troubles. Never did I think that our troubles in the Middle East was of our own making and what I mean by that is, we betrayed our religion by becoming nationalists. We Muslims of the Middle East aided the British in destroying the Ottoman Calipha who were the rightful Muslim rulers at the time. After the Calipha fell, the single Muslim nation which stretched from Morocco to Afghanistan was now broke up into small weak nations ruled by tyrant who were traitors who were put into power by their British masters. From that time to now we are still suffering and will continue to suffer until we follow the true teachings of Islam and become a single brotherhood by uniting into one nation as we are commanded to do. I know on this point I am repeating myself, but I feel that I must because we Muslims must be honest and admit that we are to blame for the condition we find ourselves in today. We can longer blame others for our plight we find ourselves in which is a punishment brought on to us by Allah/God do to the sickness we carry in our hearts. We don't love each other but despise one another, wishing ill will on each other and get great satisfaction when we hear about another Muslims family troubles than run around gossiping and expose each other's troubles. Many of us Muslims walk around arrogantly especially if we are doing well financially even though in most cases the money was earned through ways in which it is Islamically unacceptable. Let me not even get into the trust issue because you cannot trust them as far as you can throw them and that I am speaking from experience! I can only speak on what I know so I am speaking about the Arab Muslims here on the South Side of Chicago but there are of course many good and honest Arab Muslims amongst us but nowhere near the number of the arrogant cutthroats. Simply put we are our own worst enemy, yet we cannot see that and until we change ourselves by cleansing our hearts and clean sincere intentions, we will continue to find ourselves in the same position we find ourselves in today! Even the beautiful Sheikh/Imam of the Bridgeview mosque is not safe from their filthy gossiping which is based on total lies. We are now 2018 and the current President of the USA is billionaire Donald Trump who has been raising hell with his actions and comments that show how stupid and out of touch he really is. My being able to make that statement about Trump is a prime example of what makes this nation so great, here I can criticize the president and not worry about being put in prison and the possibility of receiving a death sentence as they do to the citizens of Arab/Muslim nations. To touch on one the President Trump's stupid and reckless actions is his decision to give my birthplace Jerusalem to the Zionist occupiers of my homeland by recognizing it as the eternal capital of the State of Israel by moving the US Embassy from the city of Tel Aviv to the city of Jerusalem. This is something no other US president has ever done nor was any willing to do since the creation of the state of Israel up until he came to power and did it. Here is another injustice in it, according to the US government I am deported out of this country back to my birthplace Jerusalem but here is the President of the USA illegally giving away my homeland to a people who are illegally occupy my it. In the 1900s the British along with the USA gave away my country to European Jews who were fleeing oppression in Europe than armed them to the teeth from that time and still do to this day. Losing our land and living under Israeli military occupation caused many of us Palestinians to become exiled, having to live in neighboring countries as refugees in makeshift camps. Many Palestinians left with the thought that when things settled as in any war they would be allowed to return to their lands which was far from the truth and are still living in refugee camps to this day. We Palestinians should be able to bring legal action against those nations for aiding the Zionists with the theft of our land.

The State of Israel has been receiving reparations for crimes committed against the Jewish people by the Germans for decades yet they themselves have been committing crimes against us Palestinians for well over 60 years while the so-called civilized world turns a blind eye. Not only are they playing blind at the UN but many nations there are directly or indirectly supporting the Zionists with billions of dollars yearly while the USA protects them at the United Nation with its veto powers. The so-called United Nations is a sham, meaningless, corrupt and a hypocrite organization! I find myself in a difficult situation, being deported without being going to my homeland (Jerusalem) living in the USA as a deportee at the mercy of ICE having to report to them for the rest of my life yet I feel that I am maybe more American than a lot of these so-called Americans who are born in the USA. The issue of Palestine and who it belongs to is very simple, but many people have been brainwashed to believe that Palestine belongs to these modern-day Jews who are ethnically European. The argument is that this Holy Land belongs to the Jewish people because Allah/God promised it to them is 100% wrong. The truth of the matter is that Allah/God promised this land to the Children of Israel which is made up of 12 tribes, **Q.** (1) Are the Jews living in Palestine/Israel today decedents of the Children of Israel? **Q.** (2) Was the Land itself called Israel? **Q.** (3) Is the establishment of modern-day Jewish State of Israel based on religious beliefs? **A to Q.** (1) The Children of Israel were descendants Of Prophet Abraham and his beloved wife Sarah, peace be upon them both, the pair were natives of a town called Ur in a nation known as Iraq. They were a dark colored people and in no way were they European, so those occupying Palestine today could never be Prophet Abraham and Sarah's descendants because most of them are Ethnically Eastern and Western Europeans who converted to the Jewish Faith just like most Christians are not from Palestine nor are all Muslims from Arabia. On the other hand, many Palestinians are more likely to be the descendants of the Children of Israel who converted to Christianity then to Islam in and around Jerusalem, learning the Arabic language and Islamic culture hence the term Arabized Arabs. **A to Q.** (2) The name Israel belongs to a well-known character mentioned in all three religious' books (Torah, Bible and the Quran) and that person is Prophet Jacob, peace be upon him, who was given the name Israel (Prince of God) by Allah/God. In the Middle East, a land/house is always described by the family name hence you would say "Dar Judah (the house of Judah)" but that in no way mean that the land/house is called it just means that this land/house belongs to the Judah family! This is exactly the case when we hear the term Land of Israel, it simply means the land (Palestine) belonged to Israel (Jacob) peace be upon him plain and simple! **A to Q.** (3) According to Jewish Law a State of Israel can only be established when the messiah has arrived, it is common knowledge that 99.9% the Jews of today do not accept Jesus peace be upon him as the messiah and are awaiting the coming of their messiah who has yet to arrive. So, the establishment of the State of Israel is not based on religious belief and is against the command of Allah (God). The creation and establishment of the State of Israel is based on a racist ideology known as Zionism which means that only those of the Jewish faith have a right to live in the land now called Israel and there is no room for Christians or Muslims and they (Zionist) have been doing everything in their power to drive us out of our land! My immigration situation (being deported) is full of hypocrisy, how can you possibly give my country away illegally and tell me that I am illegally here. Give me my country back and I will be more than glad to head back to my beloved Al Quds (Jerusalem) you have wronged me more than I could ever have wronged you. I am more patriotic than a lot of people who were born in the US of American who are willing to destroy the US Constitution in the name of security. For them I quote Benjamin Franklin who once said: "Those who would give up essential Liberty, to purchase a **little** temporary Safety deserve neither Liberty nor Safety". What is wrong with us humans that we refuse to accept the fact that regardless of race or color we are the same. Your race does not make you superior nor does it make you inferior there is good and bad in all races and religions our down fall is our ignorance, arrogance and greediness! That is the only advice I need to give to adults because we all know what we should be doing and how we should treat others. I have many of my issues to deal with myself such as trying to stay strong and righteous for my little girl. Funny thing, when a I was living a life full of recklessness, I never thought much about dying but now I live a clean life of taking hardly any chances and I can't stop thinking about it. I don't drink alcohol or smoke cigarettes and I work out, yet I feel like crap from the stress of worrying about leaving my little girl. I talked about a lot of different things that I have lived through in this book, but I chose to leave the stories of women I was involved with out of it because I believe that should never be talked about! We men are very weak when it comes to women and I am speaking about myself first, so I ask Allah (God) to forgive me for my sins that I committed with women and what I have done against them. I feel it important to explain that when we use the name Allah because it has a stronger meaning than the word God, but it is the same entity. The Arab Christians also use the word Allah for God just as we Arab Muslims do. Jesus, peace be upon him, spoke Aramaic and in that language, he used Allah to describe God because he did not speak English so stop thinking and saying " You Muslims worship Allah" as if it is a different God. I think I have finally stumbled on to something where I can put my life experiences into use which came through a good brother named James Holmes AKA Snoop from Detroit Michigan whom I met while doing time at FCI Milan. Snoop has and is doing a lot of community work with the city of Detroit, he introduced me to a professor who teaches law and is also an advocate for prison reform. His argument from is against warehousing inmates as a punishment to educating and rehabilitating them, so they can become productive citizens when they are released back into society. Finally I would ask for forgiveness from anybody I have ever wronged whether it be family, friend or foe. Life is way too short for any of us to hold grudges against one another for silly stuff which is the case most of the time. God bless and may the coming years bring us all together in love as a single people no matter what religion or race we may belong to, Ameen.

The Holy Quran 49:10

"Humanity is but a single Brotherhood: So make peace with your brethren."

Sahih Muslim 1844

"Whoever wants to enter Paradise, let him treat people the way he would love to be treated"

I cannot end this book without mentioning the struggle of my people in Palestine Christian and Muslim alike who have suffered a great deal for many decades now, by Allah (God) your pain is my pain. We keep our prayers up and thereafter put our trust and faith in the creator Allah (God). I pray that Allah (God) grants you victory and guides the enemy into a path of justice and righteousness so all can live a life of peace and harmony especially for my brothers and sister living in Gaza, Ameen.

AFFIDAVIT OF ▉▉▉▉▉▉▉▉▉▉▉ M.F.S.

I, ▉▉▉▉▉▉▉▉▉ being first duly sworn on oath, depose and state as follows:

1. I am over 18 years of age and competent.

2. This affidavit is made on my personal knowledge and if sworn as a witness, I could and would competently testify to the facts and documents contained herein.

3. I am employed by Drake Group International as a Forensic Document Examiner. One of my duties as a Forensic Document Examiner is the examination and comparison of questioned handwriting, signatures and initials to known handwriting, signatures and initials executed upon legal documents.

4. I hold a Master of Forensic Science Degree. I interned with ▉▉▉▉▉▉▉▉, Chief Forensic Document Examiner, Arizona Department of Public Safety for three years and continued to work with Mr. ▉▉▉▉▉ until 1997. I have been in private practice since that time. I have participated in continuing education in forensic document examination on a regular basis. I am a member of numerous forensic organizations to include ASTM International. I have testified in local, state, federal courts in Arizona, California, Illinois, and New Mexico.

5. I have been retained by ▉▉▉▉▉▉▉▉ of the Law Offices of ▉▉▉▉▉▉▉▉, P.C. to conduct a forensic examination of the following documents: Q-1, a photocopy of a document entitled, "Last Will & Testament of Fouza Saadeh", page 3, dated October 16, 2008 that bears the signatures, "Fouza Saadeh". Item Q-2, a photocopy of a document entitled "Self-Proving Affidavit"; dated October 16, 2008 that bears the signatures of "Fouza Saadeh". The purpose of this examination was to determine the authorship of the questioned "Fouza Saadeh" signatures that appear upon Items Q (1-2).

6. The following documents were submitted for examination and comparison: Item K-1, a photocopy of a document entitled, "Certificate of Naturalization", dated January 26, 1995 that displays the signature of Fouza Naim Saadeh. Item K-2, a photocopy of a document beginning, "event that the said Court", undated, that bears the signature of Fouza Saadeh. Item K-3, a photocopy of a State of Illinois ID Card issued 02/28/08 to Fouza N. Saadeh, and dated for her lifetime that bears the signature of Fouza Saadeh. Item K-4, photocopy of an Illinois

Driver's License issued to Fouza N. Saadeh, No. ▮▮▮▮▮▮▮ issued 01-10-96, that bears the signature of Fouza Saadeh.

7. The factors and basis for the formulation of my opinions consist of the following: a). The principle that no two individuals share the same combination of handwriting characteristics is the basis for handwriting identification. Habit patterns that are observable and comparable in the frequent repetitions of the writing act by one individual support the identification of handwriting.

b). Common authorship can be determined only when the handwritings agree in every fundamental element and quality and display no basic differences. If two writings contain significant differences in basic execution that cannot reasonably be explained, then the identification of the handwriting cannot be supported. c.) However, another important consideration is that every person demonstrates a "natural variation" in execution of handwriting. Because an individual executes handwriting in a free and natural manner; handwriting is fluid and is not executed in precisely the same way. However, due to this natural variation in execution, these writings are not considered to be basic or fundamental differences. d.)The authorship of questioned writing can be identified with its author if the identifiable writing habits are adequately present when compared to the known writing exemplar or standards of the individual. e.) The Evaluation of questioned and known writings by the forensic document examiner is based upon the weight and significance in the execution of letters, size, slants, connecting strokes and the ratio of uppercase and lowercase forms. Attention is focused upon the letterforms known as class characteristics generally learned and conformed to a system of writing taught in school. Individual characteristics are those that are unique and rarely seen and represent the habits and modifications in an individual's handwriting as it evolves from the copybook form.

8. Based upon my education, knowledge, experience and the examination of the questioned Items Q (1-2) with the known Items K (1-4), i have arrived at the following conclusions:

a.) It is highly probable that Items Q (1-2) and K (1-4) are not of common authorship. The signatures executed upon Items Q (1-2) display a higher level of sophistication in execution and uniformity than that demonstrated in the execution of the known signatures of Fouza Saadeh.

b.) The signatures executed upon Items Q-1 and Q-2 are of common authorship.

9. The definition of the above terminology is set forth in the ASTM Standard E1658-08 as follows: The term **"highly probable"** – the evidence is very persuasive, yet some critical feature or quality is missing so that *an identification* is not in order; however, the examiner is virtually certain that the questioned and known writings were written by the same individual.

10. This opinion was solely based upon the examination of the photocopied documents as supplied to me by ██████████ the Law Offices ██████████ P.C.. I reserve the right to update, amend and/or supplement this report as new information is provided to me.

11. FURTHER AFFIANT SAYETH NOT

DATED this 6th day of September 2012.

SUBSCRIBED AND SWORN to before me this 6th day of September 2012.

Notary Public

My Commission Expires: ________

Affidavit: ██████████, M.F.S.   Page 3

EXHIBIT C
COMPARISON OF Q(1-2) TO K(1-4)

QUESTIONED:

FOUZA SAADEH

Q-1 Last Will & Testament 10 16 08

Q-2 Self Proving Affidavit 10 11 08

KNOWN:

K-1 Certificate of Naturalization 26 95

K-3 Illinois Driver's License 2 28 08

K-4 Illinois Driver's License 1-10-96

LEGEND OF DIFFERENCES BETWEEN QUESTIONED AND KNOWN SIGNATURES
1. Execution of lower case "o"; open or tented
2. Execution of lower case "u"; lack of downstroke
3. Period inserted after upper case "A"
4. Lack of consistency in execution and slant of upper case "S"
5. Upper case "D" does not extend below baseline